The Way of Compassion

The Way of Compassion

Edited by Martin Rowe

Stealth Technologies • New York

Manufactured in the United States of America.

ISBN: 0-9664056-0-9

Library of Congress Cataloging-in-Publication Data- 98-88498

To all those trying to bring about a better world

Acknowledgments

We'd first like to acknowledge the hundreds of people who have contributed to *Satya* over the years and have helped in numerous ways—without their support, the magazine (and therefore this book) would quite literally not have been possible. We have been blessed with a core readership of committed people who have taken *Satya* under their wings and dispersed it more widely than we ever thought possible. Luckily, they are too numerous to mention individually.

There are certain people whom we would, however, like to thank personally:

Julie Hughes, who offered incalculable support, story ideas, energy and commitment to this magazine for two years.

Linda Gould, who has done more than anyone to make sure that the issues were distributed widely and that our advertisers and advertisements were many and frequent.

Mia MacDonald, who offered story ideas and has been on many issues a firm and reliable editor and guiding hand.

Jeffrey Weaver, whose expertise and guidance have added greatly to the readability, appearance and continuity of the magazine.

Martin Rowe
Beth Gould

Contents

Animal Advocacy

Being an Activist

Introduction
Martin Rowe

In June 1994, my colleague Beth Gould and I began a magazine called *Satya*. The word itself means "truth" and it is one of the fundamental precepts of the Jain religion of India. The Jains believe in radical non-violence and attempt to live that way as much as possible. It was partly this principle that Mohandas Gandhi was drawing upon when he coined the word *satyagraha*, or "truth-action", to describe the kind of civil disobedience and radical non-compliance he and others used when trying to rid India of the British. What *satyagraha* meant was a fundamental commitment to peace allied with an equal commitment to confront injustice, even if it meant imprisonment or personal discomfort. These were the ideas that Dr. Martin Luther King, Jr. employed in his quest for ensuring civil rights for African Americans in the 1950s and 1960s.

Both Dr. King and Gandhi recognized that at the heart of *satyagraha* lies a belief in the inherent dignity of the human being to live his or her life free of unnecessary suffering and unnatural confinement. They understood that similarly, and simultaneously, *satyagraha* calls upon all of us—no matter how economically disadvantaged or socially disenfranchised we may be—to make a commitment to those less fortunate than us, and to draw upon all the resources available to us to make a difference. You don't need to be rich, or well-educated, or a person of privilege to be effective in what you do. You merely need to be someone of conviction—someone who understands that an injustice is being perpetrated and needs to be stopped.

For Gandhi—and perhaps for Dr. King had he lived longer—there was an irresistible correlation between the dignity of human beings and that of other-than-human life. It is no coincidence that Dr. King's wife, Coretta Scott King, and their son Dexter Scott King do not eat animal products. Gandhi himself made a commitment to vegetarianism early in his life, and made it so fundamental a feature of his existence, that to concentrate on his concern for poor human beings and ignore his compassion for animals is to grasp only half of his spirituality and half of his conviction. Gandhi knew that animals—particularly the cow—played a vital part in the village life of India, and he knew that villages were themselves the lifeblood of his vast country. To remove one, or consider one merely subsidiary to the other, would be to drain the veins that kept the body politic alive.

This is a further element of *satyagraha*. It is the recognition that "truth-action" does not only begin with the self, but begins with those around you, in your neighborhood, and fans out to encompass all things. Many of us may feel overwhelmed by the profusion of crises that seem to plague our planet; we may find ourselves asking what one person can do to tackle these seemingly insuperable problems. Both Gandhi and Dr. King would have answered, "Everything." They would also have added that, until you try, you have no idea how powerful you can be.

The Way of Compassion
The Way of Compassion is an attempt to provide a way forward for those who want to set out on the same road as Gandhi and Dr. King. It deals with the three subjects which *Satya* dedicated itself to exploring: vegetarianism, environmentalism and animal advocacy. As the articles suggest, there are many interconnections between these issues. These include biodiversity, sustainable community, human health, moral responsibility for our treatment of non-human life, and ultimately the fate of the planet.

The book is split into five sections: Philosophical and Religious Reflections, Vegetarianism, Environmentalism, Animal Advocacy and Being an Activist. In the first section, leading writers, activists and thinkers uncover some of the foundational ways of thinking that people can draw upon in order to bring about change. **James Carse** and **James Hillman** examine the resonance animals and the natural world have in our conscious and unconscious states. They argue that honoring the extraordinariness of non-human life, and committing ourselves to its service, offer not only psychological health, but a gateway to the deepest mysteries of the human condition. The next three articles explore the rich past and complex present of India—the place many think of as the home of vegetarianism and the birthplace of three world religions (Jainism, Buddhism and Hinduism) whose first precept is non-violence to all living beings. **Christopher Key Chapple** looks at the challenges facing this rapidly developing nation, and how its long history of respect for non-human life and sustainability is being challenged by its equally long history of splendor and consumption. **Muni Nandibhushan Vijayji**, a Jain monk, explains the ideas behind Jainism, often credited with turning the ancient Vedic religion of India away from animal sacrifice with its doctrine of radical non-violence, or *ahimsa*. Leading environmentalist and animal rights campaigner **Maneka Gandhi** presents the many ways she activates *ahimsa* in contemporary India and offers some blunt words on the challenges that activists both in India and around the world must face if they are to change the situation.

In their two interviews, Jewish ecotheologist **Arthur Waskow** and **Andrew Linzey** argue that both Judaism and Christianity offer a positive concept of dealing with institutional violence to the planet and those who live on it. Waskow calls for a new and expanded sense of *kashrut*—the dietary restrictions which sealed the covenant God made with the Jewish people—to make it more sensitive to the concerns of the polluted world we live in. Linzey suggests that Jesus' death on the cross expresses God's concerns for all creation—one where human beings have a unique opportunity and responsibility for the stewardship of all living things.

2

In the concluding interviews in this section, feminist vegetarian **Carol Adams** indicates some of the major challenges involved in living in a meateating world and underlines some of the ways of thinking that stop people from considering the sources of their food. **Shelton Walden** and **Dick Gregory** discuss how they became aware of vegetarianism and who inspired them. Walden, who hosts his own radio show on health and animal protection issues, reveals some of the key stumbling blocks and opportunities facing African Americans both within the animal rights movement and in creating a healthy attitude toward food within the African American community. Finally, **John Robbins** points out the inequities of our current health care and environmental crises and how we need to take personal responsibility for both if we are to avoid potentially fatal consequences in the future.

The section on vegetarianism is dedicated to answering some of the questions people who want to know about vegetarianism often ask of vegetarians. For me, becoming a vegetarian was an act of will which changed my thinking about many things. For **Stacey Triplett**, the issue was one of moral integrity. As an African American woman used to being the subject of thoughtless remarks about her identity, she could not accept in good conscience unexamined thinking about her own food choices. **Jason Freitag** had a more visceral response, an observation of the correlation between human and animal flesh that was all the more powerful for being so essentially unextraordinary.

Tom McGuire's piece attempts to answer that hoary chestnut of a response when vegetarians advocate their plant-based diet: "Don't plants have feelings too?" **Matt Ball** makes the case for a compassionate lifestyle based on vegan principles. He suggests that veganism involves much more than not eating any animal products. It means spreading compassion without vitriol or blame to all those who have not made the connection between living lightly on the land and not exploiting animals. Vegetarian activist **Edward Bikales** explains how easy it is to make a difference in your life and **Rynn Berry** reveals the world of fruitarians—those who strive to live by not consuming any living thing that can propagate itself. **Patrick Donnelly** argues for the importance of including whole foods in your diet, especially for those like himself who have compromised immune systems. In his second article, Berry settles another chestnut—whether Hitler was or was not a vegetarian.

Rather than attempt a complete summary of all environmental issues, the environmental section of *The Way of Compassion* concentrates on some key areas where public policy and individual action need to be addressed. **Mia MacDonald** studies the philosophical underpinnings of a globalized economy and practical impacts on the environment, indigenous peoples and the animals with whom we share the planet. She shows how the demands of a modern economy conflict with the ancient (and often sustainable) lifestyles of the Maasai and the wildebeest who inhabit the Serengeti in Kenya and Tanzania. **Philip Goff** points out how the United States' dependence on the automobile has not only severely unbalanced the natural world but continues to fracture human lives through cutting down on public space, slicing up neighborhoods and generally reducing the quality of life in cities, particularly New York.

How to live sustainably in a city is a fundamental question, as worldwide the move to cities from the country continues. In his interview, Sierra Club activist **Stephan Chenault** examines the meaning of sustainability in an urban context and how groups are working together to solve local environmental problems. **Constance Lynn Cornell** and **Kathy Lawrence** reveal the exciting developments taking place in cities—where Greenmarkets, community gardens and community supported agriculture are offering immediate solutions to the problems of disappearing local farms and energy-intensive transportation of foodstuffs around the nation, while creating a ready supply of healthful, organic food for city communities.

Another crucial issue is the production of waste. **Susan Kalev** shows how New York City has been dealing with the issue in her tour of the largest landfill in the world—Fresh Kills on Staten Island. **Howard Lyman** argues that animal agriculture is decimating the natural world through overgrazing and factory farm confinement of food animals. In her article, **Stephanie Miller** describes her relationship with her garden, while **Ying Wu** calls for a rediscovered sense of the natural world from her fellow urban students.

Finally, ecotourism has often been cited as a way for countries to protect their natural resources and boost their economies. **Jessica Graham** recognizes the problems that exist in ecotourism and shows how this burgeoning mix of business and pleasure has affected the Galapagos Islands and Indonesia.

Like issues surrounding environmentalism, animal advocacy encompasses many divergent areas of interest and concern. Like that on environmentalism, the section on animal advocacy concentrates on only a few. After **Jim Mason** and I have examined some of the key philosophical assumptions surrounding animals, I introduce one of the most contentious areas where human and animal life meet: the global patenting of plant, human and genetic material. **Stuart Newman** shows how the manipulation of human DNA poses serious threats to the environment and human beings. **Alan Berger** offers similar warnings about the dangers to humans of viral epidemics through xenotransplantation—the transfer of non-human organs into human bodies. AIDS and animal activist **Steven Simmons** argues against animal research as a suitable or effective method in the search for a cure for AIDS.

Something in the region of nine billion animals are killed every year in the United States for food. I discuss the mechanized food delivery systems that make possible such a staggering number—as well as the mindset behind it—in an article on bovine spongiform encephalopathy (BSE), commonly known as mad cow disease. **Lorri Bauston** describes how she and her partner **Gene** rescued and nurtured three animals who in turn transformed their lives.

Our relationships with animals can be more intimate and affirming than the experiencing of eating them, and this is explored in the next few articles. **Antonia Gorman** relates the extraordinary story of what her dog did after a car crash. **Vicki** and **Tony Moore** offer their brave testimony of what happened after Vicki was gored by a bull when videotaping the abuses of bullfights in Spain. To end the section, primatologists **Jane Goodall** and **Roger Fouts** recall instances in which our closest relatives—the Great Apes—have revealed themselves to be equally as compassionate and courageous as we wish ourselves to be.

The final section, on becoming an activist, presents the thoughts and deeds of those who have gone that extra mile to change people's attitudes about the other-than-human world and stop the violence. First are seven activists who tell their often horrifying experiences rescuing pigeons in the annual **Hegins Pigeon Shoot**. **Henry Spira** explains how one person can make a difference with coordinated and effective campaigns. **Lawrence Carter-Long** explores the issues of burn-out among activists and describes more fruitful ways to bring about change and live a healthy life. **Alyssa Bonilla** gets down to brass tacks, providing a detailed analysis of how she created a dog run in her neighborhood in only a few months. Finally, **Ben White** and **Rod Coronado** make an inspiring plea for all of us to follow Gandhi and King in the path of civil disobedience and offer hope for radical change.

Beyond The Way of Compassion
We designed this book to be a beginning for your journey toward bringing about change. We hope that the words you find in these pages may be cause for reflection, self-examination and action. You may not like, or even believe, all that you read. Because of that, we urge you to follow up by using the bibliography and the resources at the back of the book to learn more about issues that you are concerned about.

Beth and I have been constantly amazed at the unsung work carried out by people around the world as they struggle to create a more just and sustainable world for all creatures—human or otherwise. *The Way of Compassion* is dedicated to them, and to you—the reader—in the hope that you may find in it the inspiration to make a difference not only in your life but in the lives of all those around you.

Philosophical
and
Religious Reflections

Memoirs of a Flyfisherman
James Carse

J ames Carse is the retired Director of Religious Studies and Professor of Religion at New York University, where among other subjects he has taught classes on environmental ethics, mysticism and world mythology. His book *Breakfast at the Victory: The Mysticism of Ordinary Experience* includes a number of stories from his youth in Wisconsin and reflections on the natural world around his house in Rowe, Massachusetts.

"Beauty is always threatening because it is utterly useless.
There is nothing to be done with it but to let it be.
It threatens us with a vision of our own inutility."

In your book is a meditation on catching a large trout in a pond near your house. You were unable to kill and "clean" the fish when you saw that your children had a deeper connection to the animal, a connection you once had but had to set aside to "become a man."

When I grew up in the Middle West every boy had to pass through a deer hunting ritual. First, we had to learn how to fire a deer rifle, a powerful and dangerous gun that kicked rather painfully against the shoulder. Next, we joined the fellowship of hunters, learning their myriad ways. Handling and accurately shooting guns was only a part of it. Acquiring the appropriate attitude toward animals as existing only to provide us with the thrill of killing them was another part. So were drinking, smoking, swearing—acquired adultlike swaggering.

Most important in this ritual was the moment where we were to confront what we knew as "buck fever." Buck fever was the inability to pull the trigger when we had our first deer in the gunsight. Not to overcome buck fever was a major adolescent failure, and it was not uncommon. Buck fever, in fact, became a general term that applied far beyond hunting, to every male challenge: going into a fight, or a game, or even an examination.

As it happened, I did not come from a hunting family. We were fishermen. I did learn to shoot but fortunately I never had a deer in my gunsight. Fishing had its own version of buck fever. There is a lot of killing involved in that sport as well: running a worm on the hook or attaching a minnow to it by the lips or the dorsal fin. Gutting the fish, especially when it was still alive, was the same act of killing, only more obvious. I remember the first time I cut a fish open, scraping its guts into the water and thinking with some horror, "My God, this is life!" I passed the buck fever test, however—in a way. I gutted hundreds of fish in my youth, acquiring a style of my own. But I hated it every time.

What was the part of you that hated the killing?
It was that in me that could see the beauty of the fish. And not just the fish. We lived in an area famous for its trout streams. They were deep, dark and mysterious. Water, stained dark from the tamarack trees, hid the deeper pools where the trout lay.

That we could not see the trout, that they seemed to come from nowhere, was definitely part of the romance of the sport—if it is a sport. You simply did not know where they were until they hit your line. It was setting yourself up to surprise. It was this mystery that was being killed with the fish.

Was the experience unique every time, or was it in the repetition that the beauty and mystery lay?
It was unique each time. I can still remember certain fish I caught at certain times and places. For a period of time we had an ice-fishing house, a unique structure that is pulled onto the ice when it is safe to do so. The house is just big enough for several people to sit in. It has a wood stove, and a hole two feet square. The magic of it was that the house, without windows, was lighted from below, through the ice. That meant you could not only see into the water, you couldn't even see the surface of the water. With no light reflecting off the surface of the water, you had the feeling you were in the same element as the fish. And gorgeous colors came up through the water, water so clear you could see fish sometimes fifty feet down. You felt you were in a different realm—a world impenetrable to your experience or even your imagination. So that part was the part of me that loved the mystery and beauty and hated the killing.

What was the part that allowed you to do the killing?
It was the competitive part, the one that was all boy. It was very much bound up with my father. He had been a professional boxer, very athletic, physical, aggressive, engaging, loud and amusing—irresistible in many ways. I was even thrilled by the violence I felt in him. I was drawn into the maleness of his presence, the exuberance, even joy, of being with him. He

and my brother and I laughed a lot, touching, hitting, pushing each other. Particularly in the coldest part of the winter, when it was often below zero, there were many ways of proving your manhood. Imitating our father, we went without hats, left our coats unbuttoned and scooped ice out of the fishing holes with our bare hands. I envied his ability to break the neck of a fish when he caught it or throw it onto the ice to freeze—without a thought. I couldn't do it without a thought—the thought that I was killing something unnecessarily.

As a boy I did not understand that my father was a manic depressive. What we saw then was just the manic side. Ironically, years later, when he descended into acute depression, he attempted to kill himself by leaping into one of our favorite fishing rivers during the high water of the spring runoff. That attempt failed; the next succeeded. So he was a killer, after all. Perhaps I sensed this in my own reaction to the killing of animals.

Is that, in some ways, how you became a man?
Paradoxically, I learned that the only way I was to become a man was to give up being a boy proving himself. Now I can see that this is what my father was doing. Due to the peculiar and sad features of his own childhood, he spent his life proving that he was not a loser. But once you enter into that way of thinking there will never be enough proof; the more you try to convince yourself you are no longer the loser you know yourself to be, the more you reinforce that view of yourself. Even as a kid, though I could not have articulated it at the time, I could see the contradictory nature of the competitive way of proving your own manhood to yourself. So I tried to allow that other self—the side that was fascinated by mystery—to surface and be dominant.

Did this happen automatically?
No, it wasn't automatic. It took years; years of struggle. There was nothing like a decisive moment or a sudden conversion. Although I remember a rather dramatic crossing of the line when one day I decided to stop eating meat. Once I made the decision, I realized, "Hey, I hate this shit. Why am I eating it?"

I'm interested in where this killing part comes from. Do you think it is envy of the beauty of the natural world?
Beauty is always threatening because the only thing you can do with beauty is to let it be. Once you make use of what you consider beautiful, its beauty is gone. Kant is right about this: We see something as beautiful only when we see its uselessness. As soon as you say, "Oh, this would look great on my wall," it becomes useful as a decoration or ostentation, and its beauty is lost. If your attitude toward the world is one of exploitation, domination, manipulation or competition, beauty becomes a natural enemy.

11

There is a story you tell in the book about a mouse in your cottage who becomes a brief, although fearless, companion. You find the mouse staring directly into your eyes. What did you see?

The mouse's existence clearly doesn't have the level of consciousness of a human's, but the question remains as to what that level of consciousness is and how we make sense of it. I thought the only way I could make sense of it is to say the mouse is living in a dream, but a dream from which it never awakes. We too live in a dream, except at a higher level. So the question for us is whether we can wake from this level to one higher. This may mean waking "down" as well as "up." In *Breakfast at the Victory* I suggest that we wake to deeper levels of the self when we open ourselves to the mystery in the presence of animals. I find the silence of the Buddha powerful in this respect; it is a silence that approaches that of animals, a silence that does not need to speak.

What was the difference between the eyes of the mouse, and the eyes of your cat Charlie?

The mouse's gaze was more stark. Because there was something slightly recognizable in Charlie's eyes, I thought it was possible I could even imagine what Charlie was thinking. I couldn't imagine what the mouse was thinking. It was too distant, more alien, more like a fish than a cat. The mouse had no expression on its face, its eyes were no more than two black dots. It had all the elements of a face, but it wasn't a face. And yet it was looking out of a kind of consciousness and directly into my eyes.

What do you extrapolate is our responsibility toward animals based on those observations?

Our responsibility is to take this awareness of our incomprehension seriously. The fact that I don't know what's going on with the mouse prevents or protects me from the arrogance I would normally experience or express in dealing with animals. The fact that I don't know what they're thinking means I don't know what I am doing when I decide what to do with their lives.

So, theoretically, if you could find out what a mouse was thinking by cutting open his or her head, do you feel the knowledge you would gain from that is not the knowledge that you get from just looking at the mouse?

Whatever the mouse's knowledge consists of, it is deeper than anything I can know. What is awesome to me is that my knowledge is as unavailable to the mouse's as it is to mine, or to any other being's. I think of the creatures that live in and around my house—ants, centipedes, snakes, flies, mosquitoes, woodchucks, grubs—and remind myself that each of them possesses a knowledge that is forever asleep to all the others and that it is as true for me as for them.

And is this what makes them creatures of God?

They are creatures of God for us so long as we encounter the mystery of their being. The Sufis paid special attention to the ants. As one of them said, if this small being were to remove its black cloak the glory of God would shine forth in such splendor that "the monotheists of the whole world would be put to shame."

What would you say to the accusation that ascribing to animals this knowledge is merely being anthropomorphic?

It would be anthropomorphic only if we thought we could have access to the knowledges of other beings. We are all limited knowers. It is taking those limits seriously that is the essence of mysticism. This is why mysticism is compatible with radical environmentalism and vegetarianism. It is the way we can express our respect for the mystery of other beings. That recognition does not rest with just protecting other beings, but also creates a deeper sense of our own mysteriousness to ourselves.

Learning from Animals

James Hillman

J ames Hillman is a leading archetypal psychologist and author of many books, including *Suicide and the Soul*, *Kinds of Power* and *The Soul's Code*, which reached the top of the *New York Times* bestseller list. His essay "Going Bugs" is a classic exposition of the meaning of bugs in the human psyche. Hillman examines the role that bugs—insects and creepy-crawlies—play in dreams and how human reaction to them is symptomatic of larger concerns about animals and the natural world. These themes are explored further in his book *Dream Animals*, with 35 paintings by Margot McClean. Hillman lives in Connecticut, with bugs, ducks and chickens.

"There is something extremely valuable in caring
for an animal. That's a lesson of the heart:
it's a service, a ritual service."

In "Going Bugs," you highlight four aspects of bugs that figure in the human consciousness: their multiplicity, their monstrosity, their autonomy and their parasitism. What is important about these aspects?
It is particularly the parasitical aspect: that a tiny bug can change your behavior radically; and that bugs—such as fleas, flies, crabs and maggots—seem to live off other forms of life. The multiplicity is a threat to any kind of consciousness that is identified with unity and singleness. So the very fact that there are billions of ants, and hundreds of thousands of aphids, and other kinds of things all looking exactly alike, swarming and flying in such huge amounts, makes the individual identified with singleness and singularity feel very threatened.

You have said that insects in dreams suggest the psyche's capacity to go beyond its humanistic definitions. What do you mean by that?

The bug takes you beyond the human as the model of formal beauty. As long as you follow the Bible and say, "Man is created in the image of God," then the question is, "What about bugs?" When God actually shows himself in the Book of Job, or at least reveals his power and his capacity, he shows himself as Behemoth and Leviathan—two animals. I think that the idea that Man is the model of how God literally looks is highly narrow and distorted. Therefore, bugs seem monstrous. But it may be that they are not monstrous. It may be that we are monstrous if we look at things from their point of view. What I am trying to do in "Going Bugs" is to get rid of this human-centered vision.

We human beings tend to see insects as monstrous. That has to do with their autonomy. One can charm a snake, supposedly, or rub the belly of an alligator and get it to do what you want, but it is pretty damn hard to get a bug to do anything you want it to do. There were flea circuses and in China there were cricket fights. But it is hard to control bugs. They have an autonomy. There are hundreds of thousands of different species of beetle. They have this enormous range of forms and images and colors and shapes. They share a fundamental structure, of course, but besides that they have a range of variation way beyond our understanding.

Bugs represent the extreme ranges of imagination. You see, the imagination extends beyond the human will. There is more to the imagination than my mind or my will. Again, we are human-centered: we think that things begin and end with us. So we call bugs freaky or autonomous, because their extension is greater than ours—in their whole panoply, that is. It is not that each single bug is greater, because each single bug has its own small path of habit, but it feels as if bugs are always pursuing their ends which cross ours. They seem to do things we don't want them to do: it is part of their autonomy. I'm not saying they do do that; I'm saying that's how we perceive them. That is why we don't like them. We get annoyed trying to catch or swat a fly, because it is going its own damn way and it's unpredictable.

Is that why we use the term "going bugs" for going mad?

One of the sources is the feeling that one is falling apart into multiple pieces, breaking down. Very often, bug images carry the idea of psychotic breakdown.

In Western culture we associate bugs with disease and death. Why do we have that association?

Other cultures see bugs as originating and creative—the Navaho for example. For the Jains in India, all life is holy and it doesn't matter what kind of life it is. There is the whole Christian destruction: first of all the alienation from nature, and secondly our alienation from the underworld, turning Hades into Hell. Hades was a realm in the Greek world, and in the Christian world it became Hell, a place where the damned go. That has left some heavy traces on us. We've moralized a lot of the world, particularly in the last two thousand years. We've moralized nature and moralized animals.

As long as the bug represents the underworld—the earth, the dark, the buried and, ever since the Bible, as Beelzebub, "Lord of the Flies"—then pesticides become a scientistic way of harrowing Hell, of getting rid of that underworld.

Why did you choose dreams of various people's response to animals and bugs in particular to focus upon?
I've collected animal dreams for 30 or 40 years. I had a huge collection for a while and used to lecture on the dreams a lot. But I wanted particularly to pick out the bugs because they are the most maligned and there is the most to be learned there. Take that multiplicity for a minute. If you abandon the idea that everything must be unified into singleness, then you could look at the multiplicity of these hordes and swarms, and so on, as a collective soul—as a soul that can work as a beehive or an anthill in which many, many pieces all function with a soul that is not necessarily fixed to one single thing.

How do we change our attitude towards bugs without "going bugs"?
Two of the dreams in "Going Bugs" involve a man getting down on his knees and trying to see the world as the bug does, through its eyes. While of course you can't do that literally, there are some gestures that are important. One is bowing down, giving up the superiority that looks down upon the bugs. This gesture expresses a certain interest in all things that are not human. Another is that Man is no longer, as Protagoras [480-411 BCE] said, "the measure of all things." We have a very narrow cosmos. The bugs penetrate and break through the walls and come up from the hidden corners and threaten the narrowness of our cosmos.

This only threatens our sanity if our sanity is identified with the narrow cosmos: what my will can do and what my reason can control. The first step for change would be an accommodation: a softening of the human border so it becomes a little fuzzier. Children understand. They play with bugs, they put them in matchboxes. They love caterpillars, they let them crawl all over their hands. Some kids even enjoy spiders. As you get older and get more willful and rational and controlled and let your ego define your personality, you become more estranged from the animals. You have fewer animal dreams. A child is not as threatened by the bug as we are. That says something.

So it is not really going crazy. It is the adult vision that makes it seem like we are going crazy. Suppose we are already crazy and the bugs are our deliverers?

What have you learned from your ducks and chickens?
One thing that is extremely important is the need to serve an animal (in my case by getting up in the morning and walking about 50 yards in January on ice to carry their water and make sure that the door is open so they can walk out of

their little house if they want to). It is a service that is extraordinarily valuable. I think it's what people feel when they have a dog and they take him or her for a walk, or if they have a horse and they comb her or him and muck out the stalls. There is something extremely valuable in caring for an animal. That's a lesson of the heart: it's a service, a ritual service. The kept animal is utterly dependent on you. If you don't go out there with water, they will die.

People who serve in a hospice may feel similarly. There is a leveling, a lowering of oneself, where all one's important matters—making the phone calls, going to the bank—are begun and ended by letting the chickens and the ducks out and putting them to bed at night. It is very similar I suppose to a mother with a child.

An animal cannot thank you. The thankfulness is in their living: that they live and come out into the daylight in the morning. That is the moment of their thankfulness. It's a pleasure that they experience and you experience as well—an ineffable sharing of something. Also, you learn the peculiarities of human beings within the animal world. The animals are like walking metaphors of scratching, pecking, pushing, showing off, domination and anxiety: all kinds of things we think are human are going on in their world as well. In that way, therefore, the tribal myths, which say that animals taught human beings everything we know, are true. There is a great deal of metaphoric, imagistic language that we have learned from animals.

Another thing I have discovered is that the life of the animals is not quite as terror-filled as the animal shows on television seem to suggest. I hold in suspicion the angle that everything is in constant danger and constant competition, that there are predators out to get you every minute, and that animal life is all camouflage and threat. I do not think the animals themselves live wholly that kind of life. They also live an extraordinarily symbiotic life with one another and their environment.

The Land of Plenitude

Christopher Key Chapple

Christopher Key Chapple teaches courses on Sanskrit, Religions of Asia and contemporary religious and environmental ethics at Loyola Marymount University, Los Angeles. He is the author of *Non-Violence to Animals, Earth and Self in Asian Religions.*

"One of the things that strikes a visitor to India is the permeable boundaries between the human and the animal. There is an intimacy with the animal realm that is almost inconceivable to us."

Should we blame the West—and Western religious values—for India's environmental problems?

Environmentalists have blamed our current ecological crisis on the Bible, particularly the biblical concept of dominion over the Earth. Similarly, there are aspects of Hindu tradition that downgrade the material world and declare it to be illusory. However, for the most part, our environmental problems arise from the rise of technology in the 1700s and the advent of manipulative consumerism since the Second World War, particularly in America. In India, colonialism delayed technological development until this century. Recent changes in economic policy (away from the Gandhian model) have allowed an increase in consumerism in India in the past decade. The rush toward materialist consumerism in India can be seen as quite alarming. But there are people who are critical of the rise of pollution in India and are re-examining Hindu tradition in an ecological light and resurrecting the sense of the importance of nature that is so eloquently expressed in Hindu text and ritual.

India has its indigenous system of understanding the natural world: the five elements. It begins with earth, water, fire, air and space. In the Tantric systems and in Sankhya, there is a beautiful correlation between the human body and the human senses and experience of the world. With the earth is the correla-

18

tion of smell, with water taste, with fire sight, with wind touch, and with space hearing. This is very beautiful, but it is something that is so much a part of the culture that people need to be reminded that this can be reinterpreted to allow us to perhaps think more critically and more carefully about the burgeoning development that is literally choking urban India at present.

Is consumerism in India specifically justified within the Hindu tradition or is it just a Western imperial value which has taken over?
Here I'm going to talk in bold, universal concepts, but one of the basic drives of the human being is to seek comfort. Another mainstay is to celebrate. And one of the great celebrations of India has been wealth. Part of the reason why Marco Polo went in search of the East was that the East was so fabulous. If you tour through India, the great tourist places are the palaces. There was just a splendor: a splendor of sensuality, of tapestry, of food, an incredible bounty, and this bounty and this emphasis on extravagance and wealth is supported by the texts. In Indian tradition—the *Laws of Manu*, the *Dharmashastra* tradition—there are four goals. The very first goal is wealth (*artha*). There are goddesses that are worshipped in order to accumulate wealth and India has always been rather unabashed about wealth. To have wealth is valued and virtually any human culture given the opportunity will do what it can to increase its comfort and its wealth. Since the introduction of the Western model, this has been made accessible to a far greater number of people than ever possible before thanks to technology.

On the one hand people in India are celebrating. They are celebrating a level of comfort that has never before been experienced—across classes. This is perhaps cause for celebration, and Indians are being quite vociferous in critiquing the notion that Western environmentalists should have any say in the nature of Indian consumption. Ramachandra Guha, who is a leading thinker in this area, has critiqued the Western environmentalist program saying that essentially it is yet another form of imperialism. This thinking has led to India's refusal to participate in voluntary emissions programs to stem global warming.

Guha's critique came out about ten or 15 years ago, however, and people are now realizing the urgency of the problem. In New Delhi pollution levels top out routinely at 400 or 500 particulates per million, while in Los Angeles, when it is 200, children are advised not to go outside. In India, people live day after day in two and a half times that level without any such restriction. It is not at all uncommon in a city such as New Delhi to see people wearing filters or even gas masks just to get through the day. New Delhi is second only to Mexico City in terms of air pollution. Only in 1997 did India pass legislation mandating catalytic converters for the cars which are being consumed at an alarming rate, particularly in cities like New Delhi. You see fewer cars as you go further south, but in New Delhi the traffic is overwhelming and consequently the air pollution is staggering.

Part of the problem is that India cannot really afford the latest in technology. Many of the cars burn kerosene, a very dirty sort of fuel, and for most people who are moving into the middle class—and India's middle class is the largest in the world at this point—the first step is to get a motor scooter, and motor scooters are very unclean. Their cumulative impact on the environment will be very negative. This is one of the realities that Indians grapple with.

How does, therefore, the developed world approach the developing world to reawaken the spiritual and cultural aspects of these societies without being accused of neoimperialism?
One of the beauties of India is its resourcefulness, and another legacy that India has is Mahatma Gandhi. Mahatma Gandhi, of course, advocated a philosophy and lifestyle based on simplicity that many people of the older generation recall and have in fact experienced. Many grassroots movements have been born in India: the Chipko movement in the Himalayan region has helped protect trees; the Narmada Dam activism in the central part of India, spanning the states of Uttar Pradesh and Gujurat, has successfully—at least for now—rolled back a 30-year standing plan to dam an area of India that is 800 miles wide and expands 200 miles from north to south. With the erection of just one dam, tens of thousands of people have been displaced, uprooted, and been forced to move into cities, into a totally marginalized experience. These people have found a voice, and they have found ways to lobby, to advocate that their traditional lifestyle not be disrupted, and for now the dams have been stopped. No Western intervention was involved with either instance, and this is an example of environmentalism rising from the people who are intimate with the land.

What has been your direct experience of how animals are treated in India?
One of the things that strikes a visitor to India is the permeable boundaries between the human and the animal. In Western culture people will keep a dog or a cat, and maybe a cockatiel or parakeet. But if a person sees even an ant or a spider inside the house they do all they can to remove that being. In India, animals are everywhere. Animals are in the streets, animals wander in and out of people's houses. Birds fly through people's windows and take food from their table. There is an intimacy with the animal realm that is almost inconceivable to us.

Then there are the cows, of course.
The cow, as everyone knows, is deemed sacred and is integrated into the daily life of Indians in a way that has been criticized by the West. But Western scholars have studied the cow and have discovered that the five gifts of the cow are crucial for the sustenance and maintenance of India's people. The first two gifts of the cow are—and this is traditional from the Hindu texts—the gift of milk (which is the most obvious) and the gift of urine (used as a cleanser due to its

high ammonia content). The third gift of the cow is dung, an important source of fuel. Most cooking fires—both in rural and in urban India—for the poorer people are drawn from cow dung, which is gathered by women and shaped into patties and sold. So it's also an economic resource. The last two gifts of the cow are generally associated with low-caste people, but when a cow dies (presumably a natural death) the meat of the cow will be eaten by certain classes or castes of people, and then those castes will take the skin of the cow and process it for leather. Those two items would be only used by the low castes.

What about wild animals?

Seventeen percent of the forests of India still remains. India has vast stretches of land under cultivation and is roughly a third of the size of the United States, but it supports a population more than three times that of the United States. It is quite remarkable that 17 percent of India's land is still forested. One of the issues of preservation of habitat for the tiger as well as the elephant is that 70 to 80 percent of the human population (which will reach a billion within a few years) is rural-based, and sustenance-based. This means that women have to travel great distances, depending on which state they're located in, to gather firewood and haul water. They are also having to cultivate greater and greater areas, although the advances in water technology have lessened the pressure for deforestation for the purposes of agriculture. But Ramachandra Guha has pointed out that the model of the forest preserve as a museum—which is essentially the ideology of Yosemite and Yellowstone, where you fence the people out, you let them camp there, but vast tracts of land become off-limits to human beings—is impossible in India. The key to effective conservation in India is the integration of the human into the landscape.

One wonderful strategy is illustrated by the Periyar preserve, which is in the hills of Kerala, in the Western Ghats, where the state of Kerala abuts the southern state of Tamil Nadu. This is a mountainous area where a century ago the British built a dam that created a lake several miles long. The British established a preserve that is now maintained by the Indian government. It has 700 elephants in the wild. Hundreds of people go through the preserve every day on a boat. From the boat you can watch the elephants, otters, wild boar and birds in a state of near intimacy, far more intimately than, say, in the San Diego Wildlife Park in California. The animals are totally free. That preserve includes a couple of dozen tigers as well.

I cite the instance of Periyar, because the preserve has created a delightful way for people to be in that landscape in an unobtrusive manner. But sadly, a number of the tribal peoples in that area have been drawn into the cities and are slowly beginning to lose their intimacy with the flora and the fauna. With that loss of native culture there is a diminishment of human contact with the healing powers of those plants, and that's really a great loss.

I'm also thinking of the Jain tradition. The Jain tradition emphasizes non-violence. Throughout their history, Jains have organized successful campaigns in India to limit and restrict the sacrifice of animals within the Vedic sacrifices of Brahmanic Hinduism. They have also criticized the Maharajahs of India for the rampant, wanton destruction they were bringing about through their hunts. Part of what brought the British to India was the lure of the hunt and the desire to share the grandeur and the glory of the Maharajahs who measured their success in the number of skins they could collect and the number of heads of wild beasts they could mount on the wall.

The Jains went to the Maharajahs and Sultans who ruled vast areas of India and said, "This isn't okay; these are living beings." And they were successful in convincing the Mughal emperor Akbar to declare hunt-free zones.

This had been done with Ashoka many centuries before.
Ashoka united much of India under his rule and took to heart the Buddhist teachings. The first Buddhist teaching as well as the first Jain teaching is not to injure life. This was posted on stones throughout India, and it became the standard within the Ashokan empire to give shelter to animals, to provide hospitals for animals and to plant trees and bushes along the roadways that were beneficial and medicinal for both humans and animals.

What do you think is going to happen in India in 50 years?
I think that the sheer resource limitations will force technology to recast itself in a more ecologically friendly manner. But this will only take place after more catastrophes such as the explosion of the Union Carbide chemical factory at Bhopal which injured and killed hundreds of people, as well as diminished air quality. The lure of economic growth and entering the global consumer marketplace is very compelling and it's moving very quickly. But, on the other hand, as India chokes, as communities in the developed world reject the idea of expanding and expanding their dump sites, as people begin to reconsider the cancer rate and to reconsider diet, as this information becomes more and more available and percolates throughout people's consciousness, I think there will be increasing changes.

But does the developing world need to make all our mistakes again?
When I look at America, I see a need for people to gain an intimacy with their environment that people in the not-developed world take for granted. In India, even in the urban areas, even among the middle class, due to their rituals and their upbringing, the people are maintaining an intimacy that I think will bring them into an environmental awareness faster than we've experienced in the West. Also, the birth of the environmental movement in India—which is perhaps the most vital environmental movement in the world today—owes a great debt to the tragedy in Bhopal. Bhopal killed thousands and woke people up to the reality of industrial ravage. Out of that the work of Anil Agarwal and

the Center for Science and Environment gained a high profile. Virtually every day in any part of India the newspaper will have multiple stories that have some ecological and environmental message. You cannot say the same of the United States. In the United States, the press is in the service of perpetuating a certain economy, a certain world view. That's not the case in India.

How do you integrate your insights into your personal life as both a teacher and as an individual?

My wife and I trained for 12 years with Gurani Anjali, founder and director of the Yoga Anand Ashram in Amityville, Long Island. She grew up in India during the time of Gandhi and studied classical Yoga as a young girl. In her teachings, she emphasizes the five central disciplines of Yoga: non-violence (*ahimsa*), truthfulness (*satya*), not taking what does not belong to you (*asteya*), exhibiting or observing sexual restraint (*brahmacharya*) and limiting the extent of one's possessions (*aperigraha*). On a weekly basis we experiment with these five in combination with other spiritual practices (*sadhanas*). These disciplines continue to provide a basis for our decision-making and have helped inform our life as a family negotiating contemporary America.

For example, one challenge in our life includes the automobile. We live in Los Angeles, a conglomeration of suburbs. Our vehicles were chosen by virtue of their gas-mileage. That decision certainly stemmed from a concern for *aperigraha* as well as *asteya*. We want to use as little gas as possible; if we take too much, even if we can afford it, we would in a certain sense be stealing a resource. I live close enough to the university where I teach that I generally bicycle to work. This helps in three ways: cycling keeps my body healthy, less space is taken up on campus because I leave my car at home, and a fuel is conserved.

How do you convey yogic values to children?

Our children attend school with some very wealthy kids. We try to let our kids know that it is okay not to have as much stuff as other kids do and that there are advantages to living in a smaller house. Originally, the homes in southern California were small bungalows, modeled after cottages in India and the Mediterranean. The older homes (including ours) emphasize outside space as much as inside space. In the course of 30 years, the southern California home has grown much larger. Most new homes generally come with a three-car garage; they occupy virtually all the lot and allow very little access to the outside. This is both sad and ironic, because southern California has such a gentle and mild climate.

The larger homes also tend to isolate children from their parents. Some kids have their own play rooms, their own televisions, their own phones, computers and fax machines. All this diminishes their human contact. The manipulation of the video game or the manipulation of 100 channels on the television cannot replace the value of conversation.

Besides strictly limiting television and Internet access, we make it a point to eat together every night when possible. We also try to sit down together every Sunday night around a candle and talk about simplicity, non-violence and why we are vegetarians. We check in with one another to see how we are doing and what we are involved with. It is wonderful to hear some of the insights that the kids bring to the table. Our children have learned to take pride in simplicity, though they are understandably awed and sometimes dazzled by the people who live in palatial mansions and who have several sport utility vehicles which I call "suburban assault vehicles." Hopefully our kids will have some influence on their friends.

What are your students' concerns about the environment?
On one hand, my students are concerned with getting their careers underway. They want to buy cars, raise children, own houses and so forth. But they are also very concerned about having meaning in their lives. We have an active Sierra Club unit on our campus, as well as a Free Tibet group and various other organizations. Many of our students do volunteer work through agencies such as the Jesuit Volunteer Corps during the year after graduation. They see the importance of developing a philosophy of life that emphasizes quality rather than the quantity of things they can acquire.

Is this an experience of all races?
In California, we talk about ethnicity and multiculturalism. Los Angeles county by the year 2012 will be 68 percent Latino. The county has more than nine million people and possesses an amazing blend of cultures. When I arrived in California nearly 15 years ago, each of these groups was fairly discrete, with the Samoans living in one area, Koreans in another area, African Americans living in South Central, Hispanics downtown and in East Los Angeles, and so forth. Since that time, neighborhoods throughout southern California have become diverse. There is more cross-cultural dating and cross-cultural marriage. Twenty-five percent of the workers in California are foreign born. This makes for an exciting sense of building something new. Our students are part of this new mix. In addition, as part of our core curriculum, we require all students to complete a course in intercultural studies.

Part of the newness includes finding a way to fit into this place of beauty that respects the natural environment. A few years ago, when visiting Yosemite or Joshua Tree National Parks or the wild lands maintained by the Santa Monica Mountains Conservancy, I would see Caucasians, and occasional busloads of Japanese tourists. Now in the past few years, everyone is outside and exploring: Latinos, African Americans, Asian Americans. There is a celebration of nature that is cross-cultural and in a certain sense transcends culture. More native plants are being used in landscaping and the new architecture is beginning to open up more to the outdoors rather than closing people off. And, because of emissions standards, the air quality in southern California continues to improve. I see hope, even in the city. But it is hard to live in California and not be optimistic.

Non-Violence in Action
Muni Nandibhushan Vijayji

Many people unwittingly regard Jainism—the religion of ten million Indians and an increasing number of devotees worldwide—as a branch of Hinduism. The Jains, however, maintain, not without cogent archeological evidence, that Jainism is the parent religion of India. Mahavira, the most recent of the 24 *jinnas* (victors), is considered the historical founder of Jainism, and, with the Buddha, is credited with having abolished animal sacrifice and introducing the doctrine of *ahimsa* (non-injury) into the Vedic religion. Forty-four year old Muni Nandibhushan Vijayji lives at the Santinath Jain temple in Bombay. He has been a priest since he was 15. A master of many languages—he speaks Gujarati, Marathi, and Hindi—the Muni has a reading knowledge of Sanskrit, Prakrit, and Maghadi (the language of Mahavira and the Buddha) and considerable fluency in English.

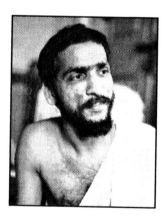

"We should be unstinting in our efforts to care
for all life forms—even stones, soil, trees, water and air,
which by the lights of Jainism are also sentient beings."

Why did you become a priest so young?
There are two reasons why one would want to become a *sadhu* (male priest)—one is unhappy with the world and desires to escape from it, or one meets a guru who inspires one to follow his example. In my case it was the latter. After school, I used to go to hear a Jain guru who persuaded me through his words and his example that I could only make spiritual progress if I were to become a *sadhu*. So at the age of 15 I left school and became a *sadhu*; I ceased my formal education, but in a sense my education really began when I left school.

Are women allowed to become priests?
Yes, in fact the majority of Lord Mahavira's followers were women, which was more than 2,000 years ago. The Jain priesthood has always been open to women. We call our female priests or monks *sadhuis*. As a rule the *sadhuis* don't speak in front of men; the *sadhus* speak before male and female audiences; however the Jain Acharya or Guru Maharaj (head priest) may appoint a woman to speak at Jain assemblies.

Are the Jains still prohibited from eating such root vegetables as potatoes, carrots and radishes as well as garlic and onions?
It is a cardinal Jain precept that one should never kill any form of life. It is our belief that while these root vegetables are growing underground, they have an infinite number of organisms attached to them. By uprooting them, one is disrupting the lives of those organisms and killing them. This is contrary to the first Jain precept against taking life. That's why we don't eat root vegetables. Our stomach is not a burial ground for dead bodies.

How do you deal with mosquitoes, termites, bed-bugs and crop-destroying pests?
According to Jainism, even these bugs have souls; so one must deal with them very gingerly.

What if you were besieged by a cloud of mosquitoes one night?
I would sweep them away with my *rajoharam* (whisk broom). If they really got bad, I would sleep under a mosquito net; but there is a difference between my killing them and their committing suicide. [*Laughter*]

Is the Jain layman as strict in his dietary habits as a Jain priest?
No, not everyone is so strict. There are different levels, but everyone is a strict vegetarian. We never wear leather, but some of our garments are made from wool. We justify that by reasoning that wool grows on top of the animal; so that to remove it is not causing the animal any deprivation. Anyway, artificial fabrics are now rendering the wearing of wool obsolete.

Did the concept of *ahimsa* originate with the Jains?
It began with Jainism. Jainism goes so far as to say that you should be concerned not only for the well-being of people, animals and bugs, but also for the well-being of the soil, the water and the air: *ahimsa* extends to all of nature. Jainism has always been very ecology-minded. We should be unstinting in our efforts to care for all life forms—even stones, soil, trees, water and air, which by the lights of Jainism are also sentient beings.

But aren't some beings more sentient than others? How would you weigh the life of a man against the life of a stone?
Jainism divides the world into five classes of beings whose membership in each class is determined by the number of senses that each being possesses. The highest class

is that of the five-sensed beings, which comprises people and the higher animals such as monkeys, parrots, dogs, horses, elephants, pigs, etc. The next class consists of four-sensed beings who are thought to lack the sense of hearing; they include the larger insects such as flies, bees and grasshoppers. The next class comprises three-sensed beings such as moths, ants, mosquitoes, etc., that lack the senses of hearing and seeing. The fourth group consists of two-sensed beings such as mollusks, crustaceans, worms, etc., who have only the senses of touch and taste. The final group, of one-sensed beings, includes trees, rocks, water, wind and fire—these too are sentient beings and as Jains we have an obligation to treat them with the same respect and care that we accord to any other life form.

Do the Jains hold the view that one can be reincarnated in a higher or lower life form?
Basically, your karma in this lifetime determines what you will become in your next lifetime. If you've been a slaughterer in this lifetime, then you may be slaughtered in the next lifetime. There are no levels of incarnation; one life form is not held to be higher or lower than another. All are sacred.

What is a typical meal for a Jain monk?
The food must be fresh. We cannot eat food that has been stored overnight.

Is that because leftover food attracts more micro-organisms, more bacteria, hence more life-forms?
That's correct. If I want to eat something, I will go to a Jain home and I will eat the food that has been prepared for me—but as I said, it must be fresh and it cannot contain root vegetables. It's considered an honor for a Jain family to provide sustenance for a Jain monk. They invariably try to give us more food than we can eat in order to obtain more blessings.

What are some of the rules that govern your life as a Jain priest?
When we travel we must walk barefoot everywhere. We are not permitted to touch a woman; we are not allowed to touch money; we never eat after sunset; twice a year I must pluck out all the hair on my face and scalp.

Why do you pluck out all your facial and scalp hair?
To increase *parishaha* (endurance of pain). *Parishaha* strengthens the spirit and reduces karma.

You don't touch money. Is money considered to be intrinsically evil?
No, money has the potential to be either good or evil; but, it is so volatile that we cannot run the risk of touching it for fear of contamination.

Do the Jains still make it a point to pursue innocent professions such as commerce and teaching in order to avoid jobs which necessitate killing life forms?
In the old days, this was strictly true; but nowadays many Jains are not so

careful about the sort of work they do so long as it pays them a good salary. Unfortunately, they don't realize that if they fail to follow the precepts of their religion, even in the workplace, they will never gain enlightenment.

Jains are not permitted to own pets—is this because it would be an intrusion in their lives, a meddling with their karmic destiny?
As a rule Jainism discourages the keeping of pets; however, if you decide to keep a pet, you are not really committing any great infraction of the rules. But we feel it is best not to interfere in the lives of animals. They should be allowed to live free and unimpeded. Of course, when animals have been mistreated or abandoned, we believe in looking after them. We have a long tradition of establishing hospitals and rest-homes for animals. Jains all over India make a practice of going to slaughterhouses to try and rescue animals that are about to be butchered. For thousands of years we Jains have operated special institutions that are called *pinjarpols* for the care and protection of helpless and decrepit animals. There is scarcely a single town in Rajasthan or Gujurat that doesn't have a *pinjarpol*. We take care of stray cows, pigs, goats, sheep, birds and insects—all creatures, irrespective of economic considerations. We keep veterinarians on hand to look after the animals regardless of cost.

Do you think Jain ethical principles will spread throughout the world?
Jainism is a very deep and demanding religious philosophy. There is only a select group of people who are lucky enough to have it as their religion and are capable of practicing it. Even the "Three Jewels" of Jainism—right thinking, right knowledge and right practice—are too difficult for most people to follow. Jainism is particular to India, which is a very sacred place. In India there is religion in every grain of sand.

Ahimsa with Attitude
Maneka Gandhi

Maneka Gandhi is the widow of Sanjay Gandhi, son of Indira Gandhi, former prime minister of India. Although she is a member of one of the most famous families in the world, it is her work that makes her remarkable. Gandhi is an animal rights and environmental activist. She was minister for environment in the coalition government of V. P. Singh from 1989 to 1991. In 1998 she returned to parliament as minister of welfare in the coalition government headed by the Bharatiya Janata Party, where she has started an Animal Welfare Department.

"I just respect the right of this animal to be.
And not to be interfered with, not to be genetically impaired,
not to be used, not to be forcibly made pregnant like the cow is,
not to be herded up and down. Just let it be."

How did you get interested in animals and the environment?
I actually started by losing an election. Until then I was a common-or-garden person. I fought an election and lost at the age of 28 [in 1984]. So when I lost, I started thinking: "Suppose I'd won? What would I have given to India? Why was I fighting this election to begin with? To give something, not take something." I came to the thought that I should do what was important for me, and what was important for me was my son. What was I doing for him? I was putting away all the material possessions for him, his cutlery, his crockery, his linen, his education, his marital life, his jewelry. But if I couldn't leave him a glass of water, what was the point of all this? Or if I couldn't let him cross the street, or if he never saw a park to play in, or if he couldn't breathe without wheezing, or if he was ill every second day: I thought that I must do something. So I started traveling in India, and I said, "Let me not impose my views." I started seeing:

What is it that people want? How have they developed? What should happen? And from there I came into the environment. I discovered the word "environment" for myself, and studied and learned and read a lot, traveled a lot. Then I became the minister for environment, and found that the word "environment" was misspelled on the ministry's letterhead! When I became minister, India had no laws for the environment—none.

How did animals become central to your ideas about the environment?
I'd always been an animal person and, when my husband died, I opened an animal hospital the same year in his memory, which I run. But I'd never thought of fitting it into an agenda. For me it was something I did because I loved animals. But the more I studied in the environmental movement, the more I thought: "Why should animals be separate, and especially in a country where animals run the country?" If I remove the cow, we're all dead. It's a cow dung economy; it's not an open or closed or democratic or communist economy. If you remove the cattle from it, you might as well pack it all in, because there's nothing else. If you remove the cow, you need buses to bring things to market, and you don't have them. If you remove the cow, you need gas cylinders to cook on, which you don't have. If you remove the cow, you need pesticides and fertilizer. If you remove the cow you need something other than milk. Everything ties in right back to the cow, the buffalo, the bullock, the horse, the camel, the elephant, the dog—which is one of the biggest scavengers of the city—and the vulture, another big scavenger. Everything has its place, except Man. So then I thought that since nobody else is going to do it, I must bring animals into the environmental movement.

Can you describe the scope of the work you do?
I run an NGO [non-governmental organization] called People for Animals, which is an umbrella organization for practically all the animal work in India. We make shelters ourselves and fund other shelters. I also go around India and set up shelters. I get land from state governments and try and arrange money; I get animal groups organized to run the shelters. We have shelters coming up in lots of parts of India. We also put cases in court against animal cruelties. For instance, I had a case in court against using animals in the circus. And I had another one for zoos selling animals to the circus. We won a case against the slaughterhouse in Delhi which had to shut down because it was perpetuating so much cruelty. I'm the chairperson of the SPCA, and that involves inspections. I have 75 inspectors who patrol Delhi and have the power to give summonses. We prevent cruelties. We catch trucks which are overloading meat animals. I'm setting up another animal shelter for People for Animals which is the biggest *goshala*, or cow shelter, in India. It will have about 10,000 cows. It's already got about 600 cows, the stray cows of Delhi.

What are some of your current campaigns?

We are working on something called "Artists for Animals," in which we're making every film star sign a pledge that they won't work with animals. It's getting to be too much: they're shooting pigeons on screen, tripping horses, and they have tigers with their mouths sewn up, fighting with these macho stars. Then I have taken on the stopping of dog killing. Two to three million dogs are being killed every year in India because they are strays, supposedly to stop rabies. It has no effect whatsoever on rabies. So now we are trying to stop that program and replace it with sterilization and vaccination.

You are a very well-known person in India. How do you use that notoriety to further your causes?

I do a column called "Heads & Tails" every week for about 30 newspapers, and that's been collected into a book. I have two TV shows, one also called "Heads & Tails." It's the *ahimsa* show, in the sense that it shows animal cruelties, and shows people who are doing good work. It shows what you can do. I have another TV show on the environment, a six-minute show every week after the news on Sunday, which says that, for instance, when you use aluminum foil, you kill the tiger. The bauxite is mined in the Bihar forest. The Bihar forest houses the tigers; the big cat is killed first when mining starts. It shows you the interrelationships, the house of cards effect; how the aluminum was mined and where.

Was it hard to start work on these issues in a developing country, where there are so many pressing human needs?

For me, it wasn't a decision that was made looking at anything except the need—whose need was greater? And then, who would take it up? You know, it's very easy to do work with children, because that's politically correct. If I hadn't come into animal rights and environmental activism, quite honestly, nobody would have. It has to be one person who's confident enough to say, "I don't care what you say, it has to be what I know to be true." People in politics say, "You don't do for people, you do for animals? Where will your votes come from?" Really, the work has a vote multiplier effect, because you're seen as good.

You are the most visible person in India, in all of the developing world, doing work like this. How much support do you find for your work?

Well, I have a great deal of support. What kind of support it is, I don't know, because I have no idea what to do with the support! I'm learning very painfully, and it's taking a long time to be an organization person. I have about 30,000 members in People for Animals. I get about 80 letters a day, and those are work letters: "Can we donate land? Can we help?" But the point is, how does it translate? The setting up of bureaus and units is coming, but it's coming very painfully. State governments are very supportive, in the sense that if I want something, I get it. I don't know whether it's the work I do or who I am, but if I want land, I get it; if I want the government to stop something, it's done.

How important is vegetarianism to you and the work you do?
I came to the environment, then took up animals, and from there I decided that it is not just "animals' work"—I had to be vegetarian. I couldn't go around saving the one cat and one dog, which is what people mean when they say "animals"; it had to be saving the meat animals, or rather preventing them from being born. So, I had to do vegetarianism. I had to do *ahimsa*, which fitted the whole thing, the whole catchall phrase "environment, animals, vegetarianism." Everything comes into *ahimsa*.

What do you think about the term "animal rights"?
I think it's very important. But it shouldn't be separated from animal welfare. In America, because you're so rich and you're so bored, you invent debates, for instance the debate about abortion. It's so nonsensical. We're amazed that you people should be burning abortion clinics and killing abortion providers. The debate is so irrelevant to the rest of the world. If you want to have an abortion, have it. If you don't want to have it, don't have it. Why do you make a thing about it? And why lobby, and why go to Congress? The right of a person to their own body is the first right, before anything else. So, the same way, now you've invented the debate between animal rights and animal welfare. How can we separate the two? My child's right is to live, therefore I must look after the child. If I were to leave a one-day-old baby and say, "Right, now it's your life's right to live, bye-bye"—it wouldn't mean anything. So, welfare is tied into rights. What I'm trying to do in India is start from a position of welfare: first welfare, then rights. If I look at a donkey on the road and it's been run down, I can't take it home. If I don't have an animal shelter, the next time I won't even look; I'll just turn my eyes away because I'm ashamed. And the third time, I won't even be ashamed. So, if I'm to nurture it, then I must have first the shelter, then I have the rights. I see no debate.

There's a lot of talk about sustainable development, particularly in poor or developing countries. Can you talk about that?
Sustainable development is only possible with environmentalism. You could have, for instance, solar-energy roofing, which may cost a little amount to begin with but will not put a strain on the city system. That would be sustainable. You could have no pesticides. If you didn't have pesticides, you wouldn't need hospitals. So you would be saving money on the hospitals, and saving money on the pesticides. There are a lot of ways to do it quite simply and easily. But we have to realize that there is no difference between development and the environment. Environmentalism is everything. All of economics should be environmentally sound first. If it's environmentally sound, it's every-which-way sound. But there's no attempt to tie this into the economics which is taught in a university. You have to tie it into what you use; it should be taught as micro-economics. Teach me environmental economics. Teach me the science of interrelated crises. In India, environmentalism is taught in schools as singing and dancing.

32

What do you think the consequences of ignoring the environment/development connection would be?

Anything that is not done correctly is going to kill us. It's Kali, the goddess, who is the ultimate revenge-taker. You hurt her and she hurts you back. It's not some big-bosomed, cow-like creature sitting around being the Earth, you know. Our main economics are going awry the minute we kill all the animals and export them. Now India is Asia's largest meat exporter. We're feeding the rest of the world, but we're not feeding them meat. We're feeding them our water, our hillsides, our land. One slaughterhouse is using 16 million liters of water a day to clean its carcasses, and the meat is all exported to the Middle East. The slaughterhouse is next to the city of Hyderabad, which only gets water for half an hour a day. One of the things that's underemphasized in the environmental thought process is our right of health, whereas that should be the basis of environmental work. If you create the greenhouse effect, I'm going to go down. In the Seychelles now, 50 percent of their money is going in building barricades, because sea levels are rising.

Did you feel you could do more for animals and the environment when you were minister for environment?

Yes, I did. I felt that I could do a lot. I feel I can do exactly the same amount now, but in a different way—and by working much harder. Politics is the ability to call change. When I was minister, we shut down the circuses with animals. And when I stopped being minister, the Circus Federation went to court and got a stay in court, and the case has dragged on for four years now.

What's needed to get people to make the connection between animals and human beings, to see an animal not as dinner, but as a living, feeling being?

What we need is not love. Love is such a stupid word. I keep getting called "animal lover" and I keep saying: "If I were working with old people, would you say 'old people lover'? If I were working with AIDS patients, would it be 'AIDS lover'?" I'm not an "animal lover." I'm somebody who respects life. That's all. I just respect the right of this animal to be. And not to be interfered with, not to be genetically impaired, not to be used, not to be forcibly made pregnant like the cow is, not to be herded up and down. Just let it be.

But for so many people, that's such a leap.

But that's where we begin from. If you begin from respect, then you go everywhere. Love is so trivial. People say to me when they come and visit (I've got 12 dogs): "Oh, you must love dogs." I say: "Absolutely I hate them, hate them. They occupy the whole house. I'm a guest in this wretched house." But the point is, I respect their right to be. I make no demands on them at all. And they don't make any demands on me. We kind of coexist.

Eco-Kosher
Arthur Waskow

Rabbi Arthur Waskow is director of the Shalom Center based in Philadelphia, which in turn is part of ALEPH: Alliance for Jewish Renewal. The Jewish renewal sees itself as trans-denominational, seeking to create a Judaism which responds fully to the issues of modernity. Waskow is one of the popularizers of the term Eco-Kosher[1], an idea which sees *kashrut*—the way of eating, living, and being Jewish elaborated in the Torah—extending into environmental consciousness, organic foods, ethical investment and conserving energy. This will ultimately lead to *tikkun olam*, or a healing of the world. One of his books is *Down-to-Earth Judaism: Food, Money, Sex and the Rest of Life*.

"Shabbat is the opposite of both producing and consuming.
Shabbat is about rest, repose and reflection:
That is the real opposite."

What do you mean by "down-to-earth Judaism" and "the rest of life"?
There are three different aspects. One is the usual idiomatic meaning in English: daily life, everyday life, ordinary life. The second is that my book is maybe the first in a long time—I mean centuries—to study what Jewish practice means for the Earth: an aspect of Earth-orientation, Earth-concern. That thread runs through all four of the sections: food, money, sex, and rest—that is resting, restfulness. The third is a theology which isn't imposed by the book but certainly runs through it as an important thread: a much more earthy sense of God, in which one aspect of God is the seemingly material world itself, rather than focusing on the God who is above and beyond the world.

You have talked about Eco-Kosher extending outwards of the home (the word "eco" comes from the Greek for "home"). What do you mean by that?
What I say when I talk to Jewish communities is that through both the Jewish tradition and looking around carefully—Torah is both what's written and what's visible—it is not possible to create a sacred relationship with the Earth only in the household. The way in which the whole society acts is also a form of spirituality. People often—and modern America tries to get you to—divide up spirituality and politics. I think the division works a different way. There is such a thing as individual spirituality, family or communal spirituality, and there is social spirituality. The Torah says that the whole society should stop tilling the land for a year, the Sabbatical year, every seventh year, and then again in the fiftieth year after the seventh seventh (forty-ninth) year—so two years in a row—and the same on Shabbat (the seventh day). It was the whole society which rested. It wasn't, "If you feel like it." And it wasn't just Israelites in the narrow sense. The Torah goes out of its way to say that *everybody* who lives in the land, the home-born and the foreign-born, the convert and one who is still not an Israelite though living in the land of Israel, the servants as well as the free, the animals—all, everybody, and the plants too, because you don't cultivate them or harvest them—*all* get to rest for the sabbatical period. And it's essentially the same thing for the seventh-day Shabbat.

You cannot do a serious healing of the Earth in families only. If a specific Jewish household tries on its own to get rid of 50 to 90 percent of the use of its automobile in order to reduce the impact of oil, given the structure of society there would be very little way to carry it out. This society does not affirm mass transit, bicycles or other ways of getting around which don't impact the Earth. So people who have decided in their personal lives that they want to do XYZ with their food, paper, energy supply, or automobile, have to say to this society, "Where are the bicycle routes? Where is the mass transit?" etc. That's the social change: it is talking about spirituality in society as a whole. I, at least symbolically, have talked about what it might mean for the whole society to shut down for a day in each month. Not every week—I mean Shabbat—because that is too hard. But what about once a month? Shutting down does not just mean Labor Day, or Independence Day, or whatever, where you shut down the factories and offices but power up the airplanes, television, automobiles and gas stations. You should shut down the highways, airplanes and the television, and even the Internet. What would that do, even just directly, for the protection of the Earth? I mean, there would be less use of everything, and a challenge to the assumption that only making, doing, inventing and producing matters. Producing and consuming are not opposites—except of the same coin, literally. Shabbat is the opposite of both producing and consuming. Shabbat is about rest, repose and reflection: that is the real opposite.

Judaism has always taken seriously the killing of animals and the consumption of food. Do you think we need to go beyond killing animals humanely toward vegetarianism?

I spend a lot of time in my book struggling with the content of *kashrut*—which means especially the main elements: Which meat you are allowed to eat (it does not say you are not allowed to eat meat, but *which*); secondly, a very elaborate system for slaughtering the meat you are allowed to eat; and third, the notion of the total separation of milk and meat. Those things make up 95 percent of what *kashrut* is. I struggled with the first one. It is quite clear in the Torah—it is not just the opinion of vegetarians—that the ideal vision is vegetarian. But the people insisted on eating meat. God was sad about it, and said: "If you have to, you have to. But do not eat the blood and do not rip the limbs from a living animal." The nearest I could come to any satisfying sense of its meaning is that it affirms being a sort of vicarious vegetarian: If you ate animals they were to be vegetarian animals.[2]

A number of people have been arguing in our era that vegetarianism is the most authentic *kashrut*. That is partly because what it means to rear animals for eating has changed so much that if you really applied the rules of not causing pain and not causing degradation, etc., you could not continue to eat them. And given the enormous ecological impact from the massification of both human numbers and animal agriculture, it is difficult to accept current eating patterns. In fact, what is happening as far as I can tell within most of the generation of Jews under 35 is not always absolute vegetarianism, but a radical avoidance of especially red meat, and even chicken.

What practical stage is the Eco-Kosher Project at?

Recently, we have been thinking of setting up standards for congregations as Eco-Kosher: what it means to commit themselves and establish what standards we would apply. I would want to include public advocacy standards, to change the rest of society with our own consuming standards. My sense is that in the meantime what has happened is that all over the place people are using the word Eco-Kosher and understand what it means. In Berkeley in 1995 I even bumped into an Eco-Kosher Cleaning Service, which uses only environmentally responsible cleaning agents and is advertising itself as such. The answer to your question is that the idea has been spreading and the organizing of specific commitments and standards is beginning.

Christianity and Animals
Andrew Linzey

Rev. Dr. Andrew Linzey is International Fund for Animal Welfare Professor of Theology at Mansfield College, Oxford University, England. He is the author of a number of important books on Christianity and animals, most notably, *Christianity and the Rights of Animals* (1987) and *Animal Theology* (1995).

"In God's eyes, all creatures have value whether we find them cuddly, affectionate, beautiful or otherwise. Our own perspective—in a way—is neither here nor there. Theology, at its best, can help to liberate us from our own anthropocentric limitations."

Did you become a vegetarian prior to being ordained?

Yes, though the two things are not unrelated. When I was in my teens I had a series of intensely religious experiences. They deepened my sense of God as the creator of all things. And they also deepened my sensitivity toward creation itself so that concern for God's creatures and animal rights followed from that. Some people think I'm an animal rights person who just happens, almost incidentally, to be religious. In fact, it's because I believe in God that I'm concerned about God's creatures. The religious impulse is primary.

Have you exerted any influence on the Church of England's position on animal rights?

The Church of England is a very liberal, diverse community in which people have a wide range of views on a whole range of issues from sexuality to war. There are some signs of light. For example, in 1992, 41 bishops signed a pledge not to wear fur because of the cruelty inflicted on animals. I'm very proud of bishops because of their moral stance. But there are also many signs of darkness. For example, I attended the General Synod in 1990 about hunting and factory farming on Church-owned land. I came away from the debate feeling deeply depressed—not only because the pro-animal motion was overwhelmingly rejected, but also because there was a lack of theological depth and seriousness with which the whole issue was treated. Anglicans, like most Christians, haven't really woken up to the moral issue of our exploitation of animals.

Are there any vegetarian priests in the Church of England?
Some, perhaps a handful, but they tend to be vegetarians as a matter of health rather than on ethical grounds. Of course, there is an ascetic tradition within Christianity. It is possible to make a strong argument for ethical asceticism in relation to animals, but alas most of the ascetic tradition in Christianity has been involved in a way of thinking that can only be called "world denying" rather than "world affirming." It's been concerned with denying creative pleasure—indeed with denying pleasure itself as a means to some higher spiritual state. Generally, I think asceticism is an entirely false trail in religion. What I mean by "asceticism" is asceticism for itself. There is a strong case for "ethical asceticism," that is, denying those things that harm others. But asceticism in itself, I think, is misconceived.

The first chapters of Genesis strongly suggest that God intended humans to be vegetarian. Could you comment on that?
At the heart of the Judeo-Christian tradition is the dream of peace. Many people refer to how humans are given "dominion" in Genesis 1, and that's true. But if you look at the whole saga: in verse 27, humans are made in the image of God; in verse 28, they're given dominion; and in verse 29, they're given a vegetarian diet. Herb-eating dominion is hardly a license for despotism. The original author was seeking to describe a relationship, not of egotistical exploitation, but of care for the Earth. It's extraordinary that almost 2,000 years of biblical exegesis should so often have overlooked the radical vegetarian message in Genesis 1.

Of course, it's not only in Genesis, it's in Isaiah as well (11:6). Again there is this harking back, now futuristically described as the state in which the lion will lie down with the lamb. So, it's not just in Genesis that you have this idea that peace between all creatures is God's will and that killing runs counter to that will.

But what about life after the "Fall"?
I'm not sure I believe in an historical Fall. I think the Genesis narratives reflect an ambivalence about the morality of killing in the sight of God. You need to remember that the Hebrew writers who wrote Genesis were not themselves vegetarians. What they were trying to do was interpret the world in the light of their moral intuitions of what they thought God wanted, and who they thought God was. Genesis is their poetic narrative of how the world came to be such

a desperate and violent place. Their view basically was that God's will was for peace and non-violence between all species, but that human wickedness threw the whole system into chaos—so much so that God, for example in the saga of Noah, would rather us not exist at all if we must live and be violent.

Besides humans, are animals also the object of God's wrath? Do animals share in the expulsion from Paradise and the Fall?
The whole creation suffers as a consequence. Nowadays the Jewish tradition makes a very sharp distinction between humans and animals, but I don't see this sharp distinction in Genesis 1:9. After all, humans and land animals are created on the same day (the sixth). I would say that animals are inextricably linked by their creation so that when humans go wrong, the animal creation goes wrong too.

I'm inclined to believe that creation can never be set to rights so long as humans are so terribly violent. In that sense the colossal emphasis within the Judeo-Christian tradition on the salvation of human beings makes a lot of sense. My view is that the world of creation, and especially animals, will be redeemed as a matter of course. The only question is whether humans are going to be saved because they are often so faithless and violent.

But the fate of animals is inextricably linked with that of humans, isn't it?
I am one of those people who believe that humans need to be saved for the sake of creation itself. We know so little about animals and creation. One of my pet peeves is hearing people pontificate about what animals are or are not capable of—because the truth is we really don't know. All the stuff about animals not having language, not having rational souls, not having culture, not being persons—all of these are human constructions. And I'm not sure how far any of these kinds of things matter to God even if they are true. Part of me wants to ask how we can know that God does not fundamentally value some parts of creation, or regard them as much more intimate with Herself than human beings. All uniqueness-spotting on the part of humans is bound to be self-serving. Christians have been fiendishly good of course at drawing lines between humans and the rest of God's creatures.

I think what we really need is a theocentric view. In God's eyes, all creatures have value, whether we find them cuddly, affectionate, beautiful or otherwise. Our own perspective—in a way—is neither here nor there. Theology, at its best, can help to liberate us from our own anthropocentric limitations.

What about the question of Christ's having been a vegetarian?
If the canonical gospels are to be believed, Jesus was not a thoroughgoing vegetarian nor, it must be said, a feminist nor a believer in Home Rule for Israel. We must beware of remaking the historical Jesus in our own image. I don't think the contemporary Christian case for vegetarianism depends on Jesus himself being a vegetarian.

I think we have to ask what it would have meant for Jesus to have been a thoroughgoing vegetarian in first-century Palestine. It would probably have implied some association with Manicheanism. Manicheans were almost all vegetarians not on ethical but on ascetical grounds. [Manicheans believed in the radical separation of spirit, which was good, from matter, which was evil.] But Manicheanism was inimical to the thrust of Jesus' teaching. After all, Christians confessed their belief in God who had become incarnate in flesh and blood—in the very materiality that the Manicheans thought impure. Even today one of the problems it seems to me is that Christian theology is still Manichean in a way, that is, too otherworldly, too world denying. I think it is a great mistake to oppose the flesh to the spirit. Christianity is about the enfleshment of God in the incarnation.

I like the Rabbinical saying that when we get to heaven we shall have to account for every legitimate pleasure we didn't enjoy. For myself that provides a vast agenda in the present world, and I intend to take every advantage of it. [*Laughter*]

So, in a sense, our mistreatment of animals, and our eating of their flesh, is an impediment to our pleasure.
Absolutely! It's an impediment to spiritual pleasure. That's why I think vegetarianism is implicitly a theological act. It's not about saying "No" but about saying "Yes." About enjoying the lives of other creatures on this Earth so much that even the thought of killing them is abhorrent. I think God rejoices in Her creatures, takes pleasure in their lives, and wants us to do so too. So much of our exploitation of animals stems from a kind of spiritual blindness: if we sensed and really felt the beauty and magnificence of the world, we would not exploit it as we do today.

What about the depiction of Yahweh in Genesis and in various other places in the Old Testament as delighting in the odor of animal sacrifices?
It's just conceivable that those who practiced animal sacrifice did not understand it as simply the gratuitous destruction of God's creatures. It was in some ways thought of as the liberation and the returning to God of that life back to the very life source that caused everything to be. But, of course, there's no one view of animal sacrifices even by those who practiced it. And one finds, for example in Isaiah, the contrary view—a rejection of sacrifice as cultically, if not morally, unacceptable to God. From the Christian point of view, however, the important thing theologically is that Jesus did not sacrifice animals.

Jesus was seen as the ultimate sacrifice?
It's all expressed in that incredible line: "The good shepherd lays down his life for the sheep." Now, if you think about it in context, the shepherd did not lay down his life for the sheep. The shepherd slaughtered the sheep. By saying that, a whole new dimension of understanding is opened up. It is about how "the higher" should sacrifice itself for "the lower" and not the reverse.

What about the communion ritual itself? To some anthropologists, the drinking of Christ's blood and the eating of his flesh, however symbolic, smacks of cannibalism.

Well, Christians continue to celebrate the Eucharist with bread and wine; it does not contain dead flesh. I would go so far as to say that the Eucharist is the continuing expression of how Christ replaces the blood and flesh of animals. Christ becomes the true lamb. The theology is not, "Oh well, therefore we must go on sacrificing animals, because Jesus is the true sacrifice!" No! It's that Jesus has become The Sacrifice.

Is it wrong for ecologists and animal rights advocates to blame Christianity and Judaism for the rape of the planet and the "slaughter of the innocent" for thousands of years?

My answer is yes and no. On the one hand, it's right for animal rights people to be critical and judgmental of the Christian tradition. It has been amazingly callous towards animals. Christian theologians have been neglectful and dismissive of the cause of animals—and many still are. Christians and Jews have allowed their ancient texts—such as Genesis—to be read as licensing tyranny over animals, even though, as I have said, Genesis 1:29 commands vegetarianism!

On the other hand, animal rights people sometimes look on Christianity as though it was unambiguously "the enemy." I think it is wrong to write off Christianity in this way. All religious traditions have great resources for a very positive ethic in relation to animals. I would go further and say that however awful the record of Christianity has been, Christian theology has some unique insights fundamental to valuing animal life.

From my perspective, without a sense of ultimate meaning and purpose, it is difficult, if not impossible, to justify any kind of moral endeavor. If Christian societies have been awful to animals so also have atheistic ones. To my mind it's not self-evident that one should live altruistically or generously. The Judeo-Christian tradition and other world religions have the potential to give us a vision of ourselves in the world that we so desperately need. I'm one of those people who believe that morality really depends upon vision. Acting morally is to live in response to a vision of how we should be, and the truth is that the Judeo-Christian, Buddhist, Hindu and Jain traditions do have visions of how the world could be at peace.

More fundamentally still, like all the great reforming movements, animal rights depends upon a certain perception—insight—in our case about the intrinsic worth of animals. I think reason and rational argument are important in defending this insight and showing its intellectual coherence. But the spiritual insight, I think, comes first. In other words, we are about trying to help people see animals differently. For me, animal rights is first and foremost a spiritual experience and spiritual struggle.

Living Among Meateaters
Carol J. Adams

Carol J. Adams has been working within the fields of violence against women and children and vegetarianism and animal advocacy for over 20 years. She is the author of *The Sexual Politics of Meat* and *Neither Man nor Beast: Feminism and the Defense of Animals*. With Josephine Donovan, she has edited two volumes on feminism and animal issues, *Beyond Animal Rights* and *Animals and Women: Feminist Theoretical Explorations*. One of her most recent concerns has been the way vegetarians and meateaters discuss the meaning of what they do.

"I do not think we have to defend our diet.
I think we need neither apology nor defensiveness."

How do you live among meateaters?
One way I handle it is that I now ask them about it. On the plane once I sat next to a child psychologist and we talked about the fact that I had had a vegetarian meal and he had eaten dead chicken. It was fascinating because when you say you are writing about it, you can say to people: "So tell me. You've said that you know it's ethically wrong; so what happens when you sit down to eat meat?" Instead of being seen as someone saying, "Look, you're doing something wrong; why do you keep doing this?" I get to ask a question which prompts them to reflect on the process that is cutting them off from their own ethical awareness. The psychologist talked about having a hole in his conscience and I said that I didn't think that was the case because our whole culture says it is okay. "Well," he said, "We've got a collective hole in our conscience."

Do you feel angry?

When the *New York Times* devotes an entire article about the growth of factory farms and the effect of that on the environment and people, and it completely ignores animals, I feel very angry. But I take that anger and use it interpretatively: What does this represent? What's going on here? By theorizing it I can engage it even more, because I want to try and understand it and how we change it. Personally, I realized I needed to begin negotiating with people about what they were going to order at a restaurant, and giving myself permission to say what I want to say.

Sometimes what meateaters do is so blatantly open to analysis that it leaves me dumbstruck. What I have done is take that ongoing, maddening frustration and anger and move so they do not paralyze or immobilize me. I continue to see this whole thing as a process. After all, I used to be a meateater. I'm living among people who have not completed the process that vegetarians go through.

What about your own family?

One way we have handled this is by exiling ourselves. My whole family's in the north, while I'm in Dallas. I don't go home for most of the important rituals I would usually have to sit through. I can exercise that kind of control. I did successfully negotiate a vegetarian barbecue, where the only things barbecued were Notdogs and Boca Burgers. It was a big success, but I had to negotiate that in advance. Some of the family members are very interested in vegetarianism; and some of my family members are very gourmet and controlling. So we don't talk about it.

Meateaters are very happy eating vegetarian food, as long as they don't know it. One time, I made walnut balls, and everybody was convinced they were meat. They thought I had given in—"Oh, Carol has given in. And aren't these the most delicious. . . ?" They enjoyed it so much, thinking I had served them dead animals. It was so profound to me: because it was the symbol they were holding on to. Their stomach didn't know the difference; but as long as their minds were so lost, it didn't matter what was going into their stomachs. I realized it's the symbolism of meat that holds sway.

We should remember, meateaters live among meateaters, too. Everything they do is mirrored back to them as being OK. Another way I handle that is through a feminist understanding of social process. For me it is becoming more and more profound that the way pornography mirrors back a message about who women are is the way a meateating culture mirrors back a message about *what*—not *who*—animals are. Trying to reconfigure our conceptualization is very important.

I can't say I have a blueprint for how to solve these family things. Whatever issue a family or couple has, meateating and vegetarianism become vehicles for displacing those relationship issues that have not been dealt with. This makes it even more confusing. For a couple, for instance, the meateating/vegetarian issue will end up being about control: what can be brought into a kitchen; what pots can be used. All those things become media for controlling behavior and for manipulating issues about love and affection.

Why is that?

Let's look at the usual make-up of the couple. It's usually the woman who is the vegetarian and the man who is the meateater. In her book *The Sexual Contract*, Carole Pateman talks about the wife and the status of wives. Before we ever had rights talk, she argues, before this notion of "fraternity, equality, liberty," before the social contract that was foundational to Western philosophy, there was the sexual contract guaranteeing men sexual access to women. With sexual access to women comes the idea that every man should have a wife; and one of the duties of the wife is to serve the man.

I was thinking about this in terms of meat, because so many women say to me: "I could be a vegetarian, but my husband couldn't." Clearly they are deciding his moods are so important that the women cannot meet their own needs. Meateating becomes another vehicle for self-denial by placing the husband and his needs first. This relates to the way in which women become caretakers, and end up denying their own bodies and their own needs.

There is a fear of men's anger about not having meat at a meal. I do not mean a fear of being battered, because when men batter women and use meat as an excuse, that is not what is really going on. Men are battering to establish control, and the absence of meat is just their most recent excuse. Yet, there must be a lot of women who are fearful of what the absence of meat means to their husbands, and the kind of anger that that would generate. We are talking about people without any feminist analysis. They just know that not to offer meat would create anger, and perhaps require them to examine the relationship—one in which clearly they do not have as much power.

Do you think vegetarians should talk back, as it were?

It is important sometimes to talk back. First of all, I think vegetarians think more literally than others. Vegetarians are not seeing food; we are seeing a corpse, a dead animal. Because we think literally as well as metaphorically, our attempt to move the literal issue will arouse a certain degree of hostility and distress because our culture in general wants to move away from the literal. It wants to disengage. For instance, we do not want to know where our clothes come from. We do not want to know that the clothing is being made by children or women in terrible situations. We do not want the literal truth of what and how our culture produces "products" for us to consume to be known. Secondly, I always say that vegetarians should not engage the issue of vegetarianism if there is a dead animal present and being eaten. There is just too much tension.

Meat-eaters are going to need to justify what they are doing, even if they are not conscious of it, because they are consuming at the moment.

What I am trying to do is push and say, "What makes you feel upset?" I think the process is not so much for us to say why we are vegetarians, because we are on the other side of that process. The process is to figure out what is catalytic for each person. Instead of my defending vegetarianism while people eat meat; I ask, "How is it that you can keep eating meat when you know that it is cruel?" I do not think we have to defend our diet. I think we need neither apology nor defensiveness.

In the movie *Babe*, Babe has to establish his individuality and thus his irreplaceability. He succeeds in being seen as a body with a biography, an individuality, and thus he succeeds in staying alive. But there is also a duck trying to establish his irreplaceability. It is much harder for the duck to prove his irreplaceability because ducks are seen as collective. They are collectivized, seen in mass terms even when alive. But a duck is killed and the corpse is eaten at Christmas. At the end of the movie, the credits said that there was no cruelty against animals in this film. My six year old asked, "Does that mean they ate fake meat?" I felt that was so profound, because in our culture we do not think it is cruel to eat animals. A six-year-old vegetarian can just wipe away the whole culture of apology.

What we need to do is create a wedge. The child psychologist on the plane said that something innovative takes quite a while to be accepted. He predicted that 200 years from now people would not eat animals. I said, "I don't want to wait 200 years. That's a lot of animals."

How does a feminist ethic of care think about animals?
People who eat animals are benefiting from a dominant/subordinate relationship, but our culture encourages invisibility of the structures enabling this, and invisibility of the animals hurt by this. Indeed, the animals are seen as unified masses. There is a complete denial of their individuality, so that it is not seen as subordination. We see meat as the reason why animals exist, that they are there to be eaten. But when you talk about intervening with an ethic of care, one of the things you ask is, "What are you going through?"

It is not that we must say this empathetically only to other beings who can speak our language—as a way of connecting. We musk ask this of the "dairy" cow, the cow being milked, the chicken in a laying factory, and any animal slated to be killed: "What are you going through?" First of all, we need to see the legitimacy of that question, that animals are going through something, and secondly, we need to get educated about what that experience is. We need to trust that if we place ourselves in situations to learn the answer to this question, the animals will tell us, in ways other than words.

When people talk with each other, the person with the least amount of information sets the level of discourse. Consequently, the meateater—who usually has less information about meateating than the vegetarian does—sets the level of the discourse. The question is how one brings all the vegetarian knowledge in, because of the ignorance that is determining the level of engagement. This is one of the things that is so frustrating for vegetarians. We talk about creating a non-violent world, but there is so much that is paralyzing us from maintaining that analysis because of the level of ignorance at which the issue is engaged. What needs to be addressed is precisely what is excluded by the level of discussion.

What do you say to those who say vegetarians have a hang-up about meat? Because we live in a therapeutic culture right now, everything is going to be seen as an individual hang-up rather than as a political recognition and engagement. My answer is that vegetarians don't have a hang-up about meat. We have a problem with what people are saying is food. We are stepping back a level. People also say vegetarians are puritans and ascetics, with a hang-up about pleasure (the same charge leveled at anti-pornography feminists). But there is no pleasure without privilege, the privilege of being a member of the dominant culture that is dominating women, people of color and animals. We need to acknowledge the privilege and the social structures that create privilege, and the way the privilege is rewarded with pleasure, a pleasure which actually arises from harming someone else.

It all goes back in a sense to the privilege of controlling. To raise vegetarianism as an ethical issue says to our culture's self-defined principles: "What we claim we're doing is not what we're doing."

Beyond Discrimination
Shelton Harrison Walden

S helton Harrison Walden is the host and executive producer of *Walden's Pond* on WBAI in New York. It is the only radio program of its type in the United States. For the past decade, *Walden's Pond* has aired programs on animal rights, human rights, veganism, and the environment. During this time, Walden has interviewed many of the leading lights of the animal rights movement, including Gary Francione and Anna Charlton of the Rutgers University Animal Rights Law Center, philosopher Tom Regan, ex-cattle rancher turned vegan activist Howard Lyman, and vegan nutritionist Dr. Michael Klaper, among many others. Walden has pioneered coverage of many environmental and human rights issues such as mad cow disease [see Rowe, "Mad Cow Disease"], the Oprah Winfrey/Howard Lyman trial, the McLibel trial in Britain, male and female genital mutilation, and breast cancer issues. He has also reported on the First People of Color Environmental Summit in Washington, DC, the 1992 United Nations Earth Summit, and the United Nations Conference on Sustainable Development.

"Being an African American perhaps lets me understand manipulation and abuse more. I feel no one should be exploited or abused or taken advantage of; I dislike discrimination of any kind. My circle, however, simply extends to animals."

When did you first become aware of vegetarianism?
When I was seven years old, in 1969. I attended a small, alternative private school called the Living School on East 66th Street in Manhattan. The classes were very small and the atmosphere was what you might call "laid-back." I developed a schoolboy crush on my primary teacher—she was a tall woman with long blonde hair who announced to all of us that she was a vegetarian. She took us to

47

a lot of interesting events, such as the first Earth Day celebration in 1970, and the first-run version (R-rated) of *Woodstock*, the documentary of the rock music festival that took place in the summer of 1969. Anyway, since the object of my crush was a vegetarian, I went home to my mother and boldly announced that I wanted to become a vegetarian. Well, she was not too thrilled by my declaration and she stated that it was not the best choice—that I would get sick and that it was a strange religion. Well, I felt I really had no choice, since my mother was in charge of the food supply!

Did the teacher ever tell you why she was a vegetarian?
I don't remember that clearly. I do remember there was some discussion among the students about various aspects of vegetarianism. Some of the students said they were vegetarian as well.

So your potential vegetarianism went underground!
Yes! Fortunately or unfortunately, depending on your point of view, it resurfaced when I attended Pine Forge Academy in Pine Forge, Pennsylvania in 1976. That summer, I was mugged. My mother was understandably upset. So she sent me to this school in order to prevent such an event from occurring again. This particular school was run by the Seventh-Day Adventist church, which espoused a vegetarian philosophy, albeit a lacto-ovo form of vegetarianism. So, in essence, I was a vegetarian at school, but I ate meat when I came home on holidays.

So when your mother sent you to the Seventh-Day Adventist school, she really was making sure that your potential vegetarianism *was* some kind of religion!
That is really ironic, isn't it? But my mother feared for my safety so she sent me to Pine Forge Academy; I do not think she was really aware of the food philosophy of the Adventist church. But from my earliest days, I was always a finicky eater, so this probably helped in terms of my acclimation to vegetarianism. However, I only attended Pine Forge Academy for two years. My final two years of high school were spent at the McBurney School, a private high school (now closed) on the Upper West Side of Manhattan.

It was during this time that I consciously made the move into vegetarianism. I will never forget it. It was January 1980, and following a day of track practice at Van Cortlandt Park in the Bronx a group of us stopped at the local Burger King near the park. I believe I ordered a Whopper. I sat down and took a couple of bites and it tasted really sour and rancid. I put it aside and said, "I just can't eat this." From that moment on I never consumed a piece of red meat again. Subsequently, I developed more body awareness. I began eating more grains and cereals. I continued to eat fish and chicken products; of course, these products are just as deadly as beef, but I did not know it at the time. Following high school, I attended Fordham University at Lincoln Center in Manhattan, and during that time I continued to eliminate animal products from my diet. One of the first books I read during that time was Dick Gregory's classic book *Cookin' with Mother Nature*, which had a profound effect on me. I graduated from Fordham University in 1984, still on the vegetarian path. It was around Christmas 1984 that I finally decided to drop *all* animal products from my diet and go vegan.

There was no awareness of animals as such, the decision had more to do with your own body?
Correct. My body and my health were my major focuses. But one afternoon in late 1984 I was listening to the late Barry Gray's radio program and his guest was Nancy Anne Payton from the International Society for Animal Rights. They were discussing chickens and how they were raised. I was captivated by their conversation, and as soon as the broadcast was over, I called her organization and requested information. I began to attend animal rights meetings and functions and I gradually became a convert to the cause of animal rights. Looking for a way to share some of my ideas and thoughts with other people, I decided to explore the radio field (I was an avid radio listener). In 1986, I took a radio announcing class at the Center for the Media Arts (now defunct) and began to look around for a position in radio. A friend informed me that there was a training program at WBAI Radio here in New York, so I went to the station and two weeks later I started working as a part-time announcer at WBAI.

What about the environmental side? Was that a natural corollary which fitted into place when you got involved in animal advocacy?
I was always interested in the physical environment, the Earth, and pollution on a global level. But soon after I became a vegetarian I really began to make connections with animals and the way they are treated and manipulated and the way that affects our environment as human beings. I have always tried to bring that connection together—whether it be the use of rBGH (recombinant Bovine Growth Hormone), mad cow disease, hunting, factory farming, pesticides or fishing. When *Walden's Pond* was first created in 1989, I produced a lot of programs featuring activists, the marches and what was going on within the movement. Since then, however, I have focused more on the human angle.

Why do you think that is?
That is an interesting question. I have vacillated on that issue. I became disillusioned with the animal rights movement at some point because they didn't have a broad view of society. As an African American, I bring certain perspectives to bear on the issues and the movement, and I think it isn't as broad as I would like. So I have tried to branch out on my own and integrate different viewpoints. I focus on capitalism, multinational corporations, governments, institutions, and how they affect the environment. On *Walden's Pond* and when I hosted the WBAI Morning Show between 1989 and 1992, I extensively covered all these

intersecting issues. For example, in March 1992, I interviewed Jeremy Rifkin, author of *Beyond Beef*. His book discussed the rise of the cattle culture in the United States and how the government and corporations sustain the beef and dairy industries. A few years earlier, I interviewed Alix Freedman of the *Wall Street Journal*, who wrote a brilliant three-part series on how a poorer quality of food is deposited in black and Latino communities. In my mind, there is a clear link between animal products and the terrible state of human health.

How can the animal advocacy movement become more diverse, or is it still a "white person's luxury"?
I do not think the animal rights movement has done a good job of trying to reach out to black people and making the case of why African Ameriacns should join the animal rights movement. There are some people in the animal rights movement who are really not interested in reaching out to "people of color." Frankly, I also think black people have unfairly dismissed the animal rights issue; they should see that animals and humans have some definite similarities—as Marjorie Spiegel points out in *The Dreaded Comparison*. A lot of black people feel that animals rights is a luxury that people with time on their hands and money can indulge in and which is not relevant to most black people's lives.

How do you think that analysis fits in with your "conversion"?
I feel a sense of empathy with animals. Through no fault of their own, they have been manipulated by society for its own uses—whether for food or sport. On a very personal level, I had a turtle when I was younger and I really loved that turtle. To me, a turtle is a stark metaphor. A turtle is such a vulnerable creature in so many ways, tough but vulnerable. If you turn it on its back, it cannot function. I still feel close to that turtle. African Americans as a whole have been abused in many similar ways by society. Probably, being an African American helps me understand manipulation and abuse. No one should be exploited or abused. My circle, however, simply extends to animals. This is such a cruel society, compassion is drilled out of us at an early age. We need a standard of respect and civility, and that should include animals and our environment. But that is a broad intellectual leap for a lot of people—especially people of color—given the intense pressures of life.

A company such as McDonald's can offer jobs in neighborhoods where there is high unemployment and few opportunities. What can vegetarians and animal advocates offer in return?
It is very difficult to say, "Be patient until the health food chain comes along." Enormous dollars are involved in the establishment of a McDonald's franchise. The food is fast and tasty to the consumer market, and even the lighting in a McDonald's makes it a safe place in the neighborhood. I have repeatedly addressed this on my radio program. Several years ago I was listening to WWRL, a

black-oriented radio station in New York, when the host, Bob Law, who is well known for his black nationalist rhetoric, had a program featuring Carole Riley, the owner of several McDonald's in Harlem. Ms. Riley had turned the interior of the McDonald's restaurant she owned into Afrocentric dining rooms. I was appalled by the juxtaposition of Afrocentrism and hamburgers. Here was an international corporation that has a very poor record on health and environmental issues. Black people, brought here through the slave trade, have a terrible legacy of eating "soul food," i.e., heavily fatted animal products such as pork intestines, beef and butter. To entice with kinte cloth a community that has been burdened with poor health to consume more animal products is, in my opinion, disgraceful. I called Mr. Law's program and raised these issues with him and his guest. He immediately took umbrage with my questioning him and his guest on these matters. I hung up the telephone disappointed that the focus of the program was solely money, and not the genuine health of the community, in spite of the vociferous verbiage to the contrary.

Do you feel that movements for healthy food and animal advocacy will, therefore, have to come from within the African American communities?
Not necessarily. Black people listen to a myriad of voices on health, from inside and outside of the immediate community. But there is, as far as I can see, a growing and continuing concern with health in the black community. It may not go in the direction of animal rights, but it is coming very much from a position of survival. While that may also be true of the larger society, it is even more so in the black community. I came to vegetarianism from a concern over my health, but the more I read and experienced, the more clearly I began to see the connection with animal rights.

You have a particular concern for environmental racism. Do you feel the larger environmental movement is dealing with this? And are local activities being under-reported by both the environmental organizations and the mainstream press?
Yes, there has been an under-reporting of these issues. There has always been a contempt for poor neighborhoods, regardless of race. The largest toxic dump in the United States is in a poor neighborhood in Alabama composed of both black and white people. I recently saw a photography exhibition of people in Utah and Nevada who had lived downwind of nuclear test blasts which had happened in the 1940s and 1950s. Most of the people were white, and were being devastated by the nuclear fallout. Another example is the sewage treatment plant in Harlem, which was originally to be placed on the Upper West Side of Manhattan, but was placed instead in Harlem due to political pressure. There was a bitter battle over it, but it was still built, and the smell from it still permeates the neighborhood. There has been substantial documentation on the location

of toxic waste dumps around the country, and ther is a pretty clear the correlation between their siting and the neighborhoods they are in. However, race is a double-edged sword. Race has been played like a violin by some of the so-called leaders in the environmental racism movement. For instance, Benjamin Chavis, now Benjamin X. Muhammad, former chairman of the National Association for the Advancement of Colored People (NAACP), used the issue of environmental racism to push himself into the spotlight. It was later revealed that he was lobbying for passage of the North American Free Trade Agreement (NAFTA), widely considered detrimental to working-class jobs and environmental protection in the United States, at the same time. There is still an enormous amount of work to be done. There *is* environmental racism. It is enacted against *all* races, not just black people.

What do you think communities should do to help themselves?
This may sound simplistic, but children need to experience the great outdoors, away from the concentration of concrete and asphalt. They need to see the large expanse of land and see the forests (what's left of them) and other parts of the globe. In conjunction with this, there needs to be a greater environmental emphasis in the schools. We need an awareness of what we were over time. We need to know about our planet, soil and water. We need to know everything we can know about our existence.

Do you feel the message is getting out for people to make the connection between social justice issues and vegetarianism?
I really do not know—I certainly try to place my message in the public arena. Perhaps by listening to my program, people will be inspired to become vegetarianism. Very few African Americans (with the exception of Dick Gregory) speak out on animal rights. But I have to continue to plant wholesome seeds—that is the only way to move forward.

Do you feel you are sometimes considered the spokesperson for all people of color in the animal advocacy movement?
There are all kinds of black people; I certainly do not represent all black people. At the same time, I do come to the table with a certain set of experiences and I would like to be recognized for that. But the main point is to remember the issues we are working on—the ending of animal testing and hunting, and the establishment of a vegan ethic of life—and to keep working for those goals. But we must recognize that this is part of a larger aim to make society more compassionate and healthy. That is the way I see it.

Do the Right Thing
Dick Gregory

Dick Gregory was born in St. Louis, Missouri, and has been a humorist and social activist for over 30 years. He protested the Vietnam War by fasting for two years on fruit juice. During the fast he got many letters from schoolchildren saying that they were praying for the war to end so that Gregory could eat something other than uncooked fruit! Gregory and his wife Lilian have raised their ten children as fruitarians. Once obese himself (he weighed 288 pounds), Gregory has launched a national anti-obesity campaign. His book *Natural Diet for Folks Who Like to Eat: Cookin' with Mother Nature* was a best seller when it was published in 1973.

"Americans spend over $39 billion a year trying to get slim by following the wrong diet. Eventually, they will get tired of doing the wrong things, and they will start doing the right things."

Why are you a fruitarian?

The great thing is that it goes in and out of the upper and lower colon in 22 minutes, so that in 44 minutes you get the benefits of it; whereas, with anything else, it takes four hours in the upper colon, four hours in the lower colon, and it takes approximately eight hours plus to digest it. One day, when we really research it, we will find out how much of our energy is depleted through eating the wrong foods. When you cook anything or freeze anything, you destroy the nutrients in it. If you serve a child raw fruit and vegetables without salad dressing, he or she will go for the fruit, and they will never eat anything but fruit. Salad dressing covers up the flavor of vegetables. But you need salad dressing to slip the vegetables past your tastebuds. That is why there is a trillion-dollar industry in salad dressings.

How did you become a rawfoodist?
I just figured it out. If you put one hand in boiling water, and the other in the deep freeze overnight, neither of those hands will be any good: it must be the same way with food. Freezing and cooking food destroy the nutrients in it. When you stop eating for taste and start eating for nutrition, you'll start to feel a lot better.

Did Gandhi influence your decision to become a vegetarian?
No. When I became vegetarian, I didn't know that Gandhi was a vegetarian. Ninety-nine percent of people know that Gandhi fasted, but they don't know he was a vegetarian. I knew that he prayed and he fasted, but I didn't know he was a vegetarian until I got into it. When I got through checking out Gandhi, I realized that Gandhi never fasted over 13 days in his life. Gandhi influenced me through Dr. Martin Luther King, Jr., and the idea of peaceful resistance.

Do you use fasting as a political tool?
I think it is a violation to use it for that purpose. I use it for spiritual cleansing and to help me attain higher consciousness. When you use fasting for political ends, you violate the universal order. But occasionally I use it for that because fasting is one of the greatest weapons in the arsenal of non-violent resistance. I use it to make a point. In America, we lose more people from over-eating than from under-eating. So anytime you go on a fast, even people who resent what you're doing, when they sit down to eat, have to think about you.

America is the most obese nation on earth. Yet I'm optimistic. One of the most hopeful signs is the fact that Americans spend over $39 billion a year trying to get slim by following the wrong diet. Eventually, they will get tired of doing the wrong things, and they will start doing the right things. If America would spend $39 billion on trying to stop smoking cigarettes, I would see that as a good sign.

You don't mention your diet in your one-man show. Why not?
I try to take a gradual approach and put people in a transition period. If you were a good friend of mine, and if you were a heavy smoker, and if you were in a very bad accident, I would not come to the hospital and entice you to stop smoking because the one thing that a person needs when he gets into a crisis is his crutches. Then after you recovered, I'd try to get you to stop smoking. I remember that when I was a heavy smoker, the moment something happened—bad or good—I would reach for a cigarette. When I stopped smoking, my whole nightclub act went off. I didn't realize it at the time, but I'd been using the cigarette as a prop. I'd tell a joke and the whole joke would be set to the rhythm of my smoking.

Reclaiming Our Health and Our Earth

John Robbins

John Robbins is the founder of EarthSave and author of the best-selling *Diet for a New America*, in which he details the horrific conditions for animals on factory farms and intensive farming's devastating costs to the environment and human health. He is also the author of *Reclaiming Our Health*, which examines the medical establishment's efforts to eradicate natural childbirth, midwifery and non-toxic cancer cures, all the while sponsoring tobacco, radiation and fierce personal vendettas against those practicing alternative medicine.

"If we are going to survive, if we are going to transform our relationship to ourselves and each other and the greater world, nothing is more important than each of us taking responsibility for our lives and our actions and our choices."

How should we rethink our political structures to be more responsive to environmental concerns?

We need to ask our politicians to be responsible for the greater good. The Iroquois used to talk about the responsibility to the seventh generation hence as a criterion for all their decisions. In our politics, our criterion generally is next quarter's profit or this month's election. The result is short-term profit and long-term disaster. The result is an economic policy that is devastating the biosphere, violating the web of life and rendering the Earth increasingly uninhabitable. One of the problems that we have in our political structure is the degree to which special interests dominate the thinking and the actions of politicians. It's a frightening thought from the point of view of public health.

What can individuals do, then?

Norman Cousins said that nothing is more powerful than an individual acting out of his or her own conscience who's helping to bring the collective conscience alive. I don't know that we can measure or grasp the power or the impact of an individual's function connected to a core value.

The media report a certain level of event and call that news. But there are other things occurring that the media don't notice or recognize, things that do not get validated in our culture that much, but may be even more important in the long run. If we are going to survive, if we are going to transform our relationship to ourselves and each other and the greater world, nothing is more important than each of us taking responsibility for our lives and our actions and our choices. Different ones of us have different fields of action in which we find ourselves. Some of us may be in a position of more public exposure than others. But we all interact with other people a great deal.

I think that the fundamental unit of social change is the human heart.

How do you square individual freedom with forcing unsustainable practices to change?

People don't like to be told that the way they are living is wrong. People don't like to feel criticized. Yet the way we, as a culture, are living is wrong in that it is ecocidal. As a society, we live without respect for other forms of life. We live without a sense of our interconnectedness with the rest of the Earth community. We define success in material terms, as the ability to acquire things and consume resources. We take pride in our ever-growing gross national product, not realizing that this means ever more gallons of gasoline burned, ever more toxic waste produced, ever more forests converted into shopping centers, ever more pollution and destruction of the life-support systems.

I have had cynical moments in which I have thought that the United States citizenry will only become concerned about environmental destruction when it begins to interfere with their television reception. But more and more I sense that it will be the human health consequences that follow ecological collapse that will awaken us. The depletion of the ozone layer leads directly to higher rates of skin cancer and cataracts. Air pollution causes lung cancer, emphysema, asthma and other forms of respiratory disease. Lead and other heavy metals spewed into the environment by industry produce central-nervous-system poisoning. Pesticides and other toxic chemicals cause birth defects, cancers and auto-immune diseases. So does nuclear radiation. Acid rain not only destroys our forests, it damages all kinds of crop growth, and hence directly affects crop yields, leading to more malnutrition and hunger. As the number of malnourished and hungry people in the world rises, many infectious diseases become more virulent, because these people are immune-compromised, and function as walking petri dishes.

56

Martin Luther King, Jr., once said, "We will either learn to live together as brothers,"—I would add, "and sisters,"—"or we will perish together as fools." He was prophetic, not just in terms of social justice but in terms of modern immunology and the health crisis of our time. Therefore, while it is true that the changes that are needed to create a healthy planet run in a different direction than the prevailing political and economic drift, as Bill McKibben says, "That does not mean change is impossible. All it means is that our politics is, temporarily, out of step with the chemistry and physics of the Earth."[1] Life is change. We are all always changing. And people tend to become very angry when they realize that companies and individuals have made tremendous profits through activities that destroy the health of people and the environment.

What are the connections between large corporations profiting from people's illness and the American diet?
In modern agribusiness-dominated agriculture, we have systems of producing meat that treat animals as commodities, without any regard whatsoever to their natures. The conditions are a total violation of who these animals are. Every single one of their natural instincts is frustrated: they have no space to move around, the diets they are fed are deplorable from a health point of view as well as a humane point of view, and the whole thing is propped up with a tremendous amount of pharmaceuticals. We are the only industrialized country that implants our beef cows with artificial hormones; we now inject recombinant Bovine Growth Hormone into our dairy herd. The degree of reliance on drugs in modern animal products is really sad.

Similarly, in our medical system, the body is treated as a machine rather than a sensitive field of energy, possibility and awareness. Sick people are treated as a market from which to make money, rather than human treasures to cherish and serve. In Western medicine, health is defined merely as the absence of symptoms. So there is this objectifying and exploitative treatment of the human being.

We spend more money on what we call healthcare (it is really "sickness care") in this country than any other country in the history of the world. We are also number one in malpractice suits. But we're twenty-fifth when it comes to infant mortality and it's getting worse each year. Thirty years ago, the cesarean rate in this country was only six percent. Now it is 23 percent! Nearly a quarter of the women who give birth in the United States today have their babies surgically removed from them. And the same obstetrical establishment that is responsible for this trend denounces midwives, home births and freestanding birth centers—all of which show better outcomes for mothers and babies.

Birth is an incredibly important event, because if you violate the mother–child bond, if you remove a woman from her experience of birth as a sacred act of immense power and instead make her feel that she must rely on a physician to get her baby out for her safely, you have disempowered her in her relationship with her newborn and her relationship with her own body at a profound level.

What would be your solution to the healthcare mess?
America is the only fully industrialized country in the world that does not guarantee minimum health care to every citizen. There are 42 million Americans with no medical insurance, and another 30 million who are seriously under-insured. Those numbers are both increasing. It is a scandal.

Some form of national insurance, some form of universal health care, is inevitable in this country, and I think it is a good thing. If we had universal health care, then those people who don't take care of themselves and have very high medical bills would in effect be draining the public pool. Any good system will have incentives built into it that encourage people to take good care of themselves.

I would like to see a form of universal coverage, but with a substantial deductible. The deductible would be based on income, so someone who is poor would have a much lower deductible than someone who is wealthy. The biggest cause of bankruptcy in the United States is medical care costs, whereas in Canada no one ever goes bankrupt due to illness or injury. I think we can achieve that same level of compassion and have everybody covered for catastrophes, or emergencies, or serious problems, and yet, unlike Canada, build an incentive system, whereby you pay the first bit and then co-pay for a while after that. In this way, you can't just merrily eat your bacon and eggs for breakfast and then take your cholesterol-lowering pills and think all will be well.

I would start taxing heavily all those products and activities that have been shown to be damaging to human health and to the health of the planet. The environmental polluters would pay heavily, as would the tobacco industry. We should be heavily taxing those products that are damaging. I would like to see a system wherein those activities that harm health are discouraged, so there would be fewer of them taking place. There would be less illness, less suffering and lower medical costs. Because people would be paying, by virtue of their deductibles, for their maintenance care, they would be in charge and could avail themselves of holistic alternatives, rather than being prisoners of their "benefits."

Vegetarianism

Becoming a Vegetarian
Martin Rowe

In January 1989, having shown neither much inclination nor any indication, with neither fanfare nor great enthusiasm, I decided to become a vegetarian. I moved out of my parents' house into one which I shared with two other people who also called themselves vegetarian.[1] I should be accurate here. When I say I decided to become a vegetarian, I mean precisely that: I decided to *become* a vegetarian. This involved, initially, no longer eating land and air animals. I still ate fish and, convinced, as are many of us who eat, that I would need some form of animal protein to keep healthy, I stocked up on cheese, milk and eggs.

Not that I didn't *call* myself a vegetarian, mind you. I did, and was rather pleased with myself for doing so, although I cannot quite remember *why*. Nevertheless, so self-satisfied was I, that, at an end-of-year dinner outing with my company, fate decided not only that I should choose lobster for my entrée but that the waiter would come and show me the unfortunate animal squirming in his hand before he took it away for the cook to boil it alive. A colleague asked me how I could reconcile the eating of lobster with the fact that I didn't eat other animals. I muttered something about cows being more physiologically complex, and therefore more ontologically important animals, than lobsters, and left it at that—hoping that using big words would hide the big hole in my argument (or at least in my conscience). It didn't. Within a couple of weeks I resolved not to eat sea animals anymore.

For the next few years I began to think more deeply about vegetarianism, and allied it with a growing interest in environmentalism and social justice. It was only a few years later that I became concerned about other aspects of the exploitation of animals—such as vivisection and hunting. In September 1993, I moved house again and stopped eating all animal products. I also began to reduce the amount of leather, wool and silk I wore.

That kind of personal confession about vegetarianism is likely to be the first thing you hear when dealing with vegetarians. This is because what human beings choose to eat and why is not—and cannot be—something you just keep to yourself. As everyone from anthropologists such as Mary Douglas and Claude Lévi-Strauss to the leaders of the world's great religions have realized, there is much more involved with food than sustaining the body. What is permissible to eat and what is taboo or unclean; whom one can eat with and when; the rituals of feasting and fasting—all these are bound up in things larger than the personal. Food is a cultural phenomenon and eating a social act. It can define a people and likewise tear them apart.[2]

Much of the cultural give-and-take of different societies through the ages has revolved around meat. Throughout history, human beings have been used to seeing meat and its metaphors as things of substance. Meat has been associated with power and privilege—not merely because it used to be (and still is in many places) the fare of the rich, but because we believe that we somehow take in the muscle or even the essence of the animal when we consume it. Meat is associated with celebration and its taste with texture. To the contrary, not eating meat is equated with eating only vegetables (although vegetarians can, of course, eat much more than vegetables). Vegetables—as their metaphors attest—are thought of as dull, static and unpowerful. Through metaphorical association and (unfortunately) occasional experience, vegetarian food is thought of as bland, and vegetarianism's long association with asceticism in religious traditions only adds to the feeling that vegetarianism involves self-denial and a distaste for life.

Vegetarians choose not to eat meat for many different reasons. Some do so because they do not like flesh—whether it is its taste or because it is esthetically unappealing. Others do so because they feel empathetic toward animals and thus do not consider them suitable food. Some carry these feelings forward and refuse to eat meat because of the confinement conditions under which modern farm animals live, while others become vegetarian because they recognize the burdens that modern agricultural practices have placed on the environment and natural resources upon which we all—human and non-human—depend.

In the last couple of decades, as more and more people have begun to view vegetarianism not merely as a fad but as a lifestyle possessing integrity and reason, there has been a concurrent emergence of the recognition that eating meat is at the very least deleterious for your health and at worst supporting cruel and unsustainable practices. I often hear, "Oh, I don't eat very much meat," or "I used to be a vegetarian," or "I *love* animals" used by people who want to feel engaged in the dialogue about what is good to eat without necessarily *becoming* vegetarians. What is being realized, slowly, is that all food involves a *choice*, and that it is necessary not only for vegetarians to explain their diet, but also for meateaters to explain theirs.

The growth of vegetarianism has truly been remarkable. There are over 500 cookbooks in print in the United States with the "V word" in the title, and more and more restaurants are becoming comfortable with vegetarian options. Yet there is some confusion as to what vegetarianism is, exactly. For instance, in a *Vegetarian Times* poll conducted in 1991, 12.5 million Americans, or seven percent of the population, defined themselves as vegetarian. A similar poll taken more recently for the Vegetarian Resource Group, however, found that only one percent of Americans do not consume the flesh of animals. It seems unlikely that the loss of some ten million people to meateating is solely due to the relative difficulty of maintaining a non-flesh diet in the United States today, where some of the largest advertisers in the media are fast-food meat joints. It seems much more likely that the disparity between the two polls is due to the fact that people like to think of themselves as vegetarians, and call themselves such, before they actually stop eating meat. I can understand that.

One of the reasons there are more people who claim to be vegetarian than actually are is the reaction of friends and family to those who say they have become a vegetarian. To your relatives and friends, who have known you until then as a blameless omnivore startlingly indifferent to the fate of your health, the animals or the planet, it all seems baffling. "Why?" is a question often directed at vegetarians, followed by "What do you eat?" or "What's wrong with . . . ?" or "Do you wear leather?", etc. All these questions—which are important, make no mistake about it—are often unfortunately asked by the meateater not in a tone of genuine inquiry, but aggressively. It is as if the questioner wants to catch the vegetarian and prove his or her inconsistency. In short, the meateater feels challenged by vegetarianism—even if the vegetarian has done nothing more than order the vegetable plate at a steakhouse.

We are, therefore, caught in a bind. People want to call themselves vegetarians but don't want to be held to it as a creed. If they are, they will be subjected to the kinds of questions included above. It's not fun when you are trying to do something you think is right to be made to feel like a hypocrite or morally lax by those who don't feel *they* should be made to question their habits—or, worse, don't want to do anything to change. That being said, there are those who hold vegetarianism as a creed and forget the steps and self-analysis that led them to becoming a vegetarian, and so appear self-righteous or overly aggressive. I can understand that, too.

Nevertheless, what vegetarianism is or isn't may become increasingly moot as it becomes more and more evident that vegetarianism is not just a fad associated with the alternative lifestyle of health nuts or those with sentimental attachments to animals. It may, in fact, be the only way the burgeoning world's population can be fed. It may be one way of halting the erosion of topsoil and riparian habitats, along with the draining of underground aquifers due to overly intensive animal agriculture. It may be one way of lessening the chronic rates of heart disease and cancer that afflict the developed—and, increasingly, the developing—world. It may be one way to reduce the epidemic of obesity that is widespread in industrial nations. It may be one way to stop the destruction of precious habitat—from the overgrazed prairies of the American West to the decimated ecosystems of the world's rainforests. As such, the supposed pleasures of the flesh may have to be replaced by the myriad sustainable ones of a plant-based diet.

But that doesn't mean that vegetarianism shouldn't be fun. Vegetarianism should not be about self-denial or a distaste for life. It should be celebrated in fact for what it can be: a realization of a better and more conscious self, as we recognize the multiplicity and richness of life beyond the narrow confines of our tastebuds. In this manner, vegetarianism is both encompassing and catalytic—expanding outwards to draw in all those who are in need of nurture and sustenance on this planet, and being the engine by which you can go about your daily life and interact with your fellow beings. Becoming a vegetarian won't by itself absolve you of your sins, lead to spiritual enlightenment or even make you a more attractive individual. Nor will it guarantee good health. Even though numerous studies have shown that a plant-based diet (which is low in cholesterol and high in fiber and nutrients) is better than the fatty, low-fiber one that is currently the staple of the industrialized world, there are too many other factors—environmental, genetic and economic—to make the correlation a matter of "Go vegetarian and save your life."

For me, vegetarianism was never just a matter of being healthy. It was a matter of reinvigorating the meaning of choice—especially in an area in which for 24 years of my life I hadn't even thought there was one. We live in a world full of choices and responsibilities—and these do not stop when we sit down at the dinner table. In the end, whether you become a vegetarian or not is up to you. But it's a choice that can never be deferred for long, because you always have to eat. It is my hope that by examining our choices consciously and beginning to take some responsibility for what we do, we will find ways to live sustainably and consciously on this planet.

From Not Eating Meat To Vegetarianism

Stacey Triplett

I am becoming a vegetarian. I stopped eating meat (all animals) a few months ago, but today I realized I'm becoming a *vegetarian*. Through one simple encounter. I was at a conference—you know, the typically large-room, strangers-as-tablemates, everyone-trying-to-pay-attention-to-the-intro-ductions kind of affair, when it came. The lunch was served. The others at the table would be dining on salmon, and I needed to request the "alternate" meal. I negotiated finding the hostess and getting the new plate to my table just fine, convincing myself of my "non–meateating" status. But I became a *vegetarian* when my lunch became the table topic.

I was sitting next to a woman whose granddaughter is a vegan. She began the inquiry with, "Are you one that doesn't eat anything at all, or do you eat dairy and eggs still?" I almost asked her, "One what?" because my vegetarian status was unclear to me.

I should digress to tell a bit of why I wasn't eating meat. I have vegan friends with whom, back when I was eating meat, I had always consciously avoided engaging in conversations regarding meat and its politics. That was a defensive strategy, driven purely by self-interest. When accidentally we talked about their views on the subject, I found myself in the uncomfortable role of recognizing my participation in the raising and slaughtering of animals for my consumption and then (in order not to be caught in the contradiction of my practices) beginning to defend industries that, in many aspects, are indefensible.

My "evolution" continued as I finally recognized the untenable nature of my eating meat. I didn't believe it was necessary for my survival to eat meat; on the contrary, I think my participation in a clearly abusive and in many ways unnatural industry is against the image I hold of myself as a person who values exercising my power to manifest that which I believe is right and truthful. I have always considered my life to be one in which a stance I take is supported with actions; I can get really down on people who do (or don't do) things because they *feel* like it (or don't). Furthermore, as an African American I am frequently on the receiving end of empty statements, code words, and ill-thought-out arguments which mask and then unmask racist attitudes. In my own responses to the issues around the production of meat, I recognized the same type of empty statements coming from *me*, standing in for real discussion.

The description of conditions within the animal-slaughtering industries for the workers and the animals alike made my support through purchasing meat equivalent to strike-breaking or other actions that would place me on the opposite side of those things I hold to be just. To put it another way, if I could stop buying grapes in support of the rights of farm workers, I could also stop buying meat for the good of the planet. But I wasn't sure I could do it.

Wasn't meat part of my diet for longer than I could remember? Yes: I didn't know what living without eating meat would be like. Would I always be hungry? What would I eat in restaurants? Would I have to stop going out altogether for lack of things to eat? I told myself I would try not eating meat for a while to see if I could. I didn't tell anybody (even those who had a hand in my change), just in case I couldn't live up to it.

So far, so good; by now I have told people about "not eating meat" and except for one slip (when a good friend of mine forgot and served me lasagna that I felt badly about picking to bits), I've been fine. Until today that is. Today I joined a new class (as if I'm not in enough categories already—African American, female): vegetarian. All this time, I had been "just not eating meat." I didn't tell people the political reasons I found meat to be "wrong," I just left the impression I didn't meat, and surprisingly no one asked why. Until today. My theory on why no one had wanted to know why I didn't eat meat goes back to my own past aversion to discussing the politics of my friends' vegan lifestyle with them.

So when I was "outed" by the woman sitting next to me into discussing what had been a newfound integrity regarding the choices I made about my diet, I was unsure how to handle it. I decided to try answering with honesty, all the while preparing myself for an attack. "No, actually, I do eat dairy and eggs still, but I don't eat any meat," I answered, slightly annoyed at the tone, but curious as to how this would continue. The woman then told me that her granddaughter was someone who "didn't eat anything," and that although she couldn't say it had negatively impacted her granddaughter's health, she had felt more comfortable when her granddaughter was "just a vegetarian." I asked her why she felt that way. She answered obliquely: "Well, do you wear leather shoes?" I said I did, but wondered aloud if she thought she would use me to build up a case to make to her granddaughter. Luckily for me (since I would have felt responsible for her new assault on her granddaughter's choices) she said that she wouldn't, that she was just curious, and that she hadn't really thought about why she was more comfortable with her granddaughter the vegetarian, and not the vegan.

She asked what I had eaten (pasta alfredo with vegetables) and remarked that her granddaughter wouldn't have eaten that. It was then I realized that she was wondering some of the same things about her granddaughter's diet as I had about my own when I had decided to stop eating meat. Almost relieved, I rattled off all the things her granddaughter could have eaten at the table and those that they were likely to keep in the kitchen for just such occasions. We had a pleasant exchange of recipes and ideas for main dishes that everyone can enjoy.

I guess I should have thanked her (as well as my vegan friends); in just a couple of minutes I gained a new affiliation that will enhance who I become and what I am.

From Varanasi to Vegetarianism
Jason Freitag

The city of Varanasi in India is world-renowned as a place where pilgrims go to bathe in the Ganges, or to be cremated and have their ashes placed in the river, thereby ensuring their entry to heaven. Purportedly founded by the god Shiva, it is the holiest city in India and one of the oldest inhabited places in the world. Cedar Grove, New Jersey is not. Yet, for me, the two created a particular kind of *darshan* (vision of the divine).

The dawn boat ride on the Ganges is one of those prototypical activities that are advertised in all of the tourist brochures touting India. The images of the banks of the river teeming with pilgrims in the glow of the first light of day are supposed to be a testament to the spiritual power of this most holy of holy places. As a student of India, and an ardent antagonist of prototypical images, I admit extreme skepticism. I had not gone there to find God or a guru, nor to save my soul and, in the end, neither occurred. I went in the spirit of honest discovery, to see things.

Only the first signs of the rising sun were visible, but the sky was getting brighter as we approached the river. "We" were my auto-rickshaw driver Ram and myself. When we reached the river, Ram told me that he knew a good boatman. I don't know the boatman's name, and I am not sure I ever did. He was slightly shorter than I, but much thinner. He was muscular and sinewy from all the rowing and he was missing a number of teeth. The boat was a long, wooden canoe-shaped vessel, with two or three wooden slats across for seats. There was a small puddle of dirty water sloshing around the bottom, and I was reassured to see that it didn't seem to be growing.

The stereotypical images of hundreds of people gathering on the stepped platforms leading to the river, bathing and wading next to meditating *sadhus* (holy men), are all true. In person, though, the interpretation changes radically. Children are splashing and playing, as if they are spending a day at the beach. Next to the bathers performing ablutions, there are *dhobis* (clothes washers) scrubbing and rinsing clothing. Each day, amidst the sacrificial pyres on the *ghats* (the platforms leading down to the river), ashes and garlands, children play and a steady stream of laundry soap enters the river. This is a powerful apprehension: the most sacred of places is also the most ordinary.

As we moved up the river, the boatman told me I had better take pictures in our current spot and put the camera away, since people did not like tourists to take pictures of the burning *ghat*. A few hundred yards up the river, I could see a series of four or five small fires, letting off a light white smoke. I understood, snapped the pictures, and stowed the camera in my bag. As we got nearer, I could see the pyres more clearly. They were mostly burnt out—smoldering piles of black ash and bamboo—with only one flaming brightly. I looked in the water and saw charred bamboo poles, with garlands of flowers attached, float by.

The trip had ended. The sounds of the *dhobis* pounding the soap out of clothes echoed in the background.

I had been back from India less than a week. My parents had invited my partner and me for a summer evening dinner. Cedar Grove is a middle- to upper-middle-class suburb of New York City, about 15 miles to the west. The lawns are well manicured and there are two cars in every driveway. The prototypical images of American suburbia are actually quite true. We were on the deck in the backyard. The gas grill was fired up, and my father was the grill master. He lifted the grill cover, and the very familiar smell of chicken cooking over a fire wafted across the deck. I have smelled this smell hundreds of times before. This time, however, it had more resonance—I had smelled this somewhere else, or in some other context. I could not immediately place it.

The conversation continued for a few moments—so-and-so is getting married, so-and-so is late in arriving. Then, in a gentle wave of recognition, it came to me. The smell of the chicken on the grill in Cedar Grove was exactly the same as the smell of the funeral pyres on the Ganges in Varanasi. As I began to reflect, it became clear just how much sense this made. They were both burning flesh.

Burning flesh. This is an abrasive way to describe the chicken, and an even more horrific way to refer to the funeral pyre. They share so much, though. The sacred fire of Varanasi carries out its quite ordinary daily routine. The sacred coals of the barbecue in New Jersey also carry out a quite ordinary routine. These events in their contexts are not extraordinary. They become extraordinary in their juxtaposition—when they are linked. The realization of the conjunction was not as a bolt from the blue, or a sudden vision of peace for all creatures. It was a basic and involuntary olfactory reaction that set off a chain of thoughts. It was a simple recognition of identity.

This recognition had a profound effect on my relationship to food, there is no doubt. I have eaten solely or largely vegetarian ever since, and I am acutely aware of what (in a very basic sense) I eat. This very simple association, however, led to a much more powerful thought. This realization of the equality of humans and animals illuminates the base, the profane, in the apprehension of the sacred. I do not feel like a changed man. I do not feel that I have a radically altered vision of the world, and I tell this story very infrequently. This happened quietly, in the ordinary course of life, and that is my lesson.

Let Us Eat Plants

Tom McGuire

At one time or another, vegetarians must confront the inevitable: defending what we eat against an onslaught of detractors, pessimists, naysayers and staunch advocates of the dietary status quo. George Bernard Shaw referred to these unrepentant legions as "the outside anti-vegetarian world."[1] When questioned about his standard fare of fruits, grains, nuts, seeds, vegetables and assorted plants, Shaw fired back, "Why do you call *me* to account for eating decently?"[2]

For the most part the debate rages in the spirit of enlightenment and sharing information, and the questions are reasonable, if a bit naive: Do you get enough protein? What else do you eat besides tofu? Don't you miss turkey at Thanksgiving? Why are you a vegetarian after all? The feistier, more entrenched flesh-eaters, upon hearing of the ethical considerations, scoff and trivialize the issue. However, a vegetarian is at some time obliged to fend off variations of a seriously posed question: If I am so opposed to killing animals, how can I justify "killing" plants? Flesh-eaters, it seems, are trying to turn the moral tables on vegetarians by guilt-tripping with their "plants have feelings, too" line. How can vegetarians tread the moral high ground when we, too, kill and destroy living things: plants? Up against such sophistic reasoning, how many vegetarians have felt taken to the philosophical cleaners?

The most common objection vegetarians must defend against is "Plants feel pain, too, and if all things feel pain, what difference does it make which thing we inflict pain on?"—as though harvesting garden vegetables or picking ripe cherries is tantamount to enslaving, torturing and slaughtering animals! As Gabriel Cousens, MD, author of *Conscious Eating*, says, "Our very existence causes some sort of pain on the planet, but there is a relativity to it."

No reliable scientific evidence has ever been presented which documents plants being able to feel or perceive pain. Plants do not have central nervous systems, the only bio-physiological mechanism or indicator known which would enable them to suffer a discomforting, joyless existence or experience agonizing sensations of pain. Although many point to *The Secret Life of Plants*[3] as proof positive that plants are sentient, their ability to sense and take cues from their environment, to stimulate growth and to ensure the survival of their species through strategies of natural selection are not in question here. It's their ability to sense and experience pain that we're talking about, and even if plants can feel pain in the same way that animals can, Cousens notes, "to even the most callous observer, the experiences are magnitudes different in pain and violence."[4]

The idea that one can be cruel to plants is ludicrous. You can't torture or inflict cruelty on a plant, nor deprive it of a fulfilling life. The only duty we have toward plants in using them as food resources is to water them regularly and let them grow healthily without toxifying them with chemicals and pesticides. (On this count, we fail morally.) Unlike animals, plants are naturally immobile, rooted to one small space in the earth for their entire life's duration, "to draw nutrition, propagate and rot," as Alexander Pope observed.[5]

Plants are not forced to conform to cages or pens, but the practice of confining and immobilizing animals is in opposition to their free-roaming nature. Furthermore, animals are social beings: they raise and nurture offspring, mate and bond for life in some cases, perform collective activities, and travel and move about in groups, flocks, herds and even schools. They have personalities, we give them names, we commune with them—not true with plants, unless you happen to be one of the extremely rare individuals with psychically attuned frequencies to plants' modalities.

Finally, plants, unlike animals forced into unnatural aggregations, do not pollute and defile the Earth in great numbers; rather, they sustain and revitalize the Earth in great numbers. Plants, it must be concluded, do not enjoy the same sort of communicative interaction that animals do. It is absurd to compare the unethical and violent exploitation of animals with the harvesting and eating of plants.

Peter Singer, author of the seminal *Animal Liberation*, long ago pointed out the ridiculous logic of those who accuse vegetarians of ethical breaches for our killing and eating plants. He makes the point that we must eat something, so if there is even a shred of reason to this argument, then we must choose the lesser of two evils. Hands down, that is eating plants. In a meat-based diet, ten times as many plants are "killed" as in a vegetarian-based diet. Again, the plant-eaters win!

Undeniably, plants are living entities. They play a vital role in maintaining the delicate balance of Gaia's ecosystem. But do they feel pain and emotional trauma? Do they merit the same special ethical consideration that vegetarian activists and advocates extend to animals? Theoretically, our very existence causes pain to the Earth at every level. Must we carry the same burden of guilt when we take a plant's life as we presumably would in killing an animal? Only to the extent that all life, all of the Earth and "the spirit that moves through all things," are sacred. By recognizing this and acknowledging the dilemmas and contradictions of this life, we can venture forth into this imperfect world with compassion, and begin to make choices that bring us back into a state of harmony and grace with the Earth, ourselves and all living beings. Once we begin to base our food choices on the principle of least harm and destruction, we will know, as Tolstoy knew, that the vegetarian ethic is a genuine and sincere pursuit of moral perfection on the part of our species.

Being Vegan, Living Vegan
Matt Ball

As the office manager for Vegan Outreach, I often get letters, calls and e-mail about various aspects of the vegan lifestyle. These range from questions about ingredients ("Is ketchup made with blood?") to specificity ("Why didn't you say that not all soy cheese is vegan?") to possible links with the "enemy" ("How can you promote *Vegetarian Times* when its publisher also publishes a pro-hunting magazine?").

These types of questions are in keeping with the general view that veganism is a restrictive diet, a laundry list of ingredients to avoid. However, being a vegan is much more than this. In many ways, veganism is the embodiment of *ahimsa*—the philosophy of non-violence toward and all-encompassing respect for all sentient beings. Certainly, there are many concrete, "negative" implications of choosing to live according to the understanding that the other animals with whom we share the world feel pain and desire to live. Specifically, if one does not want to cause suffering to innocent animals, one cannot pay others to raise and slaughter these creatures for "food." However, where does one stop? Animal products and by-products are in the most unlikely of places, including non-food items that almost everyone takes for granted in their everyday lives. Several years ago, *Vegetarian Times* ran an article about why it is impossible to be a vegetarian, in which it listed all the items that contain (or utilize during production) animal products or by-products. Many people, infused with the fire of the newly aware, go on a crusade to root out these animal products, in order to be completely consistent, to purify themselves and become "the perfect vegan." This process can have several severe side effects.

The most common result of the pure-vegan campaign is that the campaigner quits the entire process. I have known many people who became overwhelmed with the extent of animal abuse in this world, bogged down in ingredients, by-products, nit-picking and perceived inconsistencies. They realize that complicity is impossible to avoid unless they hang from a tree with a mask over their mouth. Since they cannot achieve perfection—avoiding all suffering—they choose to do nothing, and go back to such overt cruelty as eating animals.

Embarking on the hard-core path can keep us from being the optimal voice for the animals. As is clear to anyone who has been a long-term vegan, complicity, at some level, is difficult to avoid. We live in a world of tremendous suffering that we cannot end or even avoid (in our lifetime most everything, including fruits, vegetables and even water has been tested on animals; almost any time we use money, we may well be paying the salary of a carnivore; etc.). When they finally become aware of everything that goes on behind the scenes, some people become overwhelmed by the amount of suffering and submit to the despair brought about by their relative powerlessness. I can certainly understand these reactions, but I must say that they do not do anything to help the animals or ourselves.

We so often overlook the second half of *ahimsa*: the positive, life-embracing aspects that the philosophy entails. If we want to make our world a better place, we must accept the fact that in order to make a difference, we have to be a part of a world that is corrupt, cruel and indifferent. We cannot remove ourselves entirely from exploitation and suffering and still be a part of the change so desperately needed.

As an organization dedicated to respect for the individual, it is difficult for Vegan Outreach to advocate utilitarian outlooks. Yet the simple reality remains that it is impossible to be everything to everyone and to avoid all complicity while actively doing the most we can actively to create a better world. A good example of this is the use of film, a product which isn't vegan. Although use of film contributes to animal exploitation through the use of a processing by-product, how many people would contend that the world is worse off because of film? How many people have been moved to positive action because of photographs they have seen? How many injustices have been exposed, how many tragedies ended directly because of the use of film? This is only one example of how striving for personal absolution can run counter to active participation in the advancement of understanding, justice and compassion.

I recently received e-mail that said, in part, "I think I hate meateaters." I responded: "I must admit that I understand your feelings. When I see pictures or videos of what is done to animals, I get very angry. When I hear people say, 'But I like meat' as their final argument, I find the idea of hating them very appealing. However, I don't think this, in the end, is a productive reaction. For one, I used to eat animals. Not only did I eat them, but I did so even after I had started to consider the reality behind the situation. I wouldn't eat veal because I considered it cruel, but I continued to eat all other animals. For some reason, the connection didn't click in my head right away. I didn't want to think about it. I am glad that the vegetarians I met didn't react to me with anger and hatred, but rather with gentle prodding and education. It took me quite a while to open up to the knowledge that had always been right there, but eventually I did. Now we try to reach the people who I used to be—compassionate individuals who would eventually change if they knew, but who just don't know."

Some, if not most, people find the idea of a vegan, or even vegetarian, diet to be overwhelmingly difficult, especially students living in dorms or eating on the run. And despite the reality to the contrary, a vegan diet is not generally accepted as healthy. Confronting people struggling to change with the "vegan police" does nothing positive. Indeed, it generally creates a more negative impression of vegetarians, let alone vegans, as joyless, humorless fanatics. We must reach out to people in the same spirit of affirmation and compassion that we would like them to embrace and incorporate into their lives.

Vegan Outreach, You and the Future

There is a great deal of stress involved in our lives; as much as we would like to believe otherwise, we have only a certain amount of energy to deal with our own problems, let alone save the world. Given this, obvious animal products should be avoided, but a person's energy and efforts may well be better spent trying to get others to stop eating burgers than trying to avoid sugar bleached with bone char or trying to figure out if the monoglyceride in the cafeteria's bread comes from animals or plants.

Vegan Outreach has evolved over the years to become a very effective tool for reaching as many people as possible in a meaningful and compelling way. Feedback we have received indicates that we are succeeding: there are numerous vegans in the world today as a direct result of members' support.

Still, the most important and powerful tool we have in the journey toward justice is each one of us. Our positive example is the greatest voice we have. Our movement has advanced beyond the point where anger, slogans and sound-bites serve any further constructive purpose. In many cases, the animals won't be helped by hatred and chanting. We must realize and accept that we are in a public relations campaign. I have always contended that there are many people who cannot and will not be reached. We should ignore these people in favor of the many compassionate yet unaware people we must reach.

Certainly, we must educate people about the facts of the situation for animals (e.g., factory farms). And this article is in no way meant to encourage people to turn a blind eye to non-vegan products, e.g., to buy non-vegan soy cheese and give dairy farmers a market for their casein. But becoming angry only robs us of the happiness and pleasure each of us deserves from life. I firmly believe that each one of us, in our example, actions, attitude—our entire existence—is changing the world. Living consistently and compassionately as a vegan is an affirmation of life, a means to fulfillment and joy; these positive aspects of veganism are what we must embrace for ourselves and communicate to others.

The Vegetarian Multiplier Effect
Edward Bikales

I am a vegetarian activist who doesn't carry placards, appear on radio talk shows or even man street corner cardtables (though God bless those who do!). No, I sit inconspicuously in my office, with my short hair and tie, quietly wielding my weapons—a pen and a telephone. But, like the street corner activists, I have dealt the meat industry a very satisfying blow.

I didn't always believe it was possible. Soon after I gave up meat—partly in objection to animal slaughter—I felt disheartened to realize that my tiny refusal to eat the stuff probably wouldn't trickle back to the stockyards. In other words, no slaughterhouse would butcher one less cow or ten fewer chickens just because little old me had switched to tofu. But then I learned vegetarians can, in fact, be powerfully seditious. I've done it. I write this with bravado because I want you to understand that anyone can rip the flesh off of the meat industry.

The ho-hum nature of how I discovered the vegetarian multiplier effect is also its beauty. I began working for a large church-related organization last April. Nineteen floors, 2,000 employees, one cafeteria in the basement. I even tried eating there for the first week. There were nice vegetables on the salad bar, but—day after day—not a single meatless entrée, and I'm a big eater. So at the end of my three-month new-employee probation period, I put together a polite, one-page letter to the food service manager noting my unhappiness and afternoon hunger pangs—and suggesting a few meatless entrée ideas. I "cc'd" the building superintendent and a colleague who I learned represents our unit on issues dealing with food service. Voilà—it took all of ten minutes. When I placed a follow-up call to the food service manager the next week, he actually thanked me and said that on the basis of the letter he had already devised plans to offer a daily vegetarian entrée beginning the following week. He even read me the menu. Learning that fish isn't vegetarian seemed to cause him a little befuddlement, though he promised our aquatic friends wouldn't count in the future.

So today when I strut into the cafeteria, I watch food service dollop tray after tray of meatless entrées onto waiting dishes. A hundred or more people enjoying meat-free lunches—meals that wouldn't have been available otherwise. It happens every day, whether I'm there or not: pound after pound, ton after ton, of meat not consumed. The vegetarian multiplier effect. (Sure, the vegetarian entrée is sometimes quite eggy or cheesy, but on my moral scale that's a lot higher. And I know of at least one person in the building who has since gone vegetarian in part because it is now easier to do so, given the availability at lunch.)

Here's another success. Trapped for a week in one of those hotels-as-islands-amidst-honky-tonk-sprawl in Stamford, Connecticut, I had no car. Afterward, I sent the Sheraton management a little note decrying the fact that for those seven days the hotel restaurant menu offered but one vegetarian item—and it was out of stock all week! It didn't hurt to mention that I was conferencing there with a large organization, one whose business the Sheraton surely appreciates. I was delighted to quickly receive back a letter stating, "We appreciate your comments and certainly will make the necessary changes to accommodate your and other vegetarians' needs in the future. We have expanded our menu to include grilled vegetables with hummus and pita, a variety of soups, entrée salads and pastas."

After facing a similar conundrum at the YMCA of the Rockies in Estes Park, Colorado, and dealing with it in the same way, the management wrote, "The next time you visit our facility you will find a better variety of vegetarian entrées." So now, long after I have passed through those venerable institutions, never to return, people order and eat vegetarian meals every day without seeing the silent hand that made it possible: a simple letter. Less meat used in these large institutional kitchens means a lot less meat ordered: the vegetarian multiplier effect in action. Even if you don't work for a big organization, you can influence the restaurants you enter. Always, always make sure the staff waiting on you knows you're vegetarian. Even if it's listed on the menu, ask the maître d', the waiter, the owner: "Got anything good for vegetarians?" That way management is always aware that we are out there, and far more likely to add more vegetarian items when devising menus.

Finally, be sure all of your friends know how important vegetarianism is to you. Last year a dear carnivorous friend—without asking me—planned a vegetarian menu for her wedding reception just because I would be there. Well, it turned out that I had already made unbreakable plans for that weekend, so 200 guests forfeited their greasy steaks that night for some guy a thousand miles away. The multiplier strikes again. We can do it. We can create an environment where it is simple and safe to be vegetarian—where we have tempting choices wherever we go. And when it is easier to go without meat, millions more may join our ranks. Try it. Just pick up your pen and watch the amazing vegetarian multiplier effect take charge.

Fruitarianism
The Ultimate Diet
Rynn Berry

A growing number of vegetarians have chucked the sautéed egg-plant and batter-fried zucchini to become fruitarians[1]—those who eat only raw foods, predominantly fruit (80 percent of the diet), along with raw vegetables, soaked grains and unprocessed nuts—and they are eloquent in defense of their diet. Robert Kole[2], an instructor at Queens College, has said that as a fruitarian he enjoys an immense surge of energy that lasts throughout the day and requires fewer hours of sleep every night. As a vegan, he used to catch the occasional cold, but he has not had so much as a case of sniffles since becoming a fruitarian. While Kole did confess to a few mild cravings for cooked food, once he remembered how much better he felt on his raw food diet, he stifled his regrets.

Kole does not eat bread. "It's been baked, kneaded, yeasted, etc. All the original ingredients have been refined and cooked out of it. In Western cuisine, we take out the good stuff and cook in the bad stuff. Nuts that have been roasted in oil and salted are terrible for you, whereas raw, unsalted nuts are great. Cooked fruit and fried vegetables lose their natural goodness. Even pasta is too far removed from its natural state. The grains have been turned into a paste, then dried and cooked again before eating." Kole eschews spices as well. "When you cook the flavor out of foods, you have to put spices on top of the cooked foods. If you just eat the natural raw food with its innate flavor and goodness, you don't need spices."

Zsuzsa Blakely is an aspiring opera singer. Apart from an occasional lapse into eating cooked grains (for which she has an irrepressible craving), she has been a fruitarian for six years. Typically, she has a fruit smoothie for breakfast, for lunch a green salad with cucumber, tomatoes and red pepper dressed with a salsa–tahini sauce of her own devising, and for dinner she may have apples, dates and fresh almonds or pistachios. Being a fruitarian, she says, has not restricted her social life. She takes a fruit salad with her to work and when she meets friends at restaurants she takes along some nuts and a few pieces of dried fruit to round out the meal. Zsuzsa has no trouble maintaining her weight and feels that fruitarians reach homeostasis after they have cleansed themselves on the diet. For Zsuzsa, eating vegetables was a transitional diet between flesh-eating and the "ideal diet," fruitarianism. She believes that vegetables are sentient beings who experience pain. We may not be able to hear their screams, but in uprooting them and cutting them down we are accomplices in their destruction. Fruitarians, Zsuzsa believes, are agents of the fruit trees' propagation. In return for scattering their seeds, trees provide us with the oxygen we breathe and the food we need to sustain ourselves.

Francisco Martin, president of the Vegan Society of Spain, has been a fruitarian for ten years. Although he initially became a fruitarian by accident when he joined the raw food line at a vegetarian conference, he found the food to his taste and felt an end to sluggishness and a surge of energy. While he admits that it would be more difficult to practice fruitarianism in cold climates, he has visited rawfoodists in Finland and Lithuania who were remarkably resourceful in living on dried fruits, soaked grains and roots. Francisco has remarked that the diet's simplicity appealed to him. When he felt hungry, he said, he didn't have to waste time washing, chopping and cooking. With fruit, he just plucks, peels and eats.

An Iranian fruitarian, Mr. Javad, believes that humans are "frugivores" who should take their sustenance from fruit trees. Fruits, he argues, are formed from the tree's root system and direct sunlight to create a powerful energy packet. He never tires of his diet. Twenty-five years ago, while in Iran, he started as a rawfood vegan. Then, for a time, he was a rawfood vegan and a fitful fruitarian. Finally, three years ago, he became a full-blown fruitarian. At 62, he easily looks 20 years younger. For exercise, he climbs mountains and takes endless hikes, but says he never feels tired.

Perhaps the most memorable fruitarian I have met is Arne Winqvist. Now 81, he has been a vegetarian since the 1930s, although he regrets every year he spent eating cooked vegetables. He became a fruitarian rawfoodist at 63, and since then has experienced renewed vigor and vitality. "Once you've started on this kind of diet, you don't want to eat anything else, because fruit is the best food there is," Arne says. "Unlike with steak and other meats, our body uses little energy to digest fruits. Besides, fruit helps us efficiently get rid of harmful by-products of the digestive process like uric acid, which we flush out when we sweat or urinate." Six years ago, Winqvist started entering long distance races. He is indefatigable and hasn't had a cold since he converted to rawfood fruitarianism. "Living cells should be nourished by living food. If we put raw potatoes in the ground, they'll grow. But if we do the same with boiled potatoes, they'll just rot."

Whole Food, Big Picture
Patrick Donnelly

Vietnamese monk and peace activist Thich Nhat Hanh's charming book of meditations, *The Heart of Understanding*, begins this way: "If you are a poet, you will see that there is a cloud floating in this sheet of paper. Without a cloud, there will be no rain; without rain, the trees cannot grow; and without trees, we cannot make paper. The cloud is essential for the paper to exist." The gentle burden of Thich Nhat Hanh's song is that all things are interrelated, nothing can be separated from anything else. He begins with clouds and paper; we could begin anywhere. But there is one thing that is more emblematic than any other of the interrelatedness of all things: and that is the food we eat.

What do we see when we look deeply into the food on our plates, with the eyes of a poet? As with Thich Nhat Hanh's paper, we could see clouds, rain, sun, wind and earth, because these are the phenomena that sustain everything that lives. But we can look deeper still. Do we see food that has been brought to our tables with loving care—or food full of pesticides, preservatives, additives, antibiotics and growth hormones? Do we see food grown by methods that left the earth healthy and fecund, or food whose production depleted and poisoned the land it grew on? Do we see food that is whole, full of vitamins, minerals and vital energy that we need to support our lives and health, or food whose integrity has been diminished by processing and "refining," leaving a kind of ghost of its presence on our plates and in our bodies?

If we look deeply into our food in this way, it can become a window on the past and on the future. Do we see mostly plants on our plate, making it more likely that we will be healthy and that there will be enough food for everyone to eat? Or do we see mostly food that came from animals, which represents their suffering, and causes ours, in the form of illnesses, pollution, waste of precious resources, famine and untimely death? When we look at the food we choose to eat today, do we see justice and safety for the people that grew it, picked it, shipped it, sold it? If we are people already living with illness, is the food on our plates of the kind that will support our healing, or will it reinforce the imbalances that may have contributed to our becoming ill in the first place?

The Whole Foods Project
The Whole Foods Project is a unique organization in New York City that is dedicated to exploring these issues. We provide organic vegan meals and holistic nutrition education for people with HIV/AIDS, cancer, heart disease and other life-challenging illnesses. About 75 percent of the people we work with are living with an immune imbalance related to HIV. There are other organiza-

tions in New York and around the country that provide meals for people with AIDS. But ours is the only such organization that serves and teaches about a plant-based diet of whole grains, legumes, vegetables and fruits, grown by sustainable agricultural methods. We do this in response to the substantial and growing body of research that indicates these foods are able to prevent and heal illness, and because our own deepest instincts tell us that personal healing is not separate from the healing of the planet. We also offer a comprehensive program of nutrition education, including cooking classes, lectures and workshops, so people living with illness can learn how to find, choose and prepare health-supportive food for themselves. We offer our services to people at all stages of the immune imbalance that may be caused by HIV, because we believe that the nutritional support provided by whole vegetarian foods may prevent many from progressing to full-blown AIDS.

The Whole Foods Project serves meals in a supportive social environment that helps to lessen the isolation that can accompany serious illness. We are not a soup kitchen or a cafeteria—our guests are made welcome at large, round tables with fresh linens, flowers and candles, and are served by friendly waiters (many of whom are also clients). This creates an opportunity for people to support one another and share information about healing resources. One of our services is the Sunday Cabaret Supper, a popular monthly gathering that offers gourmet vegan food and the healing power of music and laughter, courtesy of some of New York's most talented musicians and comedians. One of our primary goals is to show by example that healthy food need not be boring, bland or—as is all too often the case—brown, so when our guests look deeply into the food we serve they have a chance to enjoy the magical colors, textures and flavors of food that was grown with respect for the Earth and prepared with love. This is an experience that beckons us to life and sustains healing.

It will seem self-evident to many that the approach to nutrition I am describing is well founded, but we have met some surprising obstacles in our work. We have been told that our emphasis on an organic, plant-based diet is elitist and unrealistic, especially for people with low incomes. We have been told that people of color are not interested in this food and won't frequent places where it is served. We have been told, by the head dietitian of a major food program for people with AIDS in New York City, that while she is herself a vegetarian and sympathizes with our approach, people simply are not capable of making the changes we are suggesting, however beneficial they might be. We have been told, by a medical advisor for a national publication for people with HIV, that it may not be responsible for us to recommend that people with HIV avoid sugar (which clinical research has shown to be immune-suppressive) because people with low incomes, who may derive as many as half their daily calories from sugary foods, would not get enough calories without it. It has been frustrating for us to watch a major AIDS-service organization in New York City spending part of its multi-million-dollar budget to recommend for people with immune imbalance the food that is making the rest of America sick: "Eat whatever you want," it says. "Enjoy your favorite foods whenever you want—and more often. Pizza for breakfast, pancakes and syrup for dinner—go for it."

Our lives have been changed by looking deeply into whole foods, so we can also see possible paths over, under and around these obstacles. We visualize that small food co-ops could be established in every neighborhood where people could have access to organic food cheaply. We see people of every color learning about and returning with enthusiasm to the health-supportive traditional diets of their ancient cultures (which in almost every instance were plant-based), leaving behind the foods that slavery and poverty has driven them to. We see holistic dietitians and whole-foods chefs working closely with people who have serious illnesses to support them through the slow, difficult and emotional process of making changes in their diet. We see people of every income being provided with correct nutritional information, and being motivated by this to make healthy choices for themselves.

From the Anglo-Saxon word *hal* came the English words happy, health, holy and whole, and we named ourselves the Whole Foods Project to associate ourselves with all those nuances of meaning. If we eat the ghosts of food, we will ourselves become the hungry ghosts of what we could be. But if we look into our plate and see wholeness, we may find that wholeness nurturing every aspect of our lives.

Living with AIDS, Living with Compassion

Health and wholeness are also being compromised in other ways. I received a catalog from a health practitioner who was proposing to organize a clinical trial of Standard Process Products nutritional supplements, the majority of which were derived from animal sources. The practitioner's aim was to determine the supplements' efficacy for people with AIDS. I reviewed the catalog and decided that participating in such a trial was not for me. I felt it was important to write him and express my feelings. I explained that ingredients like "vacuum-dried bovine and ovine spleen" and "veal-bone PMG extract" were just too much of a leap for an ethical vegetarian—especially the veal-bone extract. I informed the practitioner that veal calves live out their short lives in such atrocious agony that I didn't think I could benefit from any remedy that makes use of them.

I spoke to Joseph Antell, a salesperson at Standard Process Products, about some of my concerns. He was under the impression that most veal calves live free-range, by their mothers' side. I told him this belief didn't stand up to even the simplest investigation. Standard Process literature emphasizes that its supplements that come from plant sources are scrupulously raised by organic farming methods, but no such claim is made for its supplements based

81

on animal glands. Antell acknowledged that these come from conventional slaughterhouse by-products, because the expense and difficulty of using organically raised animals is too great. I pointed out that these products, therefore, come from animals who are themselves ill in many cases, and are likely to be tainted with the residues of pesticides, growth hormones and antibiotics. Growth hormones, especially, are substances which are biologically active in incredibly small amounts.

In my writing and teaching about nutrition for people with AIDS, I try to convey the idea that our own personal healing can't be separate from the healing of the planet as a whole. The widespread use of animal products in the standard American diet is weakening natural immunity and creating many of the degenerative diseases that are killing us, poisoning the environment, exhausting irreplaceable resources and making it difficult for many people on the planet to get any food at all. It is more than ironic and misfortunate that we make ourselves sick by overemphasizing animal products in our diet, and then demand of those same animals that they provide remedies to make us well. The most effective way—indeed the only way—of changing this situation is with our personal consumer dollars, by not buying products that sustain this system. I was informed by Joseph Antell that a quarter of a million cows were involved in making just one batch of Standard Process supplements. Most of these gentle, intelligent animals live in squalor, fear and misery their entire lives. I can only wonder as to the effect on human beings of ingesting this fear and misery. If these animals are making their glands, with all of their marvelous benefits, from a diet of plants, the question remains why we couldn't—and shouldn't—try to do the same thing.

I am certain that the practitioner's interest in promoting SPP supplements through a clinical trial comes from the best possible motivation, to help people with AIDS. In writing to him, I requested one thing: for him to investigate thoroughly where the animal products that go into SPP supplements come from. I urged him to find out how many animals are involved, where they are raised, in what conditions, what the state of their health is, what drugs and hormones are used, what the animals are fed, how they are killed and how the meat is handled after the animals are dead. I told him that, after his investigation, he may well still feel that SPP supplements made from animals are worthwhile. But at least he would have based that decision on full information. Macrobiotic teachers have a saying: "Every front has a back." The question, therefore, is: What is the back of this particular front?

Hitler and Vegetarianism
Rynn Berry

One of the comments often aimed at those such as myself who write about famous vegetarians of the past—and how many of them were paragons of virtue who practiced non-violence and compassion—is the following: "But wasn't Hitler a vegetarian?" One such example began in 1991 when I wrote to the *New York Times* commenting on the vegetarianism of Isaac Bashevis Singer and how this important feature of Singer's life had been glossed over in his recent obituary. I had interviewed Singer[1] and he had been vehement on the issue of respect for animals.

Two weeks later, under the headline "The Vegetarian Road to World Peace," the *Times* published a reply to my letter from the well-known author and *New Yorker* essayist Janet Malcolm. Malcolm remembered a comment Singer had made to a woman who noted approvingly during a meal that Singer wasn't eating the meat course and that her health had improved after she stopped eating meat. Singer had replied: "I do it for the health of the chickens."

Malcolm continued: "Mr. Singer's belief, quoted by Mr. Berry, 'that everything connected with vegetarianism is of the highest importance, because there will never be any peace in the world so long as we eat animals,' may have puzzled readers. What does eating or not eating meat have to do with world peace?

"Milan Kundera gives us the answer on page 289 of *The Unbearable Lightness of Being*: 'True human goodness, in all its purity and freedom, can come to the fore only when its recipient has no power. Mankind's true moral test, its fundamental test (which lies deeply buried from view) consists of its attitude toward those who are at its mercy: animals. And in this respect, mankind has suffered a fundamental debacle, a debacle so fundamental that all others stem from it.' "[2]

Janet Malcolm's response to my letter drew a reply from another *Times* reader. The writer castigated Malcolm for implying that the universal acceptance of vegetarianism will bring about world peace, because "Adolf Hitler was a vegetarian all his life and wrote extensively on the subject."

To me this response was all too predictable. I have yet to give a talk on vegetarianism in which the question of Hitler's vegetarianism has not been raised. Invariably, at every bookstore signing, at every lecture, on every phone-in talk show, at least one person has asked me half-mockingly: "Is Hitler in your book?" or "Why didn't you put Hitler in your book?"

Following this letter, on September 21, 1991, the *New York Times* published two rejoinders to this question. Richard Schwartz, author of *Judaism and Vegetarianism*,[3] pointed out that Hitler would occasionally go on vegetarian binges to cure himself of excessive sweatiness and flatulence, but that his main diet was meat-centered. He also cited Robert Payne, Albert Speer and other well-known Hitler biographers, who mentioned Hitler's predilection for such non-vegetarian foods as Bavarian sausages, ham, liver and game. Furthermore, it was argued, if Hitler had been a vegetarian, he would not have banned vegetarian organizations in Germany and the occupied countries; nor would he have failed to urge a meatless diet on the German people as a way of coping with Germany's food shortage during the war.

Another correspondent cited a passage from a cookbook which had been written by a European chef, Dione Lucas, who was an eyewitness to Hitler's meateating. In her *Gourmet Cooking School Cookbook* (1964), Lucas, drawing on her experiences as a hotel chef in Hamburg during the 1930s and 1940s, remembered being called upon quite often to prepare Hitler's favorite dish, which was not vegetarian. "I do not mean to spoil your appetite for stuffed squab," she writes, "but you might be interested to know that it was a great favorite with Mr. Hitler, who dined at the hotel often. Let us not hold that against a fine recipe, though."[4]

According to Robert Payne, in *The Life and Death of Adolf Hitler*, Hitler's vegetarianism was a fiction made up by his propaganda minister Joseph Goebbels to give Hitler the aura of a revolutionary ascetic: a Fascist Gandhi, if you will. Payne writes that of the claims that made up Hitler's asceticism—that he never smoked, drank, ate meat or had anything to do with women—only the first was true. Payne says that Hitler drank beer and wine often and, among other discreet affairs, kept his famous mistress Eva Braun with him in the Bergdhof. The asceticism devised by Goebbels, writes Payne, aimed "to emphasize [Hitler's] total dedication, his self-control, the distance that separated him from other men. By this outward show of asceticism, he could claim that he was dedicated to the service of his people."[5]

As to Hitler's diet, Payne notes that he loved not only sausages but caviar. He also loved sweet things, consuming vast amounts of sugar. John Toland, in his biography of Hitler,[6] says that by the time of his suicide, Hitler suffered from rotting teeth, acute gastric disorders, hardening of the arteries, a liver ailment and incurable heart disease. It seems likely that these diseases were only furthered by the ten-percent cocaine solution, strychnine-based pills and injections of pulverized bull's testicles his doctors fed him to "cure" him of his extraordinary hypochondria. Whatever the prime sources of Hitler's illnesses, he did not enjoy the robust health that has come to be associated with vegetarianism; on the contrary, his symptoms were those associated with a heavy intake of animal foods.

Defining Vegetarianism
One of the problems of defining who or who was or was not a vegetarian, is that non-vegetarians often have an elastic definition of what constitutes a vegetarian. Vegetarianism, it often seems, is a label attached to anything that falls within the spectrum of not eating any animal products on one end to cutting down on

red meat on the other. Because of this, people like Hitler—who ate fish eggs, pigeon (the squab in Lucas's recipe) and sausages—are called vegetarians. By this criterion, even jackals and hyenas, who eat fruits and vegetables between kills, could be classified as vegetarians![7]

It should be noted that the man didn't describe himself as a vegetarian until 1937. This "conversion" may have been prompted by an emotional response to the death of his niece who had been in love with him and who may have taken her own life. That at least was the thinking of Hitler's close friend Frau Hess. Toland writes: "[Hitler] had made such remarks before, and had toyed with the idea of vegetarianism, but this time, according to Frau Hess, he meant it. From that moment on, Hitler never ate another piece of meat except for liver dumplings." An article, however, published on May 30, 1937, in the *Times*, entitled "At Home with the Fuhrer," mentions that Hitler eats "a slice of ham and relieves the tediousness of his diet with such delicacies as caviar."

Dione Lucas offers a revealing analysis of that squab dish served to Hitler during his stays in Hamburg. "One of the great nuisances about eating squab," she writes, "is the dozens of tiny bones you must contend with for every morsel of flesh you get. By the time you have finished, your plate looks like a charnel house, you are exhausted and there is a lingering suspicion that the game was not worth the candle." Looking at the devastation unleashed by the sociopathic and hypochondriacal Hitler, we might say that Europe too was a charnel house, its citizens mentally and physically exhausted—if not victims of the charnel houses of the concentration camps—and that it had all in millions of ways not been worth the candle.

It is ironic that people should be so willing to gloss over the truth about Isaac Bashevis Singer's absolute commitment to the welfare of animals, yet be so willing to believe a myth about Hitler's vegetarianism. It is also ironic that my letter to the editor about Isaac Bashevis Singer's vegetarianism should have touched off a chain of letters that ended by exploding the myth of Hitler's vegetarianism. Of course, there is no cogent reason why this myth should have embarrassed a movement that contributes so much to "the health of chickens," the health of humans and the ecological health of the planet. Nonetheless, it doesn't hurt to have it finally settled on the record that while Pythagoras, Leonardo da Vinci, Tolstoy, Shaw, Gandhi and Singer were vegetarians, Hitler—who strewed bones across Europe—was not.

Environmentalism

Globalization and Its Discontents
Mia MacDonald

It was, until recently, a truth universally acknowledged that if only the poorer or "developing" countries of Africa, Asia and Latin America could be enabled or cajoled to "develop," large blots of environmental misuse and ill-use would be wiped off the planet's face. "Development" was not only the best contraceptive, it was also, by many accounts, the best steward of the Earth's resources: environmentalism and development would go hand in hand.

"Why," the argument would run, "does the Hudson River contain far less industrial pollution and human and animal waste than India's venerable Ganges?" It was the undeveloped nations' poverty that led people to treat the planet as foe, not friend. The results, at least to many in the developed countries (the U.S., Europe, Japan, Australia and New Zealand), were clear and heart-breaking: millions of infant and child deaths each year from water fouled by feces or parasites; acres of Amazon rainforest slashed and burned to make way for landless farmers; chimpanzees hunted by poor West African villagers for sale as "bush meat" in local restaurants; women in India chopping down ever smaller numbers of trees to ensure a fuel supply for family meals. If the poor weren't so poor, they wouldn't need to "act out" against their environment.

Conventional Wisdom

I was taught along these lines as a graduate student in public policy in the first part of the 1990s. I was taught that the capacity of the developed nations for technological innovation, their sturdy and effective legal and political systems and a free press would provide a formidable (perhaps invincible) bulwark against ecological apocalypse. Sure, such features of "modern" societies cost money, but they also held the promise of saving the planet. The power of the greenback could finally be put to universal service: preserving the last remnants of green on the once-verdant Earth. No need for limits on growth, as called for by iconoclastic biologists Anne and Paul Ehrlich and roundly rejected by U.S. economists and policy-makers alike. Instead, we could grow economies, lift all those poor people out of the degradation of poverty and glow more greenly at the same time.

Theorists and proponents of this panacea, however, didn't count on one thing: wealth has significant environmental costs of its own. A balance sheet rife with profit does not always mean a surplus for the environment. And, as we approach the millennium, it is difficult to see good times rolling for the planet. Indeed, the facts show otherwise. The U.S.-based Worldwatch Institute put it succinctly in a recent global factbook.[1] The world today is economically *richer* and environmentally *poorer* than ever before.

The United States, the richest and, some might argue, most technologically inventive country on Earth, is also the world's largest polluter. Each American uses between ten and 30 (data vary widely) *times* more planetary resources each year than does the average Indian. Such are the environmental costs of sustaining a way of life cherished at home, and now aspired to by most of the rest of the world's human inhabitants.

Hidden and Obvious Costs

It is true the Hudson River may be cleaner than it was 30 years ago, but the products of wealth—among them 4 X 4 sport utility vehicles (SUVs), larger houses, more and "richer" food, cradle-to-grave air conditioning, and malls both luxury and strip—put huge pressures on the planet's ecosystems. The actual costs in fuel, water, species and global warming are tidily hidden—not to mention the landfills needed to hold all our old "stuff" when we scale up to bigger and better versions. Malls do a pretty good job of eradicating fully the wetlands many of them have been built on. The golden-hued, off-road allure of SUV ads are video paeans to nature; the impacts of their low mileage per gallon, choking smoke and fouled water from oil refineries and increases in per-vehicle emissions, are not seen. As Gary Snyder, Pulitzer prize-winning Beat poet and environmentalist, has written:

> *Instead of independence, we have over-dependence on life-giving substances such as water, which we squander. Many species of animal and bird have become extinct in the service of fashion fads, or fertilizer, or industrial oil.*"[2]

The Worldwatch report makes many hidden realities visible and, depending on your tolerance level, inescapable. This litany of statistics also bespeaks a current and future truth: the environment and the myriad processes of development are fully and perhaps irrevocably intertwined. In 1997, for instance, carbon emissions and the Earth's temperature reached their highest recorded levels ever. Concentrations of carbon dioxide in the atmosphere are the most they have been for 160,000 years. In 1997, another 16 million hectares of forest were burned, chopped down, or converted to other uses. Almost half of the three billion hectares of forest that initially covered the Earth are gone. At the same time, global production of passenger cars set a new record—nearly 40 million—while half of all primate species (except human beings) are threatened with extinction. Some primate species now number only in the hundreds.

In 1997, 80 million more people joined the planet—nearly 50 million in Asia—the equivalent of a new Sweden making its home on Earth every month. And we are eating more animals. Global consumption of animal protein—strongly linked to the high rates of cancer and heart disease in developed countries and intensive use of water, land and grain—reached record highs. Two hundred and eleven million tons of beef, pork and poultry were "produced." Leading the pack in beef and veal consumption are, in descending order, the United States, Brazil, China, Russia, France, Japan and Italy. Worldwatch describes this "growing appetite for animal protein" as "the dominant distinguishing feature of dietary changes over the past half-century." The primary reason? Rising incomes.

Yet it is not all bad news. Bicycle production still beats car production hands down—by more than 100 percent—at 100 million new bicycles each year. However, the number of bicycles produced in 1996 was seven percent lower than in 1995. China, the world's major producer and user, produced seven percent fewer bikes, and declines were reported in the other four top manufacturers: India, the U.S., the European Union and Taiwan. However, bicycle use is up in several European countries. In Denmark's cities, an estimated 20 percent of all trips are on bicycles; in the Netherlands, the figure is closer to 30 percent. In Germany, bicycle use has increased by 50 percent over the last 20 years. Global sales of solar cells were up 43 percent in 1997 over 1996 levels, with increased demand coming primarily from Japan. Similarly, global use of wind power grew by 26 percent, while sales of coal and oil increased during the 1990s by just over one percent. Even petroleum companies have an eye to the future: British Petroleum and Royal Dutch Shell, the largest publicly traded oil company in the world, have committed a total of $1.5 billion to develop wind, solar and other sources of renewable energy.

The Worldwatch data seem to say that not all outcomes for the planet, humanity and other species need be dire as the march to "development" (and, one could argue, "over-development" in some of the world's industrial societies) continues. This is not to say that a sustainable planet requires three-quarters of the world's population to be consigned to poverty, eking out an existence on small plots of land with no cars, no air conditioning, no washing machines, no resource-intensive food, a small number of televisions and only limited industry.

Nevertheless, the question has to be asked whether the prevailing consumption patterns of those in the developed world can become standard for people everywhere. Many environmentalists and economists agree that the finite resources of Earth cannot support the now nearly six billion people alive, nor the 9.4 billion expected to be alive by 2030, living like Americans do in the final years of this century. So who will be denied and how? Although a series of United Nations conferences in the 1990s (specifically the Earth Summit in 1992 and the International Conference on Population and Development in 1994) have attempted to deal with these questions, the notion of limits is still mostly taboo.

Globalization, the integration of world economies and markets, has been welcomed by many as the precious fruit of the triumph of free markets and democracy over competing economic and political ideologies. Its adherents are multiple and extend across region, political affiliation, gender and class. Indeed, leaders of developed countries do not show any desire to revert to an agrarian economy, with small land-holdings and limited industrial production. Likewise, developing countries, while accepting the ideals of sustainable development and in many cases taking concrete action to see them realized, do not want their economic growth contained by the recently converted titans of environmentalism—the world's richest countries. This was clear at the Kyoto global-warming treaty talks in 1997, where developing countries rejected developed countries' demands that they, too, adopt targets for reducing airborne pollution.

The developed world, the U.S. in particular, having so successfully marketed its lifestyle globally, might be asked whether it has provided the rope by which we will hang ourselves and Earth. In Ladakh, the capital of Tibet, where most people are Buddhists with long and deep spiritual ties to the Earth, the products of globalization have taken hold. Wheat trucked in from India is popular and cheaper than wheat grown locally. Local farmers are being pushed out of the market, hastening the move from small, cooperative organic farms to chemical-intensive agriculture. As consumer goods increase, Ladakh's streets and waterways are home to the most visceral evidence of "progress"—garbage.

Risings in the South
Sometime before the new century, China—still defined as a "developing" country, with a large and still-impoverished rural population—will inherit from the United States the title of world's most polluting nation. China's industrial development and astounding economic growth over the past 20 years is lifting millions out of poverty. These are the mainly well-educated or well-connected urban folk. Many more Chinese now drive cars, own homes, use computers and eat meat on a regular basis as a result of their affluence. Hong Kong's new $20 billion airport has a baggage claim the size of New York's Yankee Stadium. But the by-products of China's development are also becoming visible, although not as easily photographed, nor so intriguing, as a young woman on a Beijing street using a cellular phone. Industrial pollutants regularly cast a haze over Beijing. Respiratory infections are the number one cause of illness and death in China. In major cities, non-polluting bicycles now give way to cars powered by leaded gasoline.

In south-central China, the largest civil engineering project in the world is underway: the construction of the Three Gorges Dam. Seen as necessary by government and international proponents to meet China's growing demands for electricity, the Dam will submerge 150,000 acres, fill the gorges with a 400-mile long reservoir, displace and forcibly resettle 1.5 million people, and threaten the survival of the already-endangered river dolphin, along with the giant sturgeon and finless porpoise. However, the dam encapsulates a dilemma of development: it will also substantially reduce China's dependence on intensely polluting and globally warming coal-powered fuel. China now burns at least 1.2 billion tons of coal each year. The Dam also provides jobs to 10,000 people, many of whom are poor and in need of employment, and it will submerge 1,500 factories. Dr. Pangloss might expect that new factories to replace them would be more environmentally friendly. And, in the clear light of day, this notion cannot be entirely dismissed.

Sustainability Pursued

China has, by some accounts, made significant progress in reducing factory pollution, increasing recycling and discouraging waste. On the other hand, Kerala, a small state of 30 million people in the southeast of India, has become a "star," cited almost relentlessly as an example of sustainable development. Health and literacy levels are high (the United Nations has certified Kerala as 100 percent literate—for both men and women—almost unheard of in developing countries). Population growth is virtually non-existent, there is limited industrial pollution, and there are several well-preserved wildlife reserves—all in a state that is twice as crowded as the rest of India.

How was Kerala's success achieved? Through massive investments in health, education and other human needs by the state government, often run by the Communist party. Some economists and planners, though, discern a down side to the Kerala model: limited industrialization. The lack of industry is pushing significant numbers of people to emigrate, and bringing calls for more development from India's central government and members of Kerala's growing middle class. Will Kerala's landscape and expansive coastline soon be fouled, as has so much of the United States and Europe, by industrial effluents, factories and massive over-building? It is not clear.

A huge port-expansion project is underway in Cochin, one of Kerala's largest cities. The Indian government and developed country corporations have been promoting production of shrimp along the Kerala coast. The shrimp industry is built on intensive use of chemical fertilizers. Shrimp produced are destined for dinner tables in Asia and Europe. Thailand's coast has already been ravaged by the shrimp industry, and investors are now moving on to Vietnam. In Kerala, stands of aquatic mangrove trees are cut down to make way for huge shrimp cultivation ponds. Mechanized fishing trawlers also now compete with artisan fishermen and -women who use people-powered wooden boats.

The allure of "modernization" has not fully taken hold, as its casualties become better known. Unions of fishworkers continue to stage strikes against the noisy, polluting and dominating trawlers. They have often won concessions from the central government, including bans on trawlers. Local coalitions of trade unions, religious, students and community leaders are working to prevent conversion of coastal lands to chemical-based aquaculture. They are also facilitating small-scale, sustainable shrimp cultivation that is free of chemicals. Local activists have also succeeded in preserving swaths of mangroves—essential to preventing the erosion of coastal soils.

Where the Pattern is Made

Throughout the developing and developed world, as in Kerala, local people and organizations are promoting and demonstrating sustainable ways of living without trashing the planet. Can they—can we—succeed? In theory, billions of local efforts could close down or convert all polluting businesses, and reject patterns of consumption that do not allow the Earth to breathe and renew. However, multiple structures in developing and developed countries restrain or dilute people power—autocratic governments, biased media, unfaithful elected politicians, increasingly powerful mega-corporations and our own desires.

The leaders we in the developed world freely elect urge developing countries to avoid the ecological catastrophes they and we have brought about. Yet we are increasingly—shamelessly—reluctant to help them create a new pattern. Global development assistance, which is money given by developed countries to developing, fell in real terms by 17 percent between 1992 and 1997 according to the Organization for Economic Cooperation and Development (OECD). This assistance is, by most estimates, at its lowest level ever. This, as the rich world continues to get richer and as the rich in it do so at higher rates than anyone else. These same leaders have failed, in many key areas, to stem our domestic tides of environmental damage. The United States Congress refuses to set higher fuel efficiency standards for American-made cars, increase energy taxes or ensure that the most highly toxic dump sites in the country are cleaned up by the corporations that despoiled them, years after Superfund legislation was enacted.

What about us, the individuals in these developed countries? We refuse to reject the over-development taking place all around us, still shopping at those new malls instead of organizing to prevent them from being built; enjoying the roominess, driving advantages and "romance" of SUVs; eating food that strains the environment; using and throwing away several paper cups each day purchased at Starbucks and other cafés (the annual garbage toll of Starbucks cups is over 100 million a year in the U.S. alone); building bigger houses; buying more and more glossy magazines printed on trees that sell us celebrities, wealth and more *stuff*; and consuming the ever-wider array of consumer products that we hardly need, but just plain want. The teak furniture (from a rainforest in Asia, most likely), the electronics, the cooking gear—and that truly amazing amount of packaging it all comes in (that mostly ends up in a landfill or incinerator).

Sustainability on $350

Despite the plenty surrounding us, and its increase daily, recent surveys of parents and teachers in the United States found that the current generation of children and teenagers is more depressed, angry, worried, sad and lonely than ever before. Psychotherapist Miriam Greenspan speculates that this collective anomie is the result of young people's escalating fears and hopelessness about the ecocide they see—despite the welter of advertising and media spectacles designed to distract them. Greenspan says that when she speaks to clients about the state of the planet as a primary source of their strongest emotions, they often sigh with relief. Someone has finally recognized and ratified their connection to their environment(s).[3]

I heard a year or so back on a radio program that to begin living a sustainable life, one that treads more lightly on the planet, Americans would have to limit their consumption of consumer goods to $350 a year. That is for everything that isn't food or housing (yes, cars, bikes and other modes of transport would have to fit under the $350 limit).

This, then, is the developed-country sustainability, and it demonstrates the challenges of achieving true *praxis* in our individual and collective relationships with the planet. Indeed, these remain the greatest challenges we face: to unite the practical and spiritual paths by which "development" can take place. In many parts of the world it is truly needed, and in most, inevitable. If we are honest with ourselves, we can only walk or bicycle down paths that allow us to live with and within a green and vibrant planet. Truly, the Earth and all species are in the balance.

The Dilemma of Development
Mia MacDonald

A quiet struggle continues in a region of southern Kenya called Maasailand, far away from most journalists, aid workers and international mediators. It is a conflict over land—an increasingly volatile commodity in a country where export crops are critical to the economy, population is increasing 3.5 percent a year and economic growth is stagnant or declining. Resolution of the conflicts will have an impact on Kenya's national goals for economic development, natural resource conservation and the tourist industry (still Kenya's largest earner of foreign currency). The social and economic interests of the Maasai people will also be affected. The Maasai are pastoral herders who still, for the most part, measure their wealth and security in cattle.

The struggle underway in Maasailand is not unique. It is among a growing number of similar dilemmas throughout the world, in both rich and poor countries, where the large question is the same: How can development be achieved in a sustainable way? How can the benefits of "development" be ensured for present *and* future generations? These questions lie behind the transformation of vast tracts of American wetlands into strip malls, or the conversion of millions of acres of Latin American rainforest into grazing land for beef cattle. Answers for the most part are elusive or amorphous; at times the larger questions about the benefits of development are obscured or even ignored. In addition, a host of complex issues and relationships are at play within each situation, circumscribing the outcome. These include: power, poverty, rights to resources, pressures for economic growth and free trade, the politics of international development assistance, and the allure of hard cash and the consumer goods it can now buy.

Maasailand Mix
In Kenya's Maasailand, the central questions revolve around land: Who owns it? What are the proper uses for it, as each faction defines "proper" or "best"? Who has the power to determine how the land will be used? The Maasai Mara National Reserve, the northern extension of the Tanzanian Serengeti, covers 1,363 square miles and is one of the top revenue-generating game reserves in Kenya. About 20 percent of tourist visits to Kenya are to the Mara, and the revenue generated by tourism in the Mara is over U.S. $11 million annually. In recent years, lands held by the Maasai on the borders of the Mara have become a center of new large- and small-scale agricultural development. These lands, which cover nearly 5,000 square miles, are central to the livelihoods of the Maasai and their still largely pastoral economy. The area is also a critical

dry-season resource for the million-plus herd of wildebeest that makes its way each year into Kenya from the Serengeti. This trek is a major tourist attraction which brings substantial revenue to both Kenya and Tanzania.

As land surrounding the Mara is developed, it is fenced off—transformed—and becomes inaccessible to the 80,000 Maasai in the region, their cattle and the wildebeest. Pressure on the Maasai to sell or convert their land to crops is increasing, from both outside and within their communities. Many Maasai have become large land-owners, concentrating on raising millet, wheat and barley. Others have sold or lost title to small parcels of land and end up cattle-less and jobless in Nairobi, Kenya's capital, or the slums that now surround many Maasai settlements. Each year, the wildebeest find less and less open land. And each year, the Maasai pastoral lifestyle and economy are increasingly less viable. In Kenya's fractious politics, the Maasai do not hold much power. The national government, and Kenya's autocratic and perennial president, Daniel arap-Moi, often use ethnic politics to maintain their hold on power. They are anxious for the Maasai to give up herding, which is viewed as backward, and settle down and be "civilized"— build homes, wear Western clothing and generally conform to Moi's definition of a "developed" Kenya. Similar pressures on the Maasai to change or, in some views, "progress," also come from international aid donors (including the U.S. and Europe) who want Kenya to achieve economic growth by focusing on exports. The traditional Maasai subsistence economy does not conform to this vision.

Land Changes Hands

Kenya's wildlife parks and reserves were set up after World War Two as a result of the strong pressure of the conservation lobby, comprised almost entirely of European colonizers. In most cases, land for these protected areas was removed from the control of local people, including the Maasai, without compensation. Seven thousand square kilometers of Maasailand were lost with the establishment of the Amboseli, Nairobi, Maasai Mara, Kitengela and Olorgesalie reserves. Twelve percent of Kenya's arable land remains protected.

In the mid-1960s, international aid donors to Kenya initiated a development program designed to make livestock production more profitable by ensuring property rights (a central prescription of many donor-funded initiatives). Maasailand was divided into "group ranches," owned by groups of Maasai and managed by an elected committee. Some large individual ranches were created simultaneously, generally by and for the Maasai elite. Implicit in this group ranch program was the transformation of the Maasai from nomadic pastoralists to sedentary farmers or ranchers who would produce goods for the cash market and international export, including wheat, barley and beef; Maasai for the most part do not eat their cattle, but use cows' milk and blood and their by-products when cattle die.

The division of land and the scramble for property rights have continued. By the early 1990s, it is estimated that well over half of group ranch lands had been subdivided into individual landholdings. Some are quite large and contain land with much potential; others are small and of marginal productivity. Many researchers have found that land distribution has been highly unequal, favoring local Maasai elites. Population growth in Maasailand is adding to the pressure to privatize land ownership. Annual population growth in Maasailand, combining births and in-migration, is between six and 7.5 percent.

Before the national parks were set up, Maasai and wildlife moved freely across open lands. Both are now constrained by park boundaries and the increasing division of group ranch lands into smaller "private" holdings. Migrating herds of wildebeest now compete with cattle for grazing land and some Maasai refer to the annual migration as "the time of cattle famine." Still, given the rapid loss of open land, both Maasai pastoralists and wildebeest are in danger. Their fates, as many Maasai observe, are not in opposition to each other, but are closely linked. If the wildebeest go, will the Maasai herders be far behind? There is a clear parallel between the Maasai and Native Americans in the U.S. West who, after the vast herds of buffalo had been decimated, were confined to reservations on land of marginal productivity, their way of life rendered extinct.

Another problem is that land development in the group ranches bordering the Maasai Mara National Reserve follows no plan. Plots as small as one acre are sold, often in areas where crop yields are highly uncertain. John G. Galaty of McGill University, an expert on the Maasai, cites the dangers of creating "a patchwork of relatively small, economically non-viable holdings in a dry land of no potential."

The Tourism Factor

The government of Kenya is committed to expanding the international and domestic tourist industry through investing in park infrastructure, training personnel and undertaking an aggressive marketing program. The Ministry of Tourism and Wildlife has been effective in gaining international funding for wildlife protection and conservation, at times when other aid to Kenya has been reduced or cut off entirely by Western donors frustrated by President Moi's autocratic and often unpredictable regime. Tourism revenues fluctuate with perceptions of Kenya's political stability, but remain the country's largest earner of foreign currency. Almost a million tourists visit each year, with gross returns of about $500 million.

Since 1989, revenue from tourism in the Mara has been shared with surrounding Maasai communities. About 25 percent of profits are returned to the Maasai, mostly in the form of schools, health clinics and water holes for cattle and crops. Many Maasai do not consider this a fair share, or sufficient to ensure conservation of the region. David Western, who took over as director of Kenya

Wildlife Services in 1994 from the flamboyant sometime paleontologist Richard Leakey, has pledged to increase the amount of money from tourism returned to communities living on the borders of national parks. Western also has a long association with the Maasai, and is sensitive to their central role in preserving the vast variety and number of animals that still roam Kenya. A priority for Kenya Wildlife Services is stemming the sale of group ranch lands by demonstrating to the Maasai the economic benefits of tourism. But the question remains: Can Kenya Wildlife Services establish projects and/or distribute returns comparable to what the Maasai can get from cultivating or selling their land?

What the Future May Hold

In view of the pressures for development, the government of Kenya may have to take strong—and politically unpopular—measures to conserve wildlife and other natural resources. These could include: incorporating more land into the national reserve system, delegating control over wildlife areas to local communities, or building fences around game parks (still a highly controversial remedy). Another option is to enlist higher levels of international aid to pay for national parks' development and preservation, and to ensure that the money reaped by tourism is returned to local communities, like the Maasai, for their use.

Halting further development in the group ranch area is opposed by local politicians, by the wealthier Maasai and by the government, which seeks foreign investment, foreign currency and a more sedentary Maasai population. For years, the national government has been playing a tough game of ethnic and tribal politics. In a country of nearly 30 million people, the 150,000 to 200,000 Maasai do not have much political clout as a people. Some observers in Kenya say that market forces must be allowed to operate freely in the region. So, if the Maasai want to sell their land and set a price, why intervene? Critics of intervention cry "paternalism"—why question the ability (and legitimacy) of a Maasai herder to decide when and for how much to sell his land?

A case can be and has been made that some form of intervention in the region could lead to more optimal outcomes than the current helter-skelter pattern. Strong arguments can be made that an integrated, participatory development plan is needed, could be implemented in a fair manner, and will allow Maasai pastoralists, wildebeest, wheat and economic growth all to survive on the borders of the Maasai Mara National Reserve. Some elements of such a plan include: zoning land group ranch lands into three categories—farm, wildlife and pastoral—based on the land's potential and the route of the wildebeest migration, and ensuring land use through subsidies and taxes. Maasai must also receive greater returns from tourism in and around the Mara. All development planning must take place in full partnership with the Maasai, not prescribed for them by either the government or international donors. In parts of Maasailand, some group ranchers are hosting tourists eager to see wildlife outside the Mara borders, and making a good profit.

In Tanzanian Maasailand, just south of the Kenyan border, geographer Rick Schroeder is working to develop local maps to guide land use in partnership with the Tanzania National Park Service, Maasai pastoralists, an ecotourism company and a local non-governmental organization. "Historically, rural Africans have been relocated out of protected areas in the interest of resource conservation," Schroeder says. His project aims to create a different outcome, while protecting both the land and the Maasai's livelihoods. "This project," he says, "explores the potential of locally produced maps to better serve the purposes of conflict resolution than official maps would."

So Goes Pastoralism...?

A range of anthropological studies have concluded that pastoralism is an efficient and ecological system of land management. It also allows for multiple uses of the land; wildebeest and other migrating wildlife, as well as tourists, can all roam across a large open range without adversely affecting Maasai cattle. In short, pastoralism is sustainable development. However, as land in Kenya becomes increasingly scarce and demands for agriculture production and exports increase, the hegemony of the prevailing "development" model forces the question: Is it inevitable that pastoralism be transformed—some would say eradicated—to make way for small- and large-scale agricultural production and other definitions of "development"?

As population growth and in-migration to Maasailand increase land pressure, some Maasai are making alternate arrangements, little by little transforming themselves. Many now seek jobs in Nairobi, or expect that their children will. "They will have to go to Nairobi to work, of course," says one Maasailand sub-chief when asked about the future of his older children. He explained that his ranch was too small to be subdivided among his many sons and daughters.

Still, as in many parts of the world undergoing the development process, if action is to be taken in Maasailand to realize development that confers rights on local communities and values the untrammeled natural world, it will have to happen quickly. The situation in the group ranch lands is changing fast and, possibly, irreversibly. "We've got very strong traditions," William Ole Ntimana, a Maasai and a former Kenyan minister of local government, says. "But now, with the education of children, we are changing. In 25 or 30 years, I think we will all be changed."

Car Culture and the Landscape of Subtraction

Philip Goff

The hit foreign film of the late 1980s *Cinema Paradiso* provides a marvelous metaphor for our current international predicament. The film demonstrates how our collective obsession with automobiles has savaged our cities and diminished our sense of place and community. The central character within the movie is the Paradiso cinema, located on a generous piazza in a small town in Sicily. The movie house and a church provide not only the dominant architectural features of the piazza, but also the heart and soul of the community. The piazza of 1954 existed as the gathering space for the town, with its open market, cultural festivals and even an outdoor movie-screening space. In the movie, people continually traverse the space by foot, bicycle and horse-drawn cart. Upon the protagonist's return to the town in the 1980s, the once glorious urban space has been usurped by modern progress. Pedestrians are scarce as cars speed across the piazza dodging the multitude of parked vehicles. The former projectionist-turned-famous-movie-director appears devastated to see the Paradiso condemned for demolition, only to be replaced with a parking lot. In the final scene, we see the theater blasted to smithereens in the background, the weeping, nostalgic crowds in the middle ground and, in the foreground, the rooftops of Fiats and Volkswagens. Although the film ostensibly presents a general critique of modern industrial society, in the forefront is the burgeoning obsession with the *machina*. The Sicilian town's identity and sense of community have been lost with the compromise of the piazza. Crucial public space has been handed over, free of charge, to the privileged few who can afford an automobile.

Unfortunately, this is the typical state of affairs in America's cities. This (d)evolution of transportation, however, has not been a natural progression. The rise of the automobile's popularity was greatly encouraged by obstinate politicians and profit-motivated corporations. Additionally, the complicity of urban planners and architects, traffic engineers, and developers cannot be ignored. Their collective post-war creation has left us with a mountain of debt, a sprawling suburbia, polluted and crumbling inner cities and a landscape devoid of farmland and forests. All in all, ours is the landscape of subtraction. Cars have contributed nothing to our urban condition, our communities or our environment. They have only taken away. What started out as a promise for a better life based on unlimited mobility has become a modern-day obsession, as solitary commuters idle in endless traffic jams, wondering where all of the cars came from.

The Compromise of Public Space

Owning and driving an automobile has become a prerequisite for conformity in our popular culture. Not to drive in America is seen as aberrant behavior. Using mass transit is for people too poor to own an automobile, or for big-city dwellers who deem the auto commute inefficient. Riding a bicycle is regarded as either a recreational act, or only as a way for children and pre-teens to get around. Walking on a country road or a suburban strip, where there is seldom a sidewalk, immediately elicits suspicion. *Surely only a lunatic or a criminal would do such a thing.* In the land of apple pie, every "normal" citizen gets around by car; after World War Two, buying a suburban bungalow was considered a patriotic act. William Levitt, the Long Island developer for whom Levittown was named, said, "The suburban homeowner could never be a communist. . . He has too much to do!"[1] The slogans "No one messes with a man's set of wheels" and "What's good for GM is good for America" possess great authority in our culture.

Indoctrination into our auto-dominated culture begins very young. Children play with toy cars and trucks. They build miniature suburbs with Tonka trucks and cranes. Every Barbie doll or G.I. Joe figurine needs an accompanying vehicle to be complete. Many children's toy vehicles are ornamented to appear like cars, even though mechanically they are similar to bicycles. Many young boys build miniature racetracks of plastic, emulating the stock-car races seen on television. By the time these children become teenagers, they will have their sights set on that sixteenth birthday with the driver's license to follow. Who can blame them? With many living in suburbs spread so thinly, bicycle trips become impractical, and mass transit is non-existent. Those privileged enough will receive a car from their parents as a gift. Most others, though, will need to work to support their new, used cars. Some will argue that they need a car to get to work. . . so that they can have money in order to maintain their cars ... so that they can get to work... And so it goes on.

One's adult life is a constant barrage of images reinforcing the "normalcy" of car ownership and use. Psychological reinforcement comes heavily from our media sources. One-third of all television advertisements are for automobiles and a great deal of newspaper space, including the weekly "automotive section," is used to present images, statistics and commentary based on cars. This prohibits a reasonable debate on our collective auto obsession, since the media's finances are so tied in with the auto industry. The government, too, is saturated with lobbyists representing the interests of the auto, oil, tire and road-construction industries, thus inhibiting extensive support for alternative transportation funding. Subtle reinforcements occur in other ways as well, e.g., the glorification of winning a "new car" as the top prize in a television game show, at the New York Marathon, or with auto company sponsorship of bicycle races, etc.

While the media continue to highlight accidents involving airplanes, trains, subways and buses, over 40,000 people a year—the same number of Americans killed in the Vietnam War—die in car accidents.[2] According to the U.S. National Safety Council, the death rate per mile traveled in a car is 18 times greater than in a train and 97 times greater than in a bus.[3] This statistic does not include non-motorists; in New York City alone, 302 pedestrians and cyclists were killed and thousands more injured by motorists in 1996.[4] Within the developing world's chaotic mix of motorized and non-motorized vehicles, the driver and pedestrian fatality rate is close to 20 times greater than in the United States.[5] Car use also adversely affects human health by promoting a more sedentary lifestyle than does, say, bicycling. Urban commuters who drive to and from work increase their levels of stress and hypertension as they long to escape traffic and arrive at work or home. Being stuck in traffic affects a worker's morale and productivity and, along with delayed delivery of goods, costs the American economy $100 billion a year, according to the General Accounting Office.[6]

Subsidizing the American Motorist

The promotion of car culture is clearly evident in the massive subsidies bestowed upon motorists to enable them to drive almost anywhere as cheaply and efficiently as possible. The true costs of driving an automobile are obfuscated, for their disclosure would certainly reduce auto use and make alternative means more attractive. This would not be compatible with the interests of the oil, car, road construction and development industries, all of whom contribute heavily to politicians on the local and national levels.

Ample cheap and free parking is a significant way in which motorists are subsidized. Real estate values in urban areas are costly, yet motorists are allowed to use up to 100 square feet of public space for the storage of their vehicles. What reserves the side of the street to be used for the sole purpose of parking cars? Could one use the space for storage instead? To put a trampoline, maybe? Could one open up a futon in a parking space and sleep overnight? What privileges car owners to eat up such valuable urban space, when others pay hundreds of dollars for apartments hardly bigger than a parking space? A non-motorist pays the same amount for his or her groceries as a motorist, despite the inflated prices to help pay for the store's enormous parking lot and free access to it.

The allotment of public space is just one of the many ways in which motorists are subsidized in our country. Charles Komanoff, an energy consultant in New York, calculates a total subsidy of $700 billion per year, averaging out to about $5.50 per gallon, through federal and state governments. He estimates that this is roughly equivalent to what the individual motorist pays for upkeep, fuel, insurance, taxes, etc. Therefore, he reasons, driving in the United States is done at half price. The other half is provided for by the taxpayer. This puts those who do not drive—the elderly, poor people and those who choose not to—at a severe financial disadvantage.[7]

According to the United States Federal Highway Administration, taxes from gas, new car purchases, and registration cover only two-thirds of the costs of building and maintaining highways and roads.[8] The remaining costs arrive via the general tax fund. To cover the myriad costs associated with driving, gas would have to cost between three and four dollars per gallon.[9] This is closer to the rate found in European countries, where the gas tax is five times greater than in the United States. (Additionally, taxes on new car purchases overseas are close to 50 percent of the cost, while in America, the rate is five to ten percent of the total cost of the new car.)[10] Considering the uproar over President Clinton's 1993 request for a ten-cent increase in gas taxes, it is easy to see why hidden subsidies need to replace a system of direct taxation.

The primary cost of a car-dependent transportation system is the construction and maintenance of highways, roads and bridges, to the tune of $140 million every workday.[11] However, there are many other ways in which motorists are getting a free ride. A significant portion of our security forces is utilized in automobile related issues: accidents, thefts, traffic control and parking enforcement. These police officers could be much better employed going after true criminals, rather than waving along rush-hour traffic or investigating a minor traffic accident. Many of these accidents add yet another burden for the taxpayer by disabling expensive pieces of public infrastructure. Destroyed fire hydrants, light poles, mailboxes, street signs, guardrails, planters, etc. become financial burdens that would be mitigated in a society less reliant on automobiles for transportation. Besides municipal police, state police units are an enormous public expense, and apprehending highway speeders seems their reason for being.

Additionally, a large portion of health care costs are related to car accidents. Oil and car companies get large public subsidies, ranging from tax breaks to oil exploration permits on public lands. Employers are allowed to deduct from their taxes the expense of providing parking for their workers, and receive tax benefits for providing company cars. They are more strictly limited when it comes to tax incentives for mass transit or bicycle use.[12] The environmental damage caused by car use—dirty air, dirty water, deforestation, etc.—is impossible to calculate, but certainly not insignificant.

Perhaps the most expensive endowment of all lies within the tangled fabric of our foreign policy. Every year, we spend billions of dollars to protect our oil tankers traveling through the Persian Gulf. We even went to war to preserve our "right" to drive wherever, and whenever, we see fit. This prompted then senator Bob Dole to say: "We are there for three letters: O-I-L. That is why we are in the Gulf. We are not there to save democracy. Saudi Arabia is not a democracy, and neither is Kuwait."[13] Meanwhile, if we had continued conserving oil after 1985 at the same rate as before, we would have eliminated our need for any oil from the gulf.[14] The industrialized world's intense reliance on petroleum has allowed it to become a pawn in international politics.

The Great Suburban Build-Out

Government and corporate encouragement of car use and suburban sprawl as support structures for our fallacious economic "growth" is nothing new. It began in earnest in 1936 with the creation of the National City Lines company, a corporate front group representing General Motors, Standard Oil, Firestone Tire and Mack Trucks. For the next 15 years, this powerful company bought out 45 streetcar and trolley systems throughout the country. By the 1950s, all 45 transit systems were completely dismantled, opening the way for private car use and increased bus service, a demand that GM was all too happy to supply. This was the sad fate of public transportation in Los Angeles, a system nearly as extensive as New York's. Eventually, National City Lines was found guilty of criminal antitrust violations. But the verdict was moot, for the great suburban build-out was in full throttle.

Meanwhile, in the 1930s, President Roosevelt's Federal Housing Authority (FHA) was created to put the construction industry back on its feet and to improve housing stock for Americans. The FHA subsidized banks through the federal treasury, therefore allowing for reduced downpayments and extended mortgages. Unfortunately, the FHA did not guarantee new loans for those who wanted to build or renovate in the inner cities. Maybe this should come as no surprise considering that one of its commissioners happened to be on the Board of Directors of the Standard Oil Company. After World War Two, the government allowed the millions of returning GIs to own homes without requiring any downpayments, and mortgage interests were made tax deductible. Thus owning was made less expensive than renting and, encouraged by the planned system of new highways, white veterans flocked to the burgeoning suburbs.

As farmland and forests were being paved over with housing developments in the 1950s, the county and state road systems were becoming overburdened. Our economy demanded more growth, and the federal government began the largest public-works project in our history: the Interstate Highway System. President Eisenhower began funding the highways after a hearty recommendation by his self-appointed commission, chaired by Lucius D. Clay, on the Board of Directors of General Motors. Forty-one thousand miles of new expressways spread over the country like a complex of veins and arteries.[15] Apologists for the vast new system insisted that the highways would quicken urban evacuation in the case of a Soviet nuclear attack and would provide enormous expanses of pavement and concrete to act as firebreaks, allowing sectors to remain unscathed.

Many companies had enormous profits to make through suburban expansion. The obvious beneficiaries were the oil and car companies, but those that produced appliances, lawn mowers, and lawn care products stood to cash in as well. One of these was General Electric, which realized that every new home was certain to need a new washer and dryer, refrigerator, stove, blender and other convenience items. GE knew that its fortunes lay within the increased unpopularity of urban apartment living. To encourage the exodus, the company sponsored exhibitions and architectural competitions to glorify the modern suburban house. Famous architects normally won the competitions, thus legitimizing of—and guaranteeing press coverage for—the single-family suburban home.

While large sums of money funded the creation of highways and airports, rail improvements were all but forgotten. Sustainable, non-polluting alternatives have never been encouraged by our government except in emergency situations such as oil embargoes. The sprawling suburbs came to a crawl after the 1973 embargo, and subsequently President Carter sought alternative energy sources and decreased automobile reliance. After the election of Ronald Reagan, the oil cartel weakened, Iran and Iraq were soon engaged in a long and brutal war, and the oil market was flooded. With cheap gas, bank deregulation and Reagan's tax policies, suburban development and car use went back into high gear throughout the 1980s. During this period, federal funding for highways nearly doubled while the funding for mass transit was reduced by ten percent.[16] In 1991, over $28 billion was spent to build, widen and maintain roads in the United States, while only a fraction was allocated for rail improvements.[17]

The ultimate fallacy of an economy and lifestyle dependent upon cheap and plentiful oil is that it is not sustainable. The figures on oil reserves by the United States Geological Survey (USGS) and the *Oil and Gas Journal* place the world's supply at 40 years. This figure is extremely conservative, for it underestimates the exploding demand for oil in developing countries.[18] Petroleum depletion could be mitigated if motorists would pay for the true costs of driving, thus making alternatives, such as trains and bicycles, more attractive. Higher taxes must be levied upon gas, registration and new car purchases, and tolls need to be increased, especially for solitary commuters. These meaures would not only offset the many subsidized costs of auto transit, but also create capital for rail improvements. The discouragement of automobile use must begin today, or we run the risk of being unprepared when the pumps run dry and "carmaggedon" is upon us.

Suburban Culture

Where half a century ago most people lived in a city or a rural location, the post-war blossoming of our car culture has allowed today's typical American to live in a suburban housing development. Ostensibly designed to preserve open space, these communities lack public open space and, due to dysfunctional zoning regulations, are spread so thinly that public transportation becomes elusive. Therefore, a car trip is the required method of transportation for every task; it is no wonder that the average American motorist drives nearly 10,000 miles a year.[19]

The need to drive everywhere increases social fragmentation and is most detrimental to those who cannot drive: the elderly, the sick, children and the poor, all of whom become completely dependent on car drivers for mobility. Ironically, many families initially relocate to suburbs for the "good" of their children, yet the children are stuck in virtual isolation and overdependence on their parents, for their communities are designed not for them but for cars. Thus, they spend a great deal of their time in front of the television or computer, which become the prime attractions in many suburbs whose landscapes are defined by housing developments, parking lots, fast-food joints and expressway off-ramps. The suburban landscape that most politicians would proudly call "growth" has greatly contributed to the deterioration of community and culture, for community has been replaced by shopping malls, and culture by television.

Zoning laws account for much of the reason suburbs look the way they do. Drafted by planning boards often representing development and business interests, many of the codes are tailored for the convenience of automobiles, as if they were the dominant life form on the planet. The main premise behind our current zoning codes is the complete and distanced separation of homes and jobs, as though we still inhabited cities of smokestacked factories and revolting slaughterhouses. With segregation rather than mixed-uses, walking or biking to perform daily errands or go to work becomes impossible and, because mass transit is so poor, a motor vehicle becomes a necessity. Additionally, the car creates the dysfunctional hierarchy of the commercial strip, the destination for so many who simply need a soda or a newspaper. Corner stores are not allowed in most suburban residential neighborhoods, nor are apartments allowed above shops and restaurants, denying mixed-use buildings, and keeping densities at a minimum.

Zoning laws regarding street design contribute to the lack of community in most suburbs. These laws deny enclosure, so necessary in making quality street spaces. The comforting feeling of enclosure is what makes nineteenth-century brownstone-lined streets so charming. For instance, compare a street in old-world Brooklyn to one that has a wide paved surface, no sidewalk, facades comprised of garages, and houses set back from the street and spaced at large intervals. Requirements for wide streets make speeds in excess of 35 miles per hour possible, and street trees and sharp curves are heartily discouraged for fear of prompting traffic accidents. Towering, alien-like street lamps block out the stars and exist so that late-night motorists can negotiate the street at higher speeds. All told, suburban zoning laws mandate an environment designed for automobile driving, with zero regard for the public realm.[20]

On the commercial boulevards, zoning requires that buildings be set back certain distances and provide large parking lots. The amalgamation of these structures resembles a gridded archipelago within a vast sea of pavement. Architecturally, these areas are as cheaply constructed as they are unsightly, and many design elements are at a scale not commensurate with pedestrians. The attempt to lure motorists reaches its most perverse extreme as gas stations and restaurants float their signs hundreds of feet in the air, begging for the attention of the speeding motorist. The suburban strip has also created its own building and spatial typologies: drive-in restaurants, enormous billboards, car washes, gas stations and new- and used-car lots.

Car Culture's Invasion of the Metropolis

The automobile's invasion of our cities has likewise had a major impact on urban architecture. As noted at the beginning, car culture has created the "architecture of subtraction," as pieces and parts of towns and cities have been eviscerated to make room for automobiles. This action has excised portions of urban fabric, taking away street definition, so important in civic space making. Buildings and entire blocks have been removed to make parking lots. Gas stations have become eyesores, and usurp large areas of space potentially used for public plazas, parks or buildings. Cars take away from the pedestrian experience of movement through a city, and dampen visual and cultural stimulation. Instead of strolling along a well-defined street with interesting shop windows and greenery, city dwellers are forced to gaze across a bleak landscape of cars.

Never before has an invention that so many people consider a necessity taken up so much space. In older cities such as Boston and New York, close to half of the ground space is reserved for the sole purpose of moving and storing cars, and in newer cities such as Los Angeles and Phoenix that figure is closer to two-thirds.[21] These inequities become quite obvious when one simply walks the streets of Manhattan. The distribution of pedestrian space compared with automobile space is heavily weighted toward the motorist, even in midtown Manhattan, where millions work, and Greenwich Village, where thousands socialize. Hundreds of people can be jammed onto narrow sidewalks, while cars stream by on four- and five-lane avenues. In the battle for urban turf, the clear winner is the automobile.

Few civic interventions compare to the destruction wrought by urban expressways. From the beginning, expressways were ostensibly built to bring commuters into the city more easily, but what they have really done is drained the city of its middle class by providing a very efficient pathway out. As highways plowed through cities in the 1950s and 1960s, dense urban neighborhoods of different ethnicities were removed and high-rise housing projects took their place. The government, responding to the surge in black migration north, built these projects to house the new arrivals and simultaneously provided highways to allow the white middle class to escape, encouraging segregation. Highways did not so much *ameliorate* traffic congestion as *create* it by decentralizing urban areas.

Expressways fracture neighborhoods and are accompanied by a host of subsequent urban predicaments. Besides introducing air and noise pollution, the highways are like stakes driven through the hearts of intact neighborhoods.

Geographically, expressways are often constructed along natural boundaries, resulting in the separation of the urban realm from rivers, lakes, bays and oceans. Not only does this deny the heritage of a city, whose economy may have been based on a local body of water, but it also prohibits public access to natural open spaces. Highways built above grade are like massive fortress walls of noise and smog, and built below grade they resemble moats, often with infrequent overpasses to further divide the community. From an economic point of view, they are quite detrimental, for the dense city fabric cleared for the widened road subtracts formerly taxable land. The malign effects of the highway reverberate from block to block, and property values plummet; a once middle-class neighborhood turns to squalor as residents flee to the suburbs on the very highway that destroyed their neighborhoods. The void is soon filled by immigrants and the economically disadvantaged. The municipality, loathing the loss of property taxes, allows the area to crumble. This scenario has played a major role in the disintegration of many of America's cities, from Los Angeles to Detroit to the South Bronx.

Culturally, the ubiquity of cars has had the largest impact on our street culture, the common bond of communities. The public space of the urban and suburban street has, for the most part, been compromised for the singular purpose of moving and storing automobiles and thus relinquished to the favored car owners of our society. Street space incubates social interaction, which becomes much more difficult when streets are filled with noisy, polluting and speeding motor vehicles. According to the late architectural historian Spiro Kostof, "The street stands as the burial place of a chance to learn from one another, the burial place of unrehearsed excitement, of the cumulative knowledge of human ways. We lose this because we would rather keep to ourselves, avoid social tension by escaping it, schedule encounters with friends and happily travel alone in climate-controlled and music-injected glossy metal boxes."[22]

In some large cities, streets have become so chaotic and polluted that separate planes of pedestrian movement have developed. Rather than confronting the real epidemic, cities and private sources have built extensive systems of bridges and underground concourses, keeping the public off the ground plane, where social intercourse traditionally occurs. These ersatz public spaces fail to bring together urban society in all its diversity. The quasi-public bridges and concourses are undemocratic, in that they allow the often private controlling body to eliminate undesirable elements, such as the homeless or demonstrators. Sadly, many have forgotten or may never know the true vitality of an authentic street culture. Disneyland's Main Street or the local mall will never be appropriate substitutes. Instead, much of the built landscape is a pathetic mass of squalor and dysfunctional planning. Yet most of us feel that it was an organic process that the shift could not be ameliorated.

Auto usage results directly in many violent crimes such as car jackings and drive-by shootings, and is often an integral part of much gang activity and violence. Interestingly, it is in large cities that rely most heavily on automobile transportation that major gang problems are most prevalent. The multitude of roads and expressways also provide convenient ways to buy drugs, pick up a prostitute, rob a store or blow up an office building. These criminal acts become more difficult in a society whose transportation needs are met by mass transit and bicycles.

The issue of access to terrorism has finally caught the attention of our federal government. After months of deliberation President Clinton ordered the closing of Pennsylvania Avenue, just weeks after the bombing of the Murrah Federal Building in Oklahoma City in 1995. Although the three-block stretch of road outside the White House has been reclaimed as public space and filled with hundreds of tourists and roller skaters, the need to apologize was still felt. Quoted in the *New York Times*, the President said that the street closing was "seen as a responsible security step necessary to preserve our freedom, not part of a long-term restriction of our freedom." To equate automobile access to a section of street with freedom is ludicrous, but, in a car-dominant society, many motorists feel that they have the "right" to drive anywhere, whether that be deep into a national park or directly in front of the White House. Maybe the President's attitude comes as no surprise to those who remember his valiant appeals to the American psyche when he declared, after the 1993 Los Angeles earthquake, that he would make freeway reconstruction a priority.

Based upon car culture's incorrigible impact on North America, one shudders to think of this becoming an international precedent. It is already happening. Since the collapse of the Soviet monolith, privatization in Europe and the opening of the Asian markets, multinational auto makers and oil companies have aggressively been trying to move into these arenas. In countries throughout Eastern Europe, car use has exploded and pollution levels are on the rise, as subsidies for public transport wane. In Brazil, annual car sales doubled from 1990 to 1995, and in São Paulo there are 4.5 million cars, twice the per capita rate of New York City.[23] The Chinese government, while vigorously pushing to modernize its country, has begun enormous road-building projects, hoping to encourage tens of millions to buy cars. Like post-war America, China seems to be blinded by the aura surrounding the automobile, and has failed to consider the consequences. Perhaps Chinese officials should try driving on a Los Angeles freeway at rush hour or biking up Sixth Avenue in Manhattan before they make such hasty decisions for their country.

The Destruction of Farmland, Forests and Wildlife

America's auto-dominated transportation matrix and the resultant suburban sprawl have eaten up more land in the past 40 years than in the previous 300, and the environmental damage has been unprecedented: diminished quality of air and water, loss of natural resources, and destruction of farmland, forests, and wildlife. The amoeba–like suburbs, left unchecked, will sprawl further into the deserts of the Southwest, the forests of the Pacific Northwest, the mountains of Colorado, the farmlands of the Midwest and the last few remaining wild places in the Northeast.

From the perspective of the use of natural resources, the automobile-oriented suburbs are perniciously inefficient. Compare the environmental impact of a car-oriented suburban community of 500 households with an urban community for the same 500 households. The land-use requirements for the former are enormous, as each house occupies a quarter- or half-acre lot and is connected by wide roads. The 500 individual homes require vast amounts of material to build and must be connected by a myriad of power, water and sewer lines, putting a strain on our dwindling natural resources. Although urban communities are not perfect, they have a much lower ecological impact considering their compact land use, efficiency of materials and infrastructure, and maintained distance from wilderness and wildlife.

The common piece of infrastructure that is necessary for all suburban and ex-urban developments is the paved road. Every square foot of pavement represents an ecological dead zone, a completely sterilized environment that allows runoff of oil, antifreeze and brake fluids into the water table. When a road is built in a remote area close to wilderness, it brings with it not only polluting and dangerous cars, but also the constant pressure of continued development. The close proximity to nature introduces items not native to a bioregion such as noise, garbage, dogs, vehicles and guns. Roads also allow hordes of hunters, poachers and trappers to drive into remote areas to exterminate wildlife. The rise in the popularity of campers and four-wheel-drive vehicles has accelerated the complete commodification of the natural world. Now we can all have a packaged environment, seen from the safety of mobile fortresses as if the planet were one big theme park. Television advertisements convince viewers that the appropriate four-wheel- drive vehicle will allow them to cross rivers, blaze through forests and drive to remote mountain vista points. Car culture has clearly brought too many people to places where they do not necessarily belong.

A great tragedy is the quantity of wild animals that are struck and killed every year by speeding automobiles. More than half a billion animals, as well as more than a quarter of a million people, are killed every year on the planet's roads and highways.[24] This is five times more creatures than are killed by the American pork industry.[25] The average American's car kills three to four vertebrate animals every year and has contributed to the endangerment of some species, most notably the Florida panther, 65 percent of whose documented deaths have been at the hands of motorists traveling through the Ocala National Forest. In Pennsylvania alone in 1985, 26,180 deer and 90 bears were slaughtered by automobiles.[26] In the Mikumi National Park in Tanzania, more animals, including baboons, wildebeest, zebras, antelopes, jackals and even elephants have been killed by cars than by poachers since the 1991 road improvements increased the maximum speed from 20 to 60 miles per hour.[27] By far the leading cause of death for endangered red wolves in northeast North Carolina is collision with automobiles.[28]

Some species are attracted to roads while others are frightened off, both of which inclinations have disastrous implications for the animals forced to deal with the intrusion of roadways. Animals averse to roads run the risk of genetic deterioration due to inbreeding created by the fragmentation of their populations, hemmed in by roads on all sides. The healthy migration of road-averse animals is also affected, and they are forced to stay in unnatural climates. The noises due to road construction and the resulting traffic can alter an animal's pattern of activity and raise their stress levels. This is especially true of birds who rely heavily on auditory signals.

Exacerbating the increase in roadkill is the unfortunate fact that many animals are attracted to the topography of a road. The dense vegetation at the sides of roads draws grazing deer and a multitude of rodents. The proliferation of rodents, along with previously killed animals, brings scavengers such as coyote and raccoon, who in turn are often struck by cars. Other large mammals come to the roadway to use it as a travel corridor. The proximity of the large mammals attracts curious and naive onlookers who frequently harass the animals or try to feed them human food. Wild animals come to the road to eat de-icing salts in the winter season, increasing the potential of a collision, and poisoning the animal due to the sodium and calcium chlorides present in the salt.[29]

Another way in which automobile ownership and use is detrimental to the environment is the vast quantities of natural resources required to sustain a transportation mode. Besides the wood, gravel, asphalt and steel used to build and maintain the planet's roads and highways, the world's 400 million cars require excessive amounts of resources and energy to create. In a culture less reliant on automobiles, the inner-city street's abandoned cars, the monumental piles of worn tires and the junkyard cache of flattened cars would be greatly lessened.

Although these days most cars can last much longer, many are passed on after only a few years, keeping car companies' profits rolling in. Complicit designers are all too happy to churn out the latest models with improved aerodynamics, racier colors, and the newest gizmos of convenience. In 1955, Harvey Earl, the head of the GM styling division, said, "Our biggest job is to hasten obsolescence. In 1934, the average car ownership span was five years; now it is two years. When it is one year, we will have a perfect score."[30]

The environmental problem most apparent to the public is air pollution. Within urban areas, cars create the most air pollution, 13 percent of worldwide carbon dioxide emissions, 28 percent of chlorofluorocarbons, and between 30 and 40 percent of nitrogen oxides, the primary chemical responsible for acid rain.[31] The Environmental Protection Agency reports that automobile air conditioners are the single largest source of ozone-depleting chemicals. Despite the fact that these days cars produce half as much carbon monoxide as they did 20 years ago—good for reducing urban smog—the amount of carbon dioxide released from cars is the same and will always be the same, for it is the inevitable byproduct of fossil fuel consumption. The invisible and odorless carbon dioxide cannot be reduced, no matter the filter or catalytic converter on the newest, most aerodynamic car, and it is this insidious carbon dioxide gas which is contributing greatly to the greenhouse effect.[32]

The profligate use of oil may, in many ways, contain the most ecologically destructive component of all: the ubiquitous oil-spill. It is ubiquitous in the sense that the Exxon Valdez disaster was not an anomaly; spills of that magnitude occur quite often and have disastrous implications on the ecology of the world's oceans. Greenpeace estimates that one billion gallons of oil are spilled directly into the oceans every year. Valdez was only the fourteenth largest spill in history, but because most of the others occurred offshore and did not immediately reach a populated land mass there was less media coverage. Accidental spills, however, represent only 13 percent of the total oil which enters the marine environment. The rest enters the oceans via the routine flushing of carrier tanks and the daily byproducts of the petroleum industry. Another 50 million gallons of petroleum seep into the world's fresh-water supply through the daily run-off from roads and do-it-yourself mechanics. Although the total number of deaths of sea creatures and birds due to oil spillage is incalculable, the toll from the Exxon Valdez incident, according to Greenpeace, led to the deaths of 5,000 otters, 200 harbor seals and perhaps half a million birds.[33]

The demand for petroleum constantly pressures the oil industry to search for oil in increasingly remote places. The oil companies' thirst for profit leaves them with little concern for the consequences of their actions. Their powerful lobbyists are constantly persuading the United States and other governments to open fragile wilderness and marine habitats to oil exploration, whether it be in a tropical rainforest, a spectacular mountain range or the Arctic tundra. When habitats are opened up for exploration, great damage is done even if oil is not found in sufficient quantities to warrant refining. Seismic studies destroy habitat and terrify wildlife, and the myriad abandoned roads are often subsequently used by logging companies to reach areas that were initially off-limits to them. The predicament can only get worse, for as Asia, especially China, develops its system of roads and opens its markets, the number of cars on the planet is expected to double by 2010.

Many of humanity's most pressing problems, such as deforestation, the loss of biodiversity, the dwindling of native cultures, global warming, the loss of communities, and water pollution can be traced to the overuse of automobiles and unchecked suburban development. Cars are here to stay and they certainly have their uses, but too many people have deemed these uses to mean every single trip, whether one mile or one hundred miles. We have been brainwashed into demanding a table in the non-smoking section of a restaurant and then, after the meal, either driving home or walking along noisy, chaotic and polluted streets. The daily bombardment of automobile images and our government's obstinate attitude toward alternatives have allowed us to accept the auto-dominated landscape that surrounds us. Until this type of behavior is curbed, our decadent lifestyle will continue to decimate communities and cities and accelerate the ongoing destruction of the natural world.

The Sustainable City

Stephan Chenault

Stephan Chenault is the Environmental Justice Committee co-chair for the Sierra Club New York City Group and on the Executive Committee of the Sierra Club New York City Group. He is also the vice-president of the board of Magnolia Tree Earth Center in Bedford Stuyvesant, Brooklyn, which offers programs for young people in the inner city to learn about, and further careers in, ecology and environmentalism. Chenault is a member of the Cooperative Ecological Community, a group of people who meet in Park Slope in Brooklyn and support each other in ecologically sustainable lifestyles.

"Everyone needs clean air and water and everyone has a feeling for nature and for other living things."

What is sustainability?

Sustainability means that people are living in a way that meets their basic needs but also provides for the livelihood and well-being of all other life forms and all natural communities on earth. A definition of sustainability for me would be that all the natural inhabitants of a forest are able to sustain their lives according to their nature. It's really sustainability of the whole natural community.

We should do everything possible to maintain ecosystems intact. That doesn't mean there won't be changes or that we won't ever use any innovative technologies. There are times when I think technology can be very helpful if used in the right way. Solar energy can be used in a way that could help to sustain the planet. Wind energy is another high-tech possibility that can be used in a sustainable way, and there are efforts to develop solar cookers and buildings with energy-efficient lighting. I am concerned about using technology in a way that sustains our environment.

How do you balance development of technology with sustainability?
Development per se is not necessarily a goal. Meeting people's basic needs is important. People should have enough to eat, to clothe themselves, to have a decent home and a decent livelihood. But the need to continuously have more and more in terms of both affluence and power over nature—this type of development as a goal in itself is not acceptable. An alternative type of development would be to be toward increased understanding of, and sympathy and communication with, other life forms. If we can have an ethic that values having a closer relationship with each other and with other life forms, and if we could appreciate other life forms more, it would certainly give a greater amount of satisfaction.

What does a sustainable city mean to you and how does it correlate with environmental justice?
First of all, cities can be a great asset for the environment and ecological systems. Having a concentration of people in cities is good in a way, because if people were spread out throughout suburbs and the countryside, we would find that those environments that were previously more lightly populated would become gradually impoverished ecologically. A sustainable city means a healthy environment, clean air and clean water. People should have access to nature and open spaces—whether it is through parks, community gardens within the city or chances to leave the city and enjoy the natural world.

A healthy environment is very key to environmental justice. Environmental justice groups are addressing issues such as air quality caused by the siting of bus depots in northern Manhattan. The siting of incinerators is certainly an environmental justice issue, as is the use of lead-based paint in minority communities.

Cities are centers of a great deal of consumption. It is important that we develop urban centers that do not consume as much. We consume huge amounts of paper that comes from both old–growth forests and rainforests, and we have a great responsibility to reduce that. New York City's boardwalks and the majority of the city's park benches are made from rainforest wood. I was instrumental with Rainforest Relief and the Sierra Club in getting city councilman Gifford Miller to introduce a bill to prohibit the city from purchasing tropical rainforest hardwood unless it was sustainably harvested and managed. Coffee is another problem. Coffee is grown on former rainforest land. There needs to be more organic coffee promoted in coffee bars. Organic coffee is grown in the shade in rainforest countries and still maintains a fair amount of biological diversity because it does not require full sunlight. I have been talking with people about starting a campaign to get coffee shops to buy more organic coffee.

116

What about in inner-city communities?

We already have programs like low-income weatherization projects, in which assistance is given to low-income people to make their homes more energy efficient. They save on their energy bills as well as save energy—a win–win situation. If we could do the same thing for compact fluorescent lighting and have programs to provide assistance for buying energy-efficient lighting, that would save both money and the environment. We also have Community Supported Agriculture and Greenmarkets. In this way, we could see a city be a vital core with a vibrant culture and arts and a high quality of life and, around the city, farms offering local produce. In this way, a city like New York would not have to import foods from California or South America that require a great deal of transportation, processing and packaging and thereby increase pollution.

Do you think the current environmental movement is essentially white and middle-class?

There is a great amount of activity among communities of color on environmental issues. Therefore, that perception is not quite accurate. If people really were involved in environmental justice issues, they would see that there is a lot of cross-fertilization between environmental justice and the environmental–conservation movement already taking place. People in the environmental justice movement in New York City work in cooperation with groups such as the Sierra Club, the New York League of Conservation Voters, the New York City Public Industry Research Group and other environmental organizations. There needs to be more communication about environmental justice and conservation, and other groups are already working together a great deal. There are problems, but they do work together quite often.

When white environmentalists worry that communities of color have too much to worry about in their daily lives to care about the environment, it can be a self-fulfilling prophecy. Mainstream environmental groups have that in their heads and, therefore, they do not go to minority groups or neighborhoods or meetings when they could. They don't go to Harlem, they don't table in minority neighborhoods. Then they wonder why there are not more minorities in their organizations. If they would do more outreach they would find that there are plenty of people who love nature. Everyone needs clean air and water and everyone has a feeling for nature and for other living things.

A Localized Food System
Creating Sustainable Communities
Constance Lynn Cornell

In 1975 the process of Western "development" infiltrated the Himalayan province of Ladakh. Until then, this isolated culture had survived and prospered in one of the highest, driest and coldest inhabited places on earth. Swedish philosopher, teacher and activist Helena Norberg-Hodge has lived with Ladakhi people for two decades and has witnessed the consequences of development. "Within little more than a decade, feelings of pride gave way to what can best be described as a cultural inferiority complex," she writes. Ladakhis are ashamed of their roots as they compare themselves and their ways with Western culture.[1]

For thousands of years the Ladakhis had provided themselves with food, shelter and clothing using little more than Stone Age technologies. Ladakhis had grown fields of grain, fruits and vegetables irrigated with glacial meltwater brought from miles away through stone-lined channels. Now food arrives by the ton from the other side of the Himalayas and is cheaper in the local bazaar than food grown minutes away. It is no longer worthwhile for many Ladakhis to farm. Western-style economic development "is making us all poorer by teaching people around the world to use the same global resources, ignoring those that their immediate environments naturally provide," Norberg-Hodge argues. "In this way, Western-style education creates artificial scarcity and induces competition."

New York State loses a thousand farms and 150,000 acres of farmland every year. As in Ladakhi culture, the last three decades of globalized conventional farming have come at a heavy ecological cost in the United States. Machines have replaced farmers and farmworkers. Pollution and pesticide use on post-harvested produce have increased as produce is transported long distances. Intensive farming depletes the soil of nutrients, pesticides run off into our waterways, and people lose sight of self-sufficiency and feel pressured to conform and live up to the idealized images and prosperity of the American dream.

Inherent in a model of self-sufficiency is the ability to produce our own food. A localized food system encompasses farming, transportation, marketing, employment and consumer interests. It puts control back into the hands of the people to determine where their food comes from. Local jobs are created and fresh food becomes affordable, attainable and secure.

As with the Ladakhi traditional economy, Americans once depended directly on family, friends and neighbors. Through a growing coalition of groups including educational organizations, community gardens, Community Supported Agriculture, and Greenmarkets, communities can reclaim their power to make decisions about where their food comes from and to support the local economy.

118

In 1973, the Green Guerillas formed to help New York City residents create community gardens. This group of volunteers uses "guerilla" tactics to make growing food in the inner city possible. Plants, fruit trees and tools that are neglected or donated, as well as materials for compost, are collected by the Green Guerillas and distributed to community members who want to start an urban garden. As Phil Tietz of the Green Guerillas asserts, "Gardeners are good people." In cities as diverse as New York City, community gardens draw together people from different cultures who may have farmed in their homelands. Currently, the future of community gardens is unstable as lots are being targeted for housing development purposes. Consequently, an opportunity for neighbors to connect and share vital knowledge about growing their own food will be lost.

Community Supported Agriculture (CSA) is a regional solution that combines supporting local farms with minimizing dependence on the conventional food system. Bill Halsey, the farmer for Greenthumb CSA, operating on Long Island, New York, says he cannot ordinarily compete with agribusiness practices and therefore his family farm is at an economic disadvantage. In CSAs, community members collectively organize to support a local farm. In groups such as Bill's, members buy shares in the farm to provide the farmer with capital before the start of a farming season. Farmers benefit by having the risks of farming shared regardless of weather and the size of the harvest. Core group committees organize members to work shifts on the farm and handle distribution dynamics. Sarah Milstein, a core group member of Roxbury Farm CSA in New Jersey, works to ensure that a variety of residents get served.

CSAs accommodate consumers' ability to pay by offering sliding-scale fees, scholarships and the option of paying weekly. Working periodic shifts on the farm or at distribution sites can further reduce the price of a share, but mainly provides an opportunity for members to gain an intimate appreciation for where their produce comes from and the work involved in growing and distributing. The ecological costs of transporting are reduced by localizing distribution sites at schools, churches or members' houses. Produce is bountifully arranged on tables at the sites and members come prepared with their own bags to package their goods. To complete the food-to-people cycle, leftover produce is typically contributed to food pantries and shelters for homeless people.

Another option for regional farmers who want to connect with New York City dwellers is Greenmarkets. Throughout Manhattan, Brooklyn, the Bronx and Staten Island, these markets provide a space for farmers to sell their goods throughout the year. Especially in the summer, the markets bustle. Fresh produce, baked goods and other produce are available. Consumers and farmers benefit by cutting out middlemen. Like CSAs, the Greenmarkets reduce the need for excessive transportation and packaging of food and also support a local economy.

In 1986, a group of farmers started the Finger Lakes Organics (FLO) growers cooperative. Instead of farmers individually contacting retailers and then driving long distances to deliver their produce to city Greenmarkets, FLO serves as a regional broker. For farmers like Dick deGraff, an organic farmer in New York State, FLO offers a vital link to city residents and makes his farm economically viable, despite the power of agribusiness.

Helena Norberg-Hodge, in referring to the Ladakhi culture, is "convinced that people were significantly happier before development and globalism than they are today. The people were well cared for and the environment well sustained. What could be more important?"

Sustainable Sustenance
Kathy Lawrence

Just Food was formed in 1995 to bring together organizations in and around New York City that are working on various food system issues such as urban gardening, organic farming, hunger and nutrition, consumer advocacy, and social justice. We started with the recognition that there is a lot already happening in the city. There are 36 farmers' markets. There are a thousand community gardens and over a thousand emergency feeding centers in New York City alone. And there are 15 urban gardening groups and six anti-hunger organizations. Yet no one was bringing all the pieces together and looking at what it takes to build a sustainable food and agriculture system that actually feeds people, keeps farmers in business, preserves the environment and provides good, secure livelihoods throughout the food chain.

In 1980 there were fewer than 50 emergency food centers in the city. Even now, with over a thousand, according to the New York City Coalition Against Hunger over 70,000 people a month are being turned away from those centers for lack of food or inability to get food to people. These numbers are just beginning to reflect the massive welfare cuts which took food stamp privileges away from legal immigrants, who make up a substantial part of New York City's population. Paralleling this dramatic increase in emergency feeding centers and the need for food is an alarming decline in farming. New York State loses on average 20 farms per week. From 1980 to 1995, New York State lost at least 20,000 farms. These are run by good farmers growing good food that's desperately needed in New York City, and for which there is a huge market. Seven or eight million people a day pull out their wallets to buy food in New York City. Where's that food coming from and at what cost?

Very few of us know where our food comes from—who's growing it, how it's grown, and how far it has traveled. That knowledge can tell us what kind of food system we are investing in every single day and for every single meal: either a globalized, industrialized and incredibly destructive and monopolistic food system, or a different kind of food system—one that really supports farmers and non-farmers alike.

Let me give you an example. New York is second only to Washington as the largest apple-producing state in the country. New York produces nine times as many apples as are eaten in the entire state, yet only 3.4 percent of the apples we eat in New York City actually come from our state. Most of our apples come from Washington, California and overseas—Chile, Argentina, and New Zealand. Most New York State apples are sold in the southern United States. This is insane! We need to take practical steps to support a healthy, strong, ecologically sound, regional food system.

Seven Practical Steps

1. Begin growing at least some of your own food, even if it consists only of herbs or lettuces on your window sill. Not only will you be taking a little bit of pressure off the industrialized food system, you will also reconnect with the cycles of growing life. You will have more respect and understanding for what goes into growing all of your food when you re-engage in even a small way.

2. Buy from local farmers. There are still more than 30,000 farmers in New York State. Find out where your farmers are and where your nearest farmers' markets are; buy from those farmers. Spend at least $10 a week on food that you know is grown or processed in your state. It's a pretty simple thing to do. Think about where your food dollars are going.

3. Join Community Supported Agriculture (CSA). CSA is a great way for you to know exactly where your food is coming from and how it's grown. With CSA you establish a direct relationship with a farmer, by paying in advance for a share in an entire season's harvest from a nearby farm. What city folks get is weekly delivery of fresh produce to a central distribution site (usually a church or community center) from June to November or December, or sometimes even through February. There are now nine CSAs in four boroughs of New York City, and Just Food is helping to develop more.

4. Talk to the produce manager at your grocery store or supermarket. Produce managers are required by law to know the origin of everything that comes into their store. Whether they post it or not, they are required to know. Demand that they get local regional products in their store. A manager from D'Agostino's recently told me that all he needed were five requests for him to stock something. Retake that power.

5. Prepare more of your own food. We need to spend more time actually engaging in the process of feeding ourselves and our families, and not waiting for an increasingly industrialized system to do it for us. Currently, we pay for the long-distance transportation of food whose nutrients have all been completely processed out, and which has been supplemented with additives and other things like fat, sugar and salt. This is not the way it ought to be. We need to work more with whole foods and reclaim responsibility for our own health, rather than expecting someone else to do it.

6. Start composting your food waste. For a start, it's not "waste"—it's essential nutrients that are being taken out of the system and put into another incredibly destructive system called landfills. I have some friends in my office: about three thousand red wiggler worms that eat almost all of my food waste. These worms create wonderful worm castings for your plants. You can buy red wigglers of your own, learn about home composting or even drop off your compostables, or read *Worms Eat My Garbage* by Mary Appelhof.

7. Support a community garden. The gardens in New York City are under tremendous attack from the city's selling off its property and from the pending deregulation of rents. Community gardens are centers of community education, community life and community space. Just Food is leading a collaborative project to boost urban agriculture in New York's low-income communities. We're bringing in organic farmers to work with gardeners to grow food in an urban setting and get more people involved in growing their own food. We can't do this if the gardens no longer exist.

Where Has All the Garbage Gone?

Susan Kalev

How we dispose of garbage can generate social conflict and spur political debate leading to class struggle. Powerful social issues of class, ethnicity and environmental policy are reflected in attitudes toward health, cleanliness and morality. Garbage affects an era's values regarding order and disorder and a society's beliefs about diet and disease.

New York City is no exception. Nineteenth-century New York was unimaginably filthy, with streets piled high with rubbish. Poisonous vapors rising from rotting food and waste were thought to cause epidemics. Some blamed the poor and their presumed immoral behavior. Not until 1897 did reformers realize that the poor were dirty for lack of water and bathrooms. Whether seen as a public or a private issue, garbage was here to stay. From 1895 to 1897, Colonel George E. Waring revolutionized solid-waste management by injecting respect and order into garbage collection. Ocean dumping (a popular solution) was abolished in 1934, recycling instituted, and energy recovery started. In the 1930s, the trend was toward incineration of garbage. So fiercely was this opposed by local residents that landfills were expanded. By 1946, 13 landfills were disposing of 80 percent of New York City's waste.

One of the most notorious of all landfills in the United States is the Fresh Kills landfill on Staten Island, New York. Since its opening in 1948, Fresh Kills—a Dutch transliteration of "fresh river"—has become not only the largest landfill in the world, but the highest point on the eastern seaboard. It is due to be closed on December 31, 2001. Currently, 800 of Fresh Kills' 2,400 acres are in use, holding the 650 tons of waste each of the 20 barges arriving at Fresh Kills carries every day. While the landfill is not the end point for all garbage—in 1994, 160,000 Christmas trees were mulched and recycled at Fresh Kills—it is still important to reduce the production of new garbage. For instance, New York Telephone helped eliminate 768 tons of paper waste in 1994 by printing telephone bills on both sides. Twice a year recomposted Christmas trees are given away to the public, and a pleasant pine scent is added to the waters circling the plant to make life more tolerable for nearby residents. Skimmer boats patrol the streams and pick up stray garbage while booms or floating barriers and marine fences catch any escaping litter. Lines of trees separate the landfill from the neighborhood and provide attractive landscaping.

The United States creates 19 percent of the world's garbage, with each of us responsible for four pounds per day. Every week the 6,400 New York City Department of Sanitation (DOS) employees use over 1,000 trucks to cover the five boroughs of New York City to collect the 14,000 tons of solid waste that go to Fresh Kills. From my house in upper Manhattan, an area covered by 96 sanitation workers, the garbage travels to a marine transfer station at 135th Street on the Hudson Pier and is loaded onto barges pulled by tugboats which deliver their cargo to the landfill on Staten Island. A typical residential building of 65 households will produce about 400 pounds of solid waste a day, all but 15 percent destined for burial. We bury not only our bodies, but also our products, the cultural creations of our lifestyles.

The Fresh Kills facility operates five and a half days a week, a cutback from the seven-day workweek due to increased recycling. Its landscape looks much like the Midwest horizon, with small grassy hills and yellow and green mounds gently sloping in the distance. The scene also has an eerie quality because, except for hundreds or perhaps thousands of gulls, the area seems quiet and deserted. In fact, Fresh Kills has two wildlife refuges and it encourages landscaping to create natural wildlife habitats. Birds sighted at Fresh Kills include bald eagles, ospreys, hawks, owls, herons, ducks and threatened species such as the red-tailed hawk and the long-eared owl. Each December the Audubon Society visits to count the 50 species of birds that eke out a living here.

Huge front-end loaders scoop up the mounds of trash which are then trucked to the actual disposal site termed the "active face." As compactors zoom over the surface to smooth out the fresh garbage, hundreds of gulls descend over the earth and shoot up just in time to avoid becoming part of the refuse. With the gulls' flapping wings and their calls, their bodies filling the horizon, and the compactors speeding back and forth, the scene has a strange beauty and excitement about it. Once the waste is deposited, it is blanketed with soil to reduce odor and to discourage scavenging wildlife. Areas that have been filled to capacity are given a final cover of four feet of soil and plastic liners, followed by three more feet of soil. A huge on-site composting facility provides compost as part of the final spread which is then seeded with grass.

Garbage disposal is a complex science involving hi-tech knowledge and engineering. For example, leachate is produced when rainwater mixes with pollutants in the refuse. A local leachate treatment plant removes these pollutants and also provides a cover system that reduces the amount of rainwater that filters through. The treated leachate is released back into the rivers. Gas-venting pipes and trenches abound in the area to prevent buildup and migration of landfill gas that is a natural by-product of organic decomposition. The primary elements of methane and carbon dioxide are both odorless gases. The methane is turned into a high energy gas by a company that leases space from Fresh Kills. The company then sells that gas back to Brooklyn Union Gas for energy to customers. How is that for recycling! This operation resembles the backdrop of a sci-fi movie—huge, shiny silver cylinders rotating, pulsing and circling amid the clamor of space machinery.

Fresh Kills has been a mixed blessing for New York City's garbage for 50 years. It has been the curse of nearby residents, the pride of sanitation workers and a model of garbage disposal for other nations. Today the debate over and search for another way of disposing of garbage continues among New York City officials, environmental advocates and carting companies to find the best site for exporting the city's waste. In the end, however, it is we who are the solution to the problem of garbage. If we reflect more fully on how we dispose of our waste—in all its forms—we will appreciate the science of disposal and how we are connected to all other beings and the planet we share.

Are We Eating Ourselves to Death?
Howard Lyman

There have never been more people on Earth. There have never been more cows on Earth, nor pigs, nor chickens. We are using more pesticides today than at any other time in history and we are losing a greater percentage of the crops. At the same time, there has never been less clean water on Earth. There has never been less available topsoil, nor fewer fish, nor fewer mature trees. There has never been less cause for optimism for the future of the human race. Our natural resources are disappearing at an unbelievable rate, and our so-called leaders offer only cosmetic solutions. The Earth's population calls for more of everything while the Earth demands time to recover from years of abuse.

The Brazilian rainforest is being destroyed to provide pasture for cattle. If this destruction continues at its present pace, this rainforest will disappear within our children's lifetime. We are losing acreage equal to the size of France every five years. This rainforest is called the "lungs of the world" by some and we are turning it into a desert. When we review history, the Romans referred to great forests of Africa that we know today as the Sahara Desert. How do you like the sound of "the Amazon Desert"? It is not only the Brazilian rainforest that is under attack. Many forests around the world are destroyed daily to provide items as frivolous as disposable chopsticks. This wanton destruction by humans cannot continue at its present pace and still allow an environment that will sustain human life.

Food-producing soil is disappearing at a shocking rate around the world. Grain production in the Great Plains of the United States causes the loss of three tons of topsoil for every ton of grain produced. Worldwide today, one person in 12 is fed with grain produced in the United States at the cost of precious topsoil. In the last 40 years, China has lost cropland acreage equal to the size of all the farms in Germany, France, Holland and Denmark combined, while its population continues to grow. The list goes on and on, while superficial solutions are proposed by comatose national leaders. The Earth has dealt with problems like this in the past. The solution has been to reduce the human population. We are running out of pristine resources to exploit, and the available options continue to shrink every day.

Human sperm count, in the time it has been recorded worldwide, has fallen over 40 percent—20 percent in just the last decade. The reproductive capability of many other species has also fallen at an astronomical rate in the past 50 years. Our rapidly diminishing resources should wake us up, but instead we are hoping someone else is minding the store. We are robbing ourselves of a future.

When we take the time to read the signs of the planet they all say the same thing: "I can take no more abuse." The oceans are becoming a wasteland of pollution in which fish can no longer survive. Underground aquifers are becoming polluted and we lack the technology to clean them. Topsoil is covering the ocean floor, and we are left with barren, non-productive fields around the globe.

World economists soothe the ears of governments with theories of least-cost production and free trade solving all the problems associated with natural resource destruction. These patchwork plans ignore the basic problem—what we are doing on the planet is totally non-sustainable. We adjust the pilot light while the forest fire is about to burn down our towns. The longer we fail to face the real problems the more difficult it will be to find solutions.

Problems such as nuclear waste disposal, clear-cutting, rainforest destruction, topsoil loss, over-grazing, water pollution, waste disposal, and air pollution represent just a few which we have failed to solve. The survival of our race will depend on achieving solid solutions for all of these problems during our lifetime. This is not a hope, it is a necessity.

I once heard a lecture by Dr. Michael Klaper, who stated that the amount of time available to begin the changes necessary to save the human race should be counted in months, not years. He believes we have fewer than 120 months in which to institute these changes or it will be too late. I believe he is overestimating the time we have. This ship called Earth cannot change course quickly. The most dangerous implement in the arsenal of the human race today is the table fork. We have difficulty convincing ourselves of its importance; instead, we hope for a scientific breakthrough that will allow us to indulge ourselves and save our race at the same time. I believe this breakthrough will never occur no matter how hard we pray. Common sense tells us when we work with nature, rather than against it, we restore our environment and improve the health of not only the Earth but also ourselves. The prescription for the health of all concerned is an organic plant–based diet.

There are many interconnected problems, but the most significant is the consumption of animal products. Mountains of animal manure, polluted water, overgrazing, rainforest destruction, declining human health, animal suffering, human hunger, soil loss and global warming can all be attributed to the human consumption of animal products. Time-wasting debates can be conducted for as long as money exists to buy phony studies that cloud the issue, but the fact remains: We cannot survive on this planet in our present numbers if we continue to consume our current quantities of animal products.

In my lifetime, I have seen animal production in the United States explode from rural family farms to factory farming. The size of this type of production is mind-boggling: chicken operations with millions of birds and beef feedlots with more than 50,000 animals. The waste and disease in these operations are monumental. We are also skating on very thin ice by limiting genetic varieties within our animal and plant species. This reduction of the gene pool is a time bomb waiting to explode just as it did in the United States in the mid-1980s, when the majority of United States corn was of just three different varieties. These few varieties all had the same vulnerability to disease and during the decade the majority of crop failed. The ability of pests and disease to exploit genetic weaknesses will always be the Achilles heel of the human food supply. The reason most species have survived as long as they have is because of the great variety within each species. This diversity is being reduced at an alarming rate. Modern agriculture has reduced the number of grain species from thousands to less than a hundred. This example is being repeated over and over. Every time we become involved in a new area of agriculture we select a few varieties and then combine them, believing that we know more than nature. In every instance in which we fail to maintain the genetic pool, our plan has a major flaw.

Unless we learn to live within our bioregion and face the basic problem of the interaction of all of the Earth's life forms, we are a species bound for extinction. Every trainload of corn shipped from Iowa farms today to animal feedlots in Texas produces about a trainload of manure. The cost of shipping this manure back to Iowa is prohibitive, so the soil-enhancing manure ends up in a pile in Texas while the farmers of Iowa must purchase commercial fertilizers so they can repeat the cycle. Our inability to return the natural resources to the soil is causing the mining of the most fertile soil and in the end we will find the added commercial fertilizer falls far short of the total soil needs. This type of production happens all around the Earth every time we ship products outside of local bioregions. We must not only recognize the problem, but also make "living the solution" an everyday habit of all who reside on the planet Earth. We can make this change if we begin with a commitment to our diet. This will be very difficult for some, but it's mandatory if we plan to see the survival of our children and grandchildren.

Although the future looks bleak, there are actions we can take—and the sooner we start, the sooner we may reverse existing trends. The selection of your individual diet is the most important choice you can make. How you spend your money as a consumer is the next. The future can be changed, but only if we start the change where it matters most: with ourselves.

Cultivating My Own Garden
Stephanie Miller

Contrary to popular opinion, more than one tree grows in Brooklyn. I have two in my own yard. This small piece of earth and I are still coming to know each other. We came together in June 1996 when my partner and I bought the house related to the yard. Often this yard is called "the garden." My first response to the garden was intimidation, having previously experienced only window-sill terra-cotta-pot herb-gardening. I was now confronted with an entire ecosystem, for which I was expected to serve as steward.

I armed myself mightily for my new responsibilities: gardening gloves with those nubby patches on the palm, a new set of tools, a handy everything-you-could-want-to-know-about-perennials book, as well as a book on composting. All of this in hand, I went to work carefully weeding, watering and deadheading, all with my safely gloved hands.

As the garden bloomed and grew in the summer sun, it began to reveal itself to me, and we entered into a conversation. I learned to track the course of the sun across the various beds; which plants needed more or less water; which had the most delicate flowers. I also learned about the destructive force of snails and slugs. I began to enjoy my gardening tasks more and more, soon realizing that those silly gloves are actually a lot more trouble than they're worth. I like the feeling of dirt on my hands, remnants hiding under my nails. And, come to think of it, that trowel can be a bother, too. Digging with my hands does the job nicely and is much more satisfying.

We began to see this outdoor space as an extension of our house, part of our living space, and as such, an opportunity for creative expression. I pored over my handy perennials book, learning about soil preferences, light needs and growing environments. I decided upon no color scheme—a garden should be an exciting, enchanting place, not a coordinated bedroom suite. With the help of a friend with an extensive background in horticulture (as well as a contact in the wholesale nursery business), we invested in new additions for the garden. I must confess to acting out the stereotype: I talked to the new plants as I nestled them into their holes—welcoming them to our spot of earth, hoping they would be healthy and content and become part of our world and we theirs.

Around the time I acquired my gardening tools, I also picked up a welding torch for the first time. Welding may seem a far cry from gardens and earth, but metal and flame have an earthiness all their own. I am beginning to envision sculpture in our garden, albeit on a very small scale. This has helped me to look at the space we call garden in an entirely new way. I begin to notice shape and silhouette, shadow and texture, where before I was overwhelmed by color and smell—of the plants, earth, birds and insects who live with us. I have begun to wonder what shapes would belong in this space, to enter meaningfully into the conversation and not screech it to a halt. It would be sculpture I could plant—maybe changing as viewed in the shifting light and new seasons. I am getting pretty far ahead of my abilities at the moment, but these ideas are the seeds out of which the final project will grow.

Before putting the garden to bed this year, I joined the ranks of gardening enthusiasts and planted flower bulbs. A friend had read in a magazine about a particular style of bulb planting that sounded as though it could yield some interesting variations on the theme, and I found myself as excited to try this as I normally would be to open the cover of a new book. I hated waiting for the appropriate cold weather to sink the bulbs. The bulb planting became a strangely social activity, as many of the bulbs were going in the front yard, encircling the flowering crab apple tree. Passers-by on the sidewalk expressed an interest, offered advice, wished me well or explained my curious antics to inquisitive children ("What is she doing hunched up under that tree, mom?").

Being a sucker for immediate gratification, this task of waiting for spring flowers and foliage does not rest easily with me. But this is perhaps the most important lesson I am currently learning from the garden: patience. I have, on occasion, been able to sit quietly on the ground and simply smell, watch and try to hear the sounds of leaves stretching to the sun and roots to the water. I have not heard them yet, but hey—I'm new at this.

The Path of Conservation

Ying Wu

In the eighth grade, I went on a four-day school trip to the Pocono Environment Education Center. When I heard that we were to spend most of our time hiking, I thought to myself, "Why would anyone want to walk around in a forest for hours?!" Having lived in a city all of my life, I'd never appreciated the beauty of nature because nature in Brooklyn is often not exactly pretty. Plastic bags take the place of leaves on trees, litter covers the sidewalks and clogs the gutters, and I hold my breath when buses go by.

On the first hike, my teacher showed our group the effects of glacial erosion, and we even found some fossils. We followed little animal footprints in the ground, and observed the constellations at night. I loved the forests we explored, the clean air we breathed, the great variety of animals and insects, the majestic waterfalls and the clear streams. I was jealous of the Native Americans because for them what I fell in love with was not just their "natural world," it was the world.

Coming from a cement-covered city, I had no feelings for the nature being sacrificed for human progress until that trip. That unforgettable trip inspired me to read books in order to learn more about environmental concerns. I was shocked to read that air pollution leads to the death of 120,000 Americans every year and that children brought up in polluted areas suffer reductions of 10-15 percent in lung capacity for the rest of their lives. I was horrified by the effects of contaminated drinking water. One particularly scary incident took place in Woburn, Massachusetts, where 19 children died because they drank water from their communities' polluted wells. The Environmental Protection Agency has found more than 700 pollutants in U.S. drinking water. Agricultural pesticides, fertilizers, animal wastes, mining operations, leaking garbage dumps, industrial and household chemicals, acid rain, sewage, and oil or chemical spills are constantly leaking into the rivers, streams and lakes that comprise the Earth's usable water.

Compelled to take action, I joined the Environmental Coalition of Stuyvesant (E.C.O.S.), Students for the Ethical Treatment of Animals (S.E.T.A.) and the Sierra Club's Land Preservation Committee and Solid Waste Committee. I also stopped eating meat because livestock are very significant contributors to water pollution, topsoil erosion, plant extinction and rainforest destruction, not to mention the fact they receive outrageously cruel treatment in the course of the mad scramble for profit.

I have met with many obstacles on this path of conservation. Many of my peers either don't care or don't believe that they are breathing harmful air and drinking poisonous water. They are not willing to walk even a few feet to throw cans into recycling bins. Others use the recycling bins as garbage cans.

This apathy and reluctance are very frustrating. I think many of my peers feel that the extent of environmental destruction is beyond correction. Others are unaware of the environmental consequences of their actions.

I believe that informing students about the very real consequences of environmental neglect, and inspiring them to take active roles, will jolt many of them out of this state of apathy. Communication through articles, editorials or meetings is the key to making others aware of their own responsibility for Earth's welfare. I have written editorials to my newspaper about the environmental damage created by incineration, which is the often-proposed answer to unsuccessful recycling programs. As the Chairperson of the E.C.O.S., I am very proud of all the Coalition accomplished in creating the Green Revolution, an environmental awareness campaign. E.C.O.S. has established a schoolwide can, bottle and paper recycling program. In collaboration with Key Club, E.C.O.S. produced the first student-run assembly in the history of my high school. A key component of the Green Revolution, the assembly included a guest speaker from the Sierra Club and the "Tin Can Man," who encouraged students to take an active part in protecting the environment. E.C.O.S. convinced the school's administration to replace all paper used in the school with 100 percent recycled paper (50 percent post-consumer waste). There are also plans for a composting program for food scraps from the cafeteria. In the community, E.C.O.S. members volunteer for the New York City Parks Department; we are involved in park cleanups at Battery Park, and we also volunteer at New York City's annual environmental festival, "EcoFest."

I hope the schoolwide recycling program will encourage my peers to take active responsibility for the planet we will soon inherit. Special–education students get involved by painting and recycling boxes and monitoring the amount of paper recycled. E.C.O.S. also sponsored a button design contest in search of the best button with an environmental message.

I know for a fact that this type of communication has at least awakened many of my peers to the environmental movement. But unfortunately this does not mean that every student in my high school is now an environmentalist. I have friends who are completely indifferent to the extinction of species and the burning of rainforests. They are indifferent because they have not yet noticed the impact of environmental neglect on their lives. But the environment needs their support, before the effects of pollution and destruction become both blatant and irreversible.

The abuse of the Earth is rapidly changing the natural environment. I believe the Earth will adapt itself to this new environment, but I'm afraid the new adaptation will be inhospitable to humankind. Perhaps like the dinosaurs who became extinct when the Earth changed its environment, humans will become extinct when the Earth changes itself according to the new environment we create. It is up to each individual to climb out of the ditch of abuse and onto the path of conservation.

Can the Galapagos Islands Survive Tourism?

Jessica Graham

It is, as usual, a busy morning on the island of Baltra. A small plane lands and a new group steps off the plane and squints at the sun. The tourists are easy to spot, laden with cameras, dressed in sturdy outdoor gear. They form a line to enter the enchanted Islands of Galapagos. Mainland Ecuadorians have come here mostly for work, to cash in on the growing tourist industry.

Some of the new visitors will board buses to the small schooners, sailboats or gigantic cruise ships that will be their homes for the next few days. These packages are pricey; some cruises can cost over $3,000 per person for an eight-day trip. Others, on tighter budgets, will stay on land and plan day trips to outlying islands.

Sixty thousand tourists will visit the Galapagos this year, for reasons as varied as their multicolored clothing. Birders, who have memorized the mating practices of the waved albatross and know its strange sword-fighting dance by heart, long to hear the click of its beak, which signifies the beginning of the ritual. The birders will search for hours on a hot, dry island just to glimpse the inflated red pouch of the male frigate bird, or the feet of a blue-footed booby. Nature photographers will lug lenses the size of suitcases up Prince Edward's steps onto a brush-covered island just to get close to the famed land iguanas. They will lie down on the ground to capture the faces of multicolored reptiles, closer than they'd ever dreamed to a member of an endangered species. Sea-lovers, snorkelers especially, will swim with flirty, human-friendly sea lions. Kayakers will paddle through mangroves, looking for giant sea tortoises lurking below the tranquil surface. Others want to trace the trajectory of Darwin's theory of evolution, which he developed after leaving this archipelago 330 miles off the coast of Ecuador. Geology buffs will marvel at the lava formations and still-active volcanoes, and study plate-tectonic theories.

All of them are here to see a world supposedly untouched by humans. On the surface, it seems that animals rule the Galapagos, but of course many other forces are at play in this remote paradise. Human invaders have been around for years. Indigenous peoples from Latin America are believed to have been the first land mammals to reach the islands. From the 16th century on, European seafarers stopped off on the lava-encrusted islands in search of rest and absconded with giant tortoises for their meals at sea. Sailors and tortoise hunters introduced new animals to the islands, such as goats and donkeys which compete with indigenous life and are today one of the greatest threats to many dwindling species. Human settlers have brought a whole range of other problems too, and their struggle to transform the islands into an environment that can sustain and nurture human life has taken its toll.

The story of the giant tortoises illustrates the multilayered impact of humans. Originally, there were 14 subspecies of the Galapagos tortoise; today three of those subspecies are extinct and another has only one remaining survivor, called Lonesome George. In the 19th and early 20th centuries, human hunters killed over 100,000 giant tortoises for meat and oil. Now the "introduced" animals threaten the tortoises. Pigs eat tortoise eggs, rats consume the hatchlings that survive, dogs eat young tortoises and goats compete for food. In order to maintain the ecosystem and ensure tortoise survival, the Charles Darwin Research Station on the island of Santa Cruz has launched several "introduced–animal eradication programs." On certain islands, the threat to the tortoise populations has subsided significantly due to the elimination of goats.

Commercial fishing is another threat to the delicate ecosystem, and established restrictions are often violated. The Worldwide Fund for Nature has recently recommended a worldwide ban on commercial fishing in and around the islands, pushing for the waters to be designated protected areas. As any well-heeled North American or European traveler will eagerly tell you, tourism brings local employment and prosperity. The tourist industry is booming with the popularity of vacations that combine relaxation with education and outdoor activities. For those Ecuadorians willing to work long hours and live for weeks at a time without their families, working on a Galapagos tour ship can be lucrative. But the stress of traveling to and from the mainland puts a strain on family relations—many men who work on the cruise ships have brought their families to live in the two cities on the islands. Since 1950, the human population in the few designated towns on the islands has increased dramatically, from 1,346 to 13,030 in 1995. The 5,000 human inhabitants of Porta Ayora, a city on the island of Santa Cruz, have left the ecosystem irrevocably altered. In the port, boat oil spreads in rainbows on the surface of the water.

For inhabitants, everything must be imported from the mainland, so shipments constantly come into the harbor. Tourists visit for a taste of town life after a few days at sea and on the animal-ruled islands. They see the giant tortoises at the Charles Darwin Research Station and then shop for T-shirts. Native plant life, once unique to the island of Santa Cruz, has been irrevocably altered by the introduction of foreign seeds. Where nothing but cacti once grew, guava trees cut their strong roots, destroying endemic plants. Inland, plowed fields yield neat farms, where fruit trees grow despite the harsh, inhospitable soil and the dry climate. Humans have shaped this island and have prospered from it, perhaps at the cost of the ecosystem. But the Worldwide Fund for Nature has said that careful management of the tourist industry, with limits on the number of visitors, should limit damage to the environment. It is hoped that visits by Northerners, on carefully delineated trails, in highly regulated areas, accompanied by a certified guide, will ensure the preservation of the archipelago—because personal contact with the animals may yield contributions to the Parque Nacional or the Charles Darwin Research Station.

At the end of another week in the Galapagos, the tourists stand in the waiting room at the airport writing last–minute postcards, napping and dreaming of sea lions. With their hundreds of rolls of film, their T-shirts and wood-carved tortoises, they will bring a little bit of an animal world home with them.

Maybe in their everyday lives at home, surrounded by faxes and computer screens, built-in pools and highways, they will close their eyes and remember a swim they took with a sea lion pup. No doubt their lives will be a little bit richer for it. Perhaps they will become financial supporters of preservation projects, and think more about the lives of animals. But, in the end, no one knows if the original inhabitants of the Galapagos can survive the waves of tourists that will continue to flock to the islands every day.

Animal Advocacy

The Dog in the Lifeboat

Martin Rowe

**"Fair is fair, Larry... We're out of food,
we drew straws — you lost."**

In a cartoon by Gary Larson of *The Far Side*, three men and a dog are sitting in a boat on a billowing ocean. By their ragged clothes and in one case heavily unshaven face, we can tell that the men have been on the sea for some days, presumably cast adrift by a shipwreck. One of the men is wild-eyed in astonishment and horror as he is addressed by one man and looked at by the other. "Fair is fair, Larry...," says the man to his fellow castaway, "We're out of food, we drew straws—you lost."[1]

Humor works by calling upon our sense of the normal and subverting it. The most obviously abnormal element in this case is that it would be assumed—it certainly is by the unfortunate Larry—that in a lifeboat situation it is the dog who should become the next meal. When I first looked at the cartoon, I assumed that the dog had drawn straws himself with his mouth (let us also assume that the dog is male). But the humor doesn't rely on that observation. Larry could be equally appalled that his fellow humans would consider only themselves to be among the community of edibles, and that it was not necessary for the dog to draw straws.

For me, however, much of the cartoon's humor lies not in the horrified face of Larry but in the inscrutable one of the dog. While the dog's face is turned toward Larry, it is not clear that he is looking at the man who drew the short straw. If his eyes are open at all, he appears to be looking off into the distance with an air that can only be described as insouciant. I have looked at this cartoon many times, and each time I have come back to the unreadable expression on the dog's face: Is it a quiet air of triumphant satisfaction, a barely concealed grin of ironic malice, or simply a calm resolve at the timeless fairness of the decision? As with many Gary Larson cartoons, this dog represents an animal world that appears more sophisticated and knowing than that of the oafish *Homo sapiens*.[2] Yet unlike other Larson animals, the dog is not anthropomorphized by being given language or acting like a human in a human setting. The dog appears to be no more than what he is: a dog on a boat.

This is where Larson has sophisticatedly brought to the fore some of the larger concerns about animals that have puzzled and worried thinkers for centuries. Put simply, the dog in Larson's cartoon seems to be *more* than "just" a dog. It may be, of course, that the dog's centrality to our vision lies in his being so inexpressive—he is a vacuum into which we pour our very human anxieties and beliefs. It may be that the dog has already been given a quasi-human status because he is a companion animal, and thus in some way part of the human family.[3] Even if the dog in this cartoon is under the protection of the men in the boat—perhaps he is a mascot or a companion animal, and thus given de facto personhood which renders him morally less distant from us—or even if Larry's behavior was literally rocking the boat and this straw poll was a pretext to get rid of the troublemaker, the dog seems *within himself* to have attained that quasi-human status that protects him from the vagaries to which humans usually submit non-human animals.

Larson forces us to own up to the prejudices that cluster around our association with what it means to be human, and our presumptions about what animals really *are*. The use of an actual lifeboat visualizes the classic argument used to force those who advocate for animals to declare their colors: your dog or Larry; your baby or your dog. The argument is, of course, inherently unfair and specifically misleading because, all things being equal, human lives in their fullest extent are likely to be more important to us than the lives of animals. On the other hand, things are very rarely equal. And this type of argument neither provides us with carte blanche to do what we like to animals, which is where those who use the lifeboat analogy seem to want to head, nor helps us with what have become known as "marginal cases."

The Argument from Marginal Cases

The Argument from Marginal Cases explores our responsibilities toward those human beings who are not, one assumes, like Larry: capable of reason or consciousness. These include—to a greater or lesser extent—those in permanent comas, the senile, those in a vegetative state and infants. All philosophical thinking about social contracts and rights which depend on the regular interaction of rational human beings (and which, therefore, exclude animals) has to take into account what to do with those human beings who cannot participate: the so-called "marginal cases."[4] Since, the argument runs, it has been shown that certain animals possess more of those characteristics we consider our own—the ability to have interests, to express desire, to be aware of their surroundings, etc.—than those human beings who are infants or mentally impaired, what right do we have to do to these animals what we do not do to these human beings, or (more shockingly perhaps) what is to stop us from doing to those human beings what we do to these animals (such as vivisecting or eating them)?

Responses to the argument have been many. Some have pointed out that we provide the unfortunates or the very young of our species with de facto rights because they are either likely to become (in the case of infants) or were (in the case of the elderly senile) fully-functioning members of society. Or, people argue, marginalized humans belong to a species characterized by rationality and due participation in moral discourse. Furthermore, to infringe upon the individual rights of incomplete or "defective" humans is to infringe upon the concerns of relatives or others (including the larger society) who might be adversely affected by such actions taking place. The problem with these responses is that they don't fully take into account the argument's ramifications. It is not enough to say that belonging to a species which *normally* has these traits guarantees these human beings rights. This is a form of "speciesism"; a circular argument that states that the criterion humans have that makes them special is that they are human. In the past, certain human beings have been all too quick to conclude that other human beings—such as black slaves or women—do not possess traits that allow them into the tent of human rights. Thinking in terms of species denies our responsibility to the individual in question.

But what about the argument that we are bound to each other in ways that predicate doing terrible things to these "unviable" or "unformed" humans? Well, as Larry in the lifeboat discovers, human beings may be more attached to their animals than to other human beings. Moreover, if Larry is acting in such a way that threatens the lives of the other beings on the boat, then we would consider it quite justifiable to get rid of him. Part of the reason ethical reasoning is so challenging is that it demands we deal with the often uncomfortable direction logic takes us in. It is another irony of Larson's cartoon that Larry is a victim of the scrupulous fairness of his fellow humans: it is their human reasoning that makes him their dinner! What the "Argument from Marginal Cases" does is recognize that the moral division between human and animal is not so absolute as we thought. Just as there are degrees of animality, shall we say, so are there degrees of humanness. The logic of the argument is such that we can only conclude that—while no-one today would countenance in all seriousness conducting experiments on human beings, whether infant or defective (although we have not always been so scrupulous)—we have no basis upon which to argue that we can do what we do to *some* animals. Where we draw the line is still an open question. Certainly, it would seem that mammals over one year old possess traits similar enough to us that we should exclude them from the violence we currently inflict on them. Others have argued that all animals with a nervous system could be excluded, given that they too feel pain.

In spite of the strength of the Argument from Marginal Cases—which is subtler and more extensive than presented here—it does not fully describe our moral relationship with non-human beings. As Frans de Waal puts it, "Have we really reached the point at which respect for apes is most effectively advocated by depicting them as retarded people in furry suits? . . . It is the inherent beauty and dignity of animals that should be the starting point" of an awareness of our responsibilities towards animals.[5] There are a number of problems, of course, with this approach. First, it is obvious that while human beings have acknowledged the beauty and dignity of animals for millennia, we have done, and continue to do, unspeakable things to them. Secondly, the argument points up our own inconsistent attitudes toward animals. The "marginal cases" argument does not depend on whether the animals are beautiful or dignified in our eyes. It confers rights on them irrespective of their utility to us. If it draws attention to the fact that we are still prejudiced in conferring rights on those creatures who are like us, so be it. It shows how, in spite of all our claims to objectivity and reason, we are still fundamentally anthropocentric—unable to conceive of the worth of another being except to the extent that it is like us.

The third problem is similar to the first: How can we trust our intuitive sense of what is beautiful or dignified? The humor of Larson's cartoon depends upon such intuitive assumptions—in this case the "truth" that animals are simply not like us. If the dog is involved in pulling a straw that helped determine Larry's fate, we like to think that the dog not only has no understanding of what pulling the straw implies, but has no comprehension of what the phrase "pulling the straw" means. The dog might copy one of the castaway's actions should the man pull the straw out with his teeth and hand the bunch on to the dog. But that only means that animals can copy. It does not mean they know *what* or *why* they are copying.

It is these assumptions about what animals *are* (and therefore what they are *for*) that have characterized the long history of human interaction with and abuse of animals. This is not the place to rehearse in great detail all the arguments explaining why it is all right to exploit animals—the enormous amount of literature produced on animal issues in the last few decades has done this much more satisfactorily than I could.[6] Suffice to say, the line of reasoning has been roughly as follows: Since there is no evidence that animals can talk the way we can, we have no reason to think that they can think the way we can. Because they cannot think like us, it stands to reason they do not possess consciousness and, more pointedly, self-consciousness. Self-consciousness allows us to experience our lives in the abstract—to give ourselves a biography, to seek meaning in our world, and to understand the world symbolically and morally. All these things animals *appear* not to do.

Aristotle, for one, recognized that human beings were animals. He also acknowledged that all beings had their own reason for being. These two observations led him to ask what non-human animals were *for*. His conclusion was that animals, like slaves, were here to serve man.[7] Aristotle's assumptions about animals were theologized by Thomas Aquinas who, like the Greek, recognized that animals were important—in his case, that they were meaningful to God. For Aquinas, however, their role in God's creation was to serve mankind, as plants were there to serve humans *and* animals. The status of animals did not permit us to worry too much about their conditions or suffering, since one could only be friends with rational creatures who could reciprocate with fellow feeling. While it was possible to love "irrational creatures" out of charity, it could only be so for "God's honor and man's use."[8]

It is strange how often those philosophers who have bothered to notice animals have allowed themselves to acknowledge, however cursorily or grudgingly, that animals are more than mere ciphers, only to turn away from a more morally engaged response to them. For Descartes, animals were merely machines with some form of animation ("chiming clocks" he called them). While they may possess some thoughts and could sense things, he wrote, they do not have that all important "I" that makes pain meaningful and converts it into that distinctly human experience, "suffering."[9] Immanuel Kant thought we had no direct duties to animals. Like Aquinas and Aristotle, he considered rationality the highest moral state. Since animals were not rational, Kant did not believe that animals were ends in themselves. That being said, Kant did not think it was right to be cruel to animals, but (rather like Aquinas) only because someone who tortured animals might graduate to doing the same thing to human beings.[10] (Ironically, this observation has received some currency recently in the study of murderers and sociopaths. Several tortured animals before they moved on to human victims.)

This is only one strain of thinking about animals in the Western philosophical tradition, and there have been writers and thinkers who have considered animals less instrumentally.[11] Nevertheless, this has been the dominant line of thought governing animals and the natural world: reason and language are the determining factors of moral worth; animals clearly do not possess these things; they are here for our use. In the last 150 years, however, this sense of the absolute divide between humans and animals has been eroded. Charles Darwin's *The Origin of Species* argued convincingly that humans not only were related to animals, but had evolved from them—that there was a continuous line back to the animal past rather than an absolute break. Unfortunately, rather than recognizing that a continuity with animals suggests that our relationship with our animal relatives is complex and subtle, Darwinism has been perverted throughout the 19th and 20th centuries to mean that human beings are like animals only to the extent we are beasts: amoral and cruel creatures of appetite. From Nazi ideologies of the pure breed of animal—human or otherwise—to racial science,[12] from behaviorism to the concept of the urban jungle, it is not the animal that has been "elevated" as much as the human who has been bestialized. Even now, we still refer to people as "animals" or "beasts" to suggest they are outcasts from civilization.

Nevertheless, in the last few decades our mindset about animals has begun to change. Through the work of ethologists in the field, and (ironically) scientists working in the laboratories, humans have discovered that many of the traits we have considered distinctly human have their analogues in the animal world. Our closest relatives, chimpanzees as well as other great apes, are (like us) tool users. They have been known to use sticks to draw termites from their nest and eat them, and stones to crush fruit and berries. Like us, they plan and work co-operatively for common ends, deferring immediate pleasure for long-term gain. This is evident in their collective hunting expeditions, in which groups create diversions and surround their prey. Chimpanzees, it has recently been discovered, have different dialects of calls depending on where they live, suggesting that it is not too farfetched to use the word "culture" when referring to chimpanzee colonies. Chimpanzees and gorillas, of course, have been taught sign-language,[13] and have proved to us their ability to symbolize and construct meaning from a fairly substantial vocabulary. It has also been observed that these primates have been able to teach sign-language to their own young—suggesting not only a sophisticated memory base, but a recognition of the utility of language.

De Waal himself has argued that our continuity with animals extends to our fundamental ability to moralize. His observations of primate colonies have led him to conclude that primates are in many ways as morally complex as we are. They lie and steal, they feign injury to gain attention and abase themselves to curry favor with their "superiors" in the pack. Like humans, they are territorial and often rigidly hierarchical in groups, yet they are also capable of altruism, of group cohesion when necessary, and forgiving of harm if suitable reparations are made. All these actions extend beyond mere species survival and biological instinct.[14] And this is not just the case with animals closest to humans. Elephants have been observed mourning the death of one of their own. Like many mammals, they look after their young and teach them survival skills—suggesting that, like us, animals are creatures of experience and learning as much as they are creatures of instinct. Animals get bored if they are not stimulated by their conspecifics or their surroundings.

144

A few decades ago such talk about animals would have been considered anthropomorphic. Anthropomorphism by some is considered the cardinal sin when describing animals, even though *not* ascribing certain animal expressions to be like ours may be as supposedly unscientific as doing so.[15] Slowly we are coming around to recognizing that the animal world is more richly various and interactive than we imagined. It is this that allows the Argument from Marginal Cases to be argued, and necessary.

Beyond Marginal Cases

De Waal's complaint about the argument, however, does touch upon something that we should keep in mind, even in the face of the need to construct a rational case as to why we should stop exploiting animals (or, for that matter, to construct a rational case to why we *shouldn't*). We relate to animals in a myriad of ways not touched upon by reason. From the Indian deities of Hanuman and Ganesha, from Anubis and Thoth, to the Native American gods Spider Woman and Coyote and the ancient Greeks' Zeus in the form of a bull or a swan to the Israelite Leviathan and Behemoth, from the dragons of ancient China to the bestiaries of the European Middle Ages,[16] from Aesop's fables to the poems of LaFontaine, from Bugs Bunny to Lassie, animals have often been our first teachers, providing us with the avenues whereby we not only seek to understand our origins but begin to think like humans. They live in our metaphors and similes, our folklore and idioms. They are our most trusted companions and the objects of our fascination, terror and awe. They can wake us from comas and sell advertising. Our cultures are filled with stories about turning into them, being consumed by them, naming them and being tricked by them.[17] Yet we only occasionally acknowledge their power. They can travel farther, climb higher, run faster, dig deeper and live longer than we can. They are stronger and more resilient, their senses of sight and smell are more subtle and the ranges wider. Many of them are a million more times more successful at populating the planet than we are. They were here long before we arrived and will be here long after we are gone. Yet we, like Larry, somehow *know* our superiority!

In the face of the sheer variety of life on this planet, it is extraordinary that we are so confident that we know what animals are and are not—and that we are content to consign the non-human world into one immovable lump of in-sentient and undifferentiated matter. There are, it is estimated, some 300,000 different *species* of beetle, 100,000 different species of mollusk, 50,000 species of arthropod. There are only 4,000 species of mammal, and we are one of them. We can have no concept of the impact or *meaning* of the five to 30 million species of animals on this planet. We simply do not know how they make possible or affect what we consider human (whether it be thought, culture or our supposed control over nature). If this seems far-fetched—that a beetle can change our way of thinking—then this only points up how denuded of animals our imaginative, physical and philosophical world has become.

Clearly, we need a new paradigm of relating to the other-than-human world. We need to acknowledge how important animals are in our lives, how the loss of the tiger (for instance) in the wild will not simply disturb the ecosystem in which the tigers live but will cause every human on the planet to experience a loss in our ability to *imagine* the world. A fragment of that which makes us human will be missing. As we decimate the species around us—species we don't even know about, whose gifts to us (whether pharmacological or spiritual) we still have not received—we diminish ourselves that much more. And the questions we pose of life—why are we here? why is there something rather than nothing?—become that much harder to answer when those who offer us our truest mirror are abused, tortured, manipulated and ultimately destroyed.

Animals on Our Minds
From Reverence to "Adult-eration"
Jim Mason

For ages, animals have been embedded in human minds and cultures throughout the world. Some thinkers, such as the late Paul Shepard, believe that when we use animals symbolically, as in art and poetry, we are using them as representatives of the natural world. It has been this way for millennia. When the temple friezes of ancient cultures depicted their soldier-warrior hero-kings slaughtering lions, the heroes were symbolically conquering the Earth, because the lion as the top predator symbolized much of nature around him.

If what Shepard and other people believe is true—that animals are this important to us and have been throughout evolution, and that they're indelibly imprinted on our brains—we must ask ourselves about the repercussions of that. We have to think about what our treatment of animals is doing to us as human beings.

We need to look at what has happened to us as we have moved from a primal and tribal existence to become what we call "modern" human beings with our so-called civilizations. This process has been going on for about eight or nine thousand years, beginning roughly with the advent of agriculture and the rise of cities, sophisticated trade and written language. What we think of as history covers only the last four or five thousand years of it.

We've reached such an advanced stage of civilization that we're wondering what we're doing to the Earth and to ourselves, now that we've just about wiped out all non-human life, especially the most spectacular animals. These animals, such as the tiger, are very impressive to people. They are deeply imprinted on the cultures of many peoples. So when the tiger is gone from Asia and the elephant from Africa, the human cultures and societies there will be ripped from their roots. It won't be Africa. It won't be Asia. They will just be places sterilized of the animals who really gave something to human lives.

What has happened during this long process is we have reversed our relationship with animals. Whereas we used to see them as powers, deities, spirits and as brothers and sisters, as a result of several thousand years of agriculture and mastery over nature we have formed a wholly different relationship. Once we started using animals as slaves, as domestic livestock, and started eradicating all animal life around our villages and cities in the ancient Middle East and other centers of "civilization," we had to reinvent our relationship with animals.

When people reinvent their relationship with the Earth they destroy the old mythology and replace it with a new one. They do the same with religions. Before agriculture we had a situation in which men and women were more or less equal, animals were important and we felt like part of the natural world. Several thousand years later, however, we've dammed up rivers to make irrigation systems, clear-cut forests to produce cropland and exterminated the big predators so that we can have livestock. And we have had to create new mythologies and new stories, to reinvent ourselves as agri-*cultures* living in mastery over nature.

We get a glimpse of this in some of the early stories in the Bible, which were beginning to be written down between 1000 and 800 BCE, but were much older than that. There we see the destruction of beliefs in not only the power of animals but the power of female deities as well. Across the world, emerging agricultural-period religions replaced the old stone–age religions that had animal-centered spirits and deities. This process has culminated in our culture: what we call Western, patriarchal culture, which is a nature-dominating, human-supremacist culture.

What does all this mean to us today? It means we really think we're entitled to master the world. It means we really think we deserve to own animals and nature and treat them as slaves. We're using the ancient power of animals to demonstrate our mastery over them. We have rituals to do this: bullfights, circuses, rodeos, zoos, hunting and the like. These are ways in which we remind ourselves of our power over animals, who in turn represent our power over nature. Now, all this is not consciously done; it is an accumulation of decades, maybe centuries, of attitudes and experiences with animals.

Take the elephant. There's probably no more dignified and powerful an animal than a great gray elephant. But when you see the animal in the circus, it's a clown, a buffoon. And this, whether coincidentally or not, is the great treat for children: we take them to the circus. We "adult-erate" them. The rodeo is another example. The rodeo evolved as a way for people to celebrate their mastery over animals. They do this by going to a public place where they have comfortable seats, soft drinks and popcorn and sit and watch people torture animals. They watch people twist the bulls' tails and wrestle them to the ground, drawing upon the power of those animals. Wild horses and wild bulls are some of the most powerful animals in the world. That's why we see them in the constellations and name so many of the powers in the sky after animal forms. The rodeo helps people feel in a very visceral way how the West was won, and how macho cowboy values have wrestled that place into civilization.

Today, more and more people are trying to challenge these ideas, using every discipline there is—philosophy, science, anthropology and history—to undo this poisonous sleep that we've induced in ourselves and which is leading us toward destruction. But animal advocates ought to be careful when they look at things such as circuses, rodeos and zoos, not just attack them on animal rights grounds and the suffering they cause to animals, but also critique their effects on humans. The activist Sue Pressman once reminded me that all the torture and display of animals in circuses and zoos is to nature education and wildlife education what pornographic films are to sex education. If we're going to have better attitudes about sex and gender and the act of love-making, we don't want to provide images that create negative, destructive and humiliating ideas. If we want to teach positive values about the natural world and our place in it, we don't want to take children to see things that repeatedly show our macho power.

Transgressions
The Patenting of Life
Martin Rowe

In 1976, Coca-Cola salesman John Moore went to the Medical Center of the University of California suffering from a rare disease called hairy cell leukemia. His doctor, David Golde, recommended removing Moore's spleen and Moore agreed. Over the next seven years, Moore returned to UC Medical Center, each time giving samples of blood, skin, bone marrow and sperm which he was told by Golde were needed to make sure Moore remained healthy.[1]

During this period, Golde noticed that Moore's body was over-producing lymphokines, important components of the human immune system. Without consulting Moore, Golde began using samples from Moore's body to create a culture of cells which produced these lymphokines. Realizing that a lot of money could be made from this cell line, Golde and his research assistant Shirley Quan got a patent for the cell line and its derivatives and entered into commercial contracts with several companies and the university. When Moore found out about this, he took Golde to court so that he could financially benefit from the profits—up to $350,000 a year in royalties. After losing an initial trial, Moore appealed to the California Court of Appeal, which found that Moore was entitled to compensation. But, on further appeal, the Supreme Court of California found that Moore had no proprietary interest in his removed cells. It did say, however, that Golde had breached his fiduciary obligations by not telling Moore how he was using his cell-line.

In its judgment, the Court agreed that, while the human body has value beyond how much it is worth to the market—and that Golde should have informed Moore of his commercial interests—granting Moore a property right for his own body would impede further scientific research. The majority wrote: "Companies [would be] unlikely to invest heavily in developing, manufacturing or marketing a product when uncertainty about clear title exists." Nevertheless, there was dissent among the judges. One minority opinion held that Moore's body was his own property, and that even though the valuable substance in question was only tissue, Moore had a proprietary right prior to its "discovery" and should be able to benefit financially from its use. Another argued that other, non-economic values, such as dignity and equity, should be considered when debating the market value of human biological materials. Yet another minority opinion said that property discourse and market value have no role when it comes to human biological materials.

150

The story of John Moore and his spleen offers clear indications of the problems posed by biotechnology when it comes into contact with commercial activity. The majority of court judgments in biotechnology cases have so far been based on assessments of how greatly the "discovery" concerned will impact the market. Courts have generally insisted that the greater good for society is contained in unfettered scientific research and development, and that courts should not stand in the way of what makes that possible—the investment of companies hoping for a dividend in the form of a breakthrough drug. When confronted with questions as to whether it is right to patent life, courts have generally claimed that these non-commercial concerns are beyond either their expertise or mandate, and that it is up to the legislative branch of the United States system of government to judge what is right or wrong.

While it is true that patent law is irreducibly connected to money, commerce and property, the question still remains whether biological materials should be patentable. The issue of John Moore seems solely confined to *human* biological material, but the link between human and nonhuman exploitation is a matter of mere degree rather than kind, and it is clear from the history of patenting that the debate is not, and could never be, confined solely to human biological material. Indeed, for a century before 1980, a wide variety of plant forms were patented. That year, in a landmark case, a patent was granted by the United States Patent Office to Anand Chakrabarty for a genetically altered bacterium capable of degrading oil. The patent was appealed and the case went all the way to the Supreme Court which ruled, five to four, that the bacterium was not a product of nature but a "human-made invention."

The Oncomouse

In 1985, the United States Patent Office conferred patentable status on plants, seeds and plant tissues, and two years later on "multi-cellular living organisms, including animals." In 1986, two researchers at Harvard University took out the first-ever patent—number 4,736,866—on a living being: in this case, a mouse. The two researchers, sponsored by a chemical company, had altered the animal's genes through the process of recombinant DNA technology or, in layman's terms, "genetic manipulation." The resulting rodent was what is known as "transgenic" (the result of mixing genes of different species to produce new entities), and carried a human breast cancer gene, or oncogene. The "oncomouse" (or, more accurately, OncoMouse™) has a predisposition to cancer, and all offspring of this creature will, it is assumed, have the same defective genetic make-up. Any products from the oncomouse are subject to royalty payments to Charles River Biotechnology Services, Bausch and Lomb Co., Mass.

In 1992, the oncomouse was accepted as a patentable being by the European Patent Office. Nevertheless, there has been resistance to the patenting of animals such as the oncomouse. The European Patent Office received 17 formal legal oppositions to the patent. A bill to place a moratorium on the patenting of transgenic animals was introduced in the United States House of Representatives in 1988, but was killed in the Senate after committee members agreed that such a moratorium would damage U.S. scientific competitiveness worldwide.[2] In 1989, the Animal Legal Defense Fund sued the patent commissioner over the oncomouse. At the end of several litigious battles, the patent remained legal. While the British and French have granted animal patents, the Danish parliament has prohibited them. After a ten-year investigation, the Canadian government denied a patent for the Harvard-produced rodents, although the case was appealed to the Federal Court of Canada.

The oncomouse is not the only genetically-altered mouse. There are at least five oncomouse strains along with something called an ImmortoMouse® at Charles River Laboratory alone.[3] Elsewhere, a strain of mouse—TIM, or transgenic immunodeficient mouse—has been developed to carry certain aspects of the human immune system. These so-called AIDS mice are susceptible to HIV infection, which normal mice are not. There are also about 200 so-called knockout mice. In these mice, in an attempt to investigate the role of a particular gene, a gene is "knocked out" from the germ line. This means that the mouse's sperm or eggs do not have the gene and therefore the progeny of the mice do not have it either.

Results of research with genetically-altered mice have been mixed. Occasionally there seems to be no effect when the gene has been "knocked out," raising the question of whether the gene is important. The results are partly inconclusive because other genes seem to step in and take over for functions of missing genes.

One of the most disturbing features of the oncomouse is that the company that holds the patent on the rodent also owns patent rights on any animal infected with the oncogene. Therefore, hypothetically, species throughout the entire animal kingdom are possible oncogene recipients. Presently, only the mouse has been genetically altered in this fashion. But myriad opportunities exist to alter this reality.

The oncomouse is among many animals currently undergoing transgenic "development." The plan is to create cows who produce more milk and pigs who have leaner meat. These developments, in tandem with the ongoing, $3 billion Human Genome Project (an attempt to map all 100,000 genes on the human chromosome) and its corollary, the Human Genome Diversity Project (which is collecting hair, blood and cell samples from 700 threatened indigenous communities), have left open not only the possibility of more John Moores, but—as has already occurred—the patenting of the genome of whole peoples. In 1993, when the Guaymi people of Panama discovered their cell line had been patented as part of the Diversity Project, they had to apply to then U.S. secretary of commerce Ron Brown and the World Trade Organization for control over their own cell line![4]

Bioprospecting

The issue here is not that global patent rights are wrong. Clearly, creativity and invention depend on people feeling secure that the products they create will not be exploited or used without their getting due payment. What is problematic is what—or who—is considered a product and therefore patentable, and that the industrialized world continues to exploit the developing world's resources, to the former's enrichment and the latter's impoverishment. Since the discovery of DNA and the rise of biotechnology, this exploitation has created a kind of "bioprospecting," as the industrialized world goes in search of products that have been used by indigenous peoples for centuries, patents them and thereby renders them off-limits to the very people who "discovered" the products in the first place.

The neem tree has been used by villagers in India for over two millennia as a natural pesticide and medicine. When chewed, its shoots protect the teeth from bacteria. For the past 40 years, Indian cottage industries have been selling neem products and Calcutta Chemicals has been selling neem toothpaste for decades. Since 1985, however, more than a dozen patents have been taken out by U.S. and Japanese companies for exclusive rights to the products of the neem tree. The motive, as *Science Magazine* states, is clear: "Squeezing bucks out of the neem ought to be relatively easy."[5]

What makes Calcutta Chemicals or the cottage industries that use the neem's products different from, say, W. R. Grace (which owns four of the patents) is that Grace is now operating under the Treaty on International Property Rights (TRIPs). TRIPs is a clause in the General Agreement on Tariffs and Trade (GATT) which aims to extend free trade and patents around the world and which itself is monitored by the unelected members of the World Trade Organization (WTO). To Indian physicist and ecofeminist Vandana Shiva, the common knowledge that had been known and "owned" by indigenous peoples for millennia is, through TRIPs, being usurped by international agreements. Multinational companies extend control over indigenous knowledge by patenting—and thus gaining exclusive commercial rights over the products, methods of production and even the ideas of those in the developing world.

International property–rights advocates argue that it is the ability to patent one's products that unleashes creativity. For Shiva, this is yet another way of blaming the developing world for its poverty (and supposed lack of creativity) and an excuse for the developed world to colonize and steal under the guise of saving the developing world from itself. Bioprospecting, as Shiva notes, is hardly surprising: Indigenous knowledge is a potential gold mine for multinational corporations. Seventy-five percent of the 120 active compounds isolated from plants and used in modern medicine were known to indigenous peoples—and comprise a market estimated to be valued at $43 billion. Indigenous knowledge is not only a gold mine, it's also a land mine on the path to global market domination. If villagers in India can produce a product for free that costs a lot to manufacture, that's bad business. So companies around the world are trying to buy up the products of trees like the neem and homogenize and monopolize markets using the tools of the WTO and TRIPs.

For Shiva and other activists for indigenous people around the world, indigenous knowledge is based in both biological and cultural diversity. It is centered in an intellectual commons where the value of an individual is not estimated solely in how he or she can be marketed; all knowledge is not defined by how much money can be made from it. Confining, commodifying, monopolizing and homogenizing knowledge and its products do not expand the wealth of knowledge in the world. Instead, the potential for new knowledge and new products is diminished. Both cultural and biological biodiversity depend on the intermingling of self-organizing systems operating in decentralized communities. The sort of globalization occurring through WTO and TRIPs—hand in hand with the ownership of genetic structures and their modification—leads to the imposition of one more powerful culture on a less dominant one. Excluded are other and perhaps better values, different ways of looking at things, and more sustainable modes of living—ones not immediately marketable for a dollar value.

Biotechnology and the destruction of biodiversity show links among the welfares of people, animals and plants. Monocultures—whether human, animal or plant—are more prone to destruction from diseases that wipe out one strain of stock. The effects of chemical pollution are more possible as more farmers worldwide use a smaller gene pool of genetically engineered crops. Should these crops become resistant to herbicides and pesticides, or fall victim to blight specific to the seed, the effects on these crops could be that much more devastating than if a healthy diversity among the seeds had been maintained. Similarly, genetically engineered organisms pose the threat of releasing new and unknown pollutants into the atmosphere. At the very least, expanding the use of genetically altered substances may create not a world free of illness and hunger, but precisely the opposite, as crops fail and newly mutated infections are let loose on the planet.

By essentially destroying indigenous cultures' ability to "own" their knowledge, the multinationals may destroy the very foundation of so much human knowledge and rip apart the delicate fabric of biodiversity itself. Across the world, indigenous peoples and the developing world as a whole are beginning to organize to confront globalization and the monopolization of the world's resources. In India, a network called Navdanya has been conserving native seeds, while a movement called Seed *Satyagraha* was launched in 1992—on Gandhi's birthday—to resist the diminishing of seed diversity being brought about through TRIPs. For Shiva, local movements like these are both the best hope and the best defense—indeed, the only alternative—to the commodification and homogenization of life. Indigenous and native peoples are the first and last conservationists. We destroy what they know at our peril.

154

Property Discourse

The fundamental principle upon which patenting of organic materials stands is that of private property.[6] The concept of property depends upon a cultural recognition of what it is possible to own and who is entitled to be an owner. One hundred fifty years ago in the United States, opposing forces debated whether slaves should be considered "property."[7] That debate, which revolved around what seems to be self-evident to us now—that African Americans are human beings with the same inalienable rights as white Americans—was only settled by a war. It seems, tragically, that we still have not learned to value individuals—whether human beings like John Moore or the Guaymi—or the animals who are slaughtered every day without even the legal acknowledgment that they are living beings.[8]

The legal reification of living matter, and its current extension into the ownership of the matter by which that living matter comes to be, presents at the very least a worrying trend. Now, it could be argued that commercial traffic in human bodies—whether slavery or prostitution—forms the world's oldest and second oldest professions. Certainly, John Moore was not outraged that his body was violated; he was outraged he couldn't make money from it: one more person who is willing to let himself be exploited if the price is right. What makes the level of exploitation so worrying is that we are dealing with the fundamental structures of the individual body and the body politic—owning the very matter of living organisms and capable of doing anything with it. If all this sounds like another apocalyptic jeremiad against scientific progress, consider that in 1988 Baylor University of Texas filed a European patent which included the genetic alteration of a human female who could eventually be used as a drug factory. An attorney representing Baylor indicated that the university wanted to make sure they had rights on the production of any drugs which came out of the woman, if humans were made patentable.

Boundary Crossing

Xenotransplantation, virulent transspecies infections—such as BSE and the Ebola virus—and the use of biotechnology to create "pharm" animals (such as pigs who could be genetically altered to "store" human hearts or cows who would produce human hemoglobin in their milk), all raise a serious issue. It is clear that the boundaries between human and animal are fluid, but messing with them is at the very least highly dangerous and at the most extraordinarily irresponsible. The moral problem, as well, cuts both ways. If we accept that the boundaries separating human and animal are permeable, surely the moral boundaries that have kept human and animal conveniently separate are also permeable. The more we incorporate animals into our bodily functions, the more the question is begged as to what is quintessentially "human."

This is why the argument often used by those who support the use of animals in scientific research—that the pursuit of knowledge (or, for that matter, the pursuit of the market) is a good in itself or will be of benefit to humans (no matter how tangential or far-fetched those benefits may be)—can never be solely a scientific issue. After all, the reason we use animals in research is because it is morally impermissible to use human beings for similar research—even though there would be the kind of absolute correlation between the subject and object of research required for complete scientific "validity."[9] Moreover, in recent years the public has become increasingly uncomfortable with the idea of experimentation on primates. So most experimentation is done on "lower" animals such as rats and mice, even though their biological systems are very different from ours, and even vary within their own species and gender.

As the spread of global diseases such as HIV and (potentially) BSE shows, we are already getting clear evidence that transgressing species boundaries is dangerous. At the very least there should be some caution about our current rush to alter the genetic structures of living organisms and the parallel commercialization of natural living material. There is an obvious continuity between species. There is also a reason why species are different from each other and why it is better to let differences coexist rather than transgress all boundaries between them.

Frankenstein's Children
Stuart Newman

S tuart Newman is Professor of Cell Biology and Anatomy at New York Medical College in Valhalla, New York. Twenty years ago he cofounded the Council for Responsible Genetics (CRG), which monitors developments in biotechnology and biological research and is concerned that they not be used for destructive purposes. He is an outspoken voice for restraint in the headlong rush toward genetic modification of living organisms and an opponent of any form of germ-line modification of humans.

"All of these issues should be widely discussed.
While they are not typical dinner table conversation, they are things
that will affect the entire human species if they are done."

What particular dangers were you looking at 20 years ago?
The technology that particularly stimulated the organization of CRG was the new capacity to take genes from one kind of organism, say a human being or a mouse, and splice them into another kind of organism. At that time, bacteria were the major host. The idea was to use this technique as a research tool to amplify certain gene segments, study them, and then use the techniques to get the bacteria to produce things bacteria don't normally produce which might be useful for research or for the pharmaceutical industry.

There are certain proteins made by humans—such as insulin—that bacteria don't make. If you put the gene for human insulin into a bacterium, the bacterium will make insulin. This has become the standard insulin, increasingly substituted for animal insulin in the treatment of human diabetes. Our concerns at that time were the crossing of species boundaries and the possibility of releasing into the environment bacteria that were making things that bacteria do not normally make.

It had been known before the late 1970s that many pathogens have their disease-causing properties because they mimic some aspect of the biology of higher organisms. Therefore, they conflict with certain systems in, say, the human host. There was thus a concern that new pathogens would be developed by these technologies. Furthermore, the prospect for the future was to take genes from one human and put them into another human, or transplant from an animal into a human. In the late 1970s this was just a theoretical possibility; now it is something that is technically possible. Gene switching between species or higher organisms, mice and rats for example, or humans and mice, now goes on.

Insulin from bacteria seems to be OK. Why shouldn't other practices?

The people who organized the Council for Responsible Genetics were ready to acknowledge in the 1970s that there would be some beneficial uses to the technology. There was simply a question of whether it was premature to embark on it because not enough was known about containment.

No one would object to using a bacterium to produce insulin rather than using insulin from animals. But if this bacterium established itself in the environment, or exchanged its insulin gene for that of a related bacterium that was already established in the environment, we could have the bacterial world populated with bacteria that are producing human insulin. The chemical industry in the period around World War Two put lots of things into the environment, the implications of which were not really understood until very recently. As a totally unforeseen consequence of the actions of the chemical industry, we now have widespread pollution not only in waterways and in the land, but also in the food chain and in packaging materials that are used for food transfer.

Very low levels of these chemicals mimic hormones in the human body and there is good evidence that they have caused sexual dysfunction, such as low sperm count, in humans. There is very good evidence that in various lakes and waterways species have been wiped out or disturbed in very profound ways. This is an example of a byproduct of the chemical industry that has gotten into the environment and seems to have caused widespread havoc.

The original intention of the researchers and people commercializing the chemicals was that there would be absolute containment. But people pour chemicals down the drain, and there are effluents from the industrial processes. Although I cannot cite any studies, because this really is not something on which people are actively doing research, it is almost impossible to exclude the likelihood that pathogens will appear because naturally established bacteria have acquired human genes. I have little doubt that there are populations of bacteria in the environment making insulin that were not able to before. It took many years for the consequences of the chemical penetration of the environment to be manifested in biological systems; this is going to happen with the bacterial world.

Why are we so short-sighted about the possible effects of gene-splicing?
Part of it relates to the way heredity has been viewed throughout history. The standard model we have is a combination of Mendelism and Darwinism. The Mendelian paradigm, after Gregor Mendel [1822-1884], is that things are inherited in what some people call a "particulate" fashion, that there is a one-to-one association between what we now call genes and particular traits. This is a very deeply set idea, and although every working biologist would say this is not exactly the way it happens for most or many traits, the ones that are studied and therefore the ones that are fixed in the mind and in the textbooks and in the popular consciousness are the Mendelian types of traits.

Then there is the Darwinian paradigm, after Charles Darwin [1809-1882]. According to this theory, the diversification that we have in the modern world of living organisms is the result of small variations, competition between marginally different organisms on the basis of better adaptation to certain functions, and then very small evolutionary changes over tremendous amounts of time. Now, I think that this Darwinian paradigm is subject to real question. I am not challenging the idea that organisms have evolved from simpler forms; no legitimate modern scientist would question that. I am questioning the Darwinian model for how this has occurred.

Just looking at the fossil record, as has been pointed out on many occasions by Stephen Jay Gould, who has done pioneering work in this area, organisms seem to have evolved in fits and starts. Major changes in organismal form occur rapidly in the history of life, and then for long periods of time there is stasis and very little change. Gould has also pointed out that if you look at the origin of multicellular organisms more than half a billion years ago, you find that all the different types of organisms emerged very rapidly after the origin of multicellularity. So there were very rapid, major changes very early and then there was a kind of locking in and culling out. This is very different from what Darwin proposed. The consequences of this are just seeping into the scientific consciousness.

Organisms today may look very much in their basic plans like the organisms of half a billion years ago, but there is a much greater sophistication in all the genetic pathways that have evolved to realize those forms. It is not as if evolution has been an evolution of form so much as it has been an evolution of genes in the service of conserving those forms.

The implications for gene-splicing are profound. It may be that you can remove a gene and things will react in such a way as to bring about the outcome. That is part of what this evolution was selecting for: the robustness of the system. But clearly these are highly integrated systems. With a machine you have replaceable parts and it is possible to attribute certain effects to certain causes. However, with an organic body you are dealing with a highly articulated, integrated system that has evolved in hierarchies and layers over huge amounts of time. The idea that one gene will have a very determinate function in this overall network of interactions is very naive. Moreover, to try to get at altering the biology of the organism by altering genes one at a time is also very naive and susceptible to accidents or mistakes.

Could the same could be said of an ecosystem?

Yes. The reason for the parallel is that both the human body and an ecosystem are generated by a historical process. If you look at the inside of a television set or the inside of a computer you don't really have to understand the history that led up to various design features in order to understand what the different parts are doing. But if you look at the kind of system that the human body is, or the ecosystem is, the elements that make it up have taken on their roles at different points in the evolution of the system. Therefore the complexity is of a different type than the complexity of a piece of machinery like a computer.

What you see more and more are proposals to use the results of gene technology to get at various human diseases and things that are considered by some people to be undesirable, and therefore defined as disease states—for example, obesity or short stature. If we have this sense, which I think is a false one, that we can reliably manipulate genes based on predictive knowledge of the connection between genes and traits, we will be trying to attain some kind of perfectibility by manipulating genes. That is the logical consequence of this genetic ideology. Even if you take a more modest view, where you say there are certain things that we can all agree are diseases, the question remains: Is it desirable to use these genetic techniques to design individuals who will be free of these diseases? Even there, there are real problems.

Gene modification has already been used on certain of the body tissues to attempt to ameliorate or attenuate the effects of certain diseases. Most of these have not worked, and there have been articles written about the disappointing outcomes. These failures, however, have mainly been for technical reasons; in principle there is no reason why by manipulating some genes known to be damaged or defective or associated with certain disease states you should not be able to bring about a partly palliated outcome. I personally think it is a legitimate strategy to use these gene-based correctives or therapies to attack some life-threatening diseases. But to say, "Well, why wait until an individual grows up with a disease? Why not from the start take human fertilized eggs and put the right genes in so that we get the right outcome?"—I think this is totally misguided. In contrast with the other procedure, which is called somatic gene therapy or gene modification, this is called germ-line gene modification. This is doing manipulations on people who do not even exist yet, with the possibility of the experiment going awry and resulting in a person who has a completely unforeseen set of diseases.

160

We do not have a scientific theory that would allow us to do it in a really predictable fashion. We do not have any social organization—nor should we—that would say that if the experiment did not work this person should be removed from the breeding pool of the population. That would be awful. The ethical problems, the technical problems and the prospects of creating new diseases undermine any justification for doing this germ-line modification procedure, I would say indefinitely. That said, there is little evidence that my concerns about this and the concerns of many other people will be addressed. In our society anything that can make money for somebody, if it is technically possible, will get done unless it is specifically illegal. I do not see any movement towards making germ-line modification illegal. Indeed, there have been articles in reputable journals written by philosophers and people concerned with bioethics arguing that human germ-line modification is probably in the cards and that there may be benefits to it. There was a recent high-profile scientific conference promoting this technique. I totally disagree with the benefits; but that it is in the cards, I don't doubt.

Within how many years?
Within ten years there will be attempts to do this, unless there is a big awakening involving large-scale social understanding, and a publicly expressed revulsion for taking this path. Otherwise, somebody is going to try it. There are also patenting issues involved. As we know, human embryos do not have Constitutional protection, nor should they. But because of that particular legal situation, human embryos can be genetically manipulated. Things that are genetically manipulated can be patented by existing patent law. And there you have it. This state of affairs has stimulated me, with the help of the social critic and consumer advocate Jeremy Rifkin, to apply for a patent on chimeric organisms that are part human and part animal.[1] We have no intention of creating such organisms, but have taken this step as a challenge to the system that permits patents on such "inventions." We would like to see appropriate laws passed to ban the patenting, and even the experimental production, of such entities. But if we are granted the patent we will use it to block such developments for 20 years while society has a chance to put restrictions into place.

All of these issues should be widely discussed. While they are not typical dinner table conversation, they are things that will affect the entire human species if they are done. These issues have the weightiness of provisions that we have against racial discrimination and discrimination based on gender. We have taken certain steps in our history to abolish things, such as slavery, once and for all. Scientists are always looking for forums to explain their latest breakthroughs and the government is always publicizing progress that's been made. On those occasions people should be questioned: "Are we heading towards germ-line modification, and other technologies of experimental human production, and what are we doing so it doesn't happen?"

161

Xenotransplants
Animals As Spare Parts
Alan H. Berger

Transplanting organs such as hearts, lungs and kidneys from human donors to human patients seems commonplace today. Unfortunately, as we all know, there is an increasing demand for these prized organs and a seemingly limited supply. Currently, there is a waiting list of approximately 45,000 patients and an annual supply of only 20,000 organs.

Our current system of human organ procurement for transplantation is not working. Only about 20 percent of potential organ donors who die "healthy" have arranged for their organs to be used to help others. This fact is remarkable given the results of a 1993 Gallup Poll. Eight-five percent of individuals supported the donation of organs for transplant and 69 percent were very likely or somewhat likely to want their organs donated after their death. Ninety-three percent were willing to donate a family member's organs if requested before death, but only 47 percent if the issue was not discussed before death.

The response from the medical community has been to regard animals as major organ donors. Without pausing to further evaluate the serious flaws in this practice, known as xenotransplantation, nor the ethical dilemmas in cross-species transplants, the alternatives available or the role of the biotech industry, the medical community is pursuing the course single-mindedly. There are a number of issues that are problematic: namely cost, ethical consideration and governmental guidelines.

Cost

In 1994, nearly $3 billion was spent on organ transplants. This cost does not include expensive follow-up care for the thousands who have already received transplants. As a society, we already have serious difficulties justifying the cost of human organ transplants. With a growing number of people lacking access to basic health care, it may not be justifiable even today to devote so much energy and so many financial resources to human organ transplants.

With xenotransplantation, the costs are even higher. According to the Institutes of Medicine (IOM) in their June 1996 report, "Xenotransplantation: Science, Ethics and Public Policy," this cost could rise to $20.3 billion if all patients in need of organs received xenotransplants. Furthermore, xenotransplantation's success rate is zero, health insurance is not available and the procedure annually benefits only a small number of people. It seems inappropriate to use limited research dollars on this type of experimental surgery when these same dollars can be used more appropriately for better methods of treatment and prevention.

One common response of the medical profession to those who apply a cost–benefit analysis to xenotransplantation is that it is not possible to measure the value of a human life simply by cost. Unfortunately that is just not true. Costly medical procedures to a limited, chosen group continually raise the overall cost of health care. These procedures also limit insurance coverage and increase insurance premiums. A result is that more and more people will not find adequate health care services available to them. The question is whether to save some patients with expensive medical procedures while possibly lose even more by denying them access to basic health care.

The Problem with Animals

There are also substantial ethical and safety questions involved in using animals. Until recently the animal of choice for xenotransplantation has been the baboon. The nonhuman primates available for use in surgical procedures are limited in number, expensive and difficult to maintain. They are also rarely Specific-Pathogen Free (SPF). Because of this, the current trend is to use transgenic pig organs (in which human genetic material has been spliced into the pig's DNA) for human transplant recipients. "Sacrificing" a baboon, an animal much closer in genetic make-up to humans, is harder for many people to accept than using organs from an animal whose parts already service human needs. To reduce their exposure to disease, these genetically altered pigs are removed from the womb by cesarean section. They are never allowed to suckle or even come in contact with their mother; instead they are hand-raised by humans wearing gloves, and maintained in a semi-sterile environment.

Ethical problems aside, perhaps the greatest risk xenotransplantation poses is exposing human populations to non-human primate viruses, and this possibility of transmission of a lethal virus has convinced many researchers to abandon primate-to-human transplants. It is now believed in the scientific community that HIV, already a worldwide catastrophe affecting as many as 30 million people, was a simian virus passed on to the human population.

There are no tests currently available to screen for all animal-specific diseases, meaning a lethal unknown virus can escape our vaccination and testing programs. The risk may be even higher if a xenotransplant actually succeeds and the patient lives a "normal" life. Even though the risk may be small, the outcome of a new virus spreading can be catastrophic. Even if pigs are SPF, this does not guarantee human safety from infectious diseases. The assumption that swine used in xenotransplantation are safer donors has not been proven. The new strains of swine flu that periodically appear may become more pronounced if pigs are used as organ donors for humans.

Professor Frederick Murphy, a virologist at the University of California, has issued a warning about the risk of spreading diseases to humans in proposed transplants of transgenic pig organs. There are four thousand known virus species and 30,000 strains and variants that infect living creatures. Trying to identify potentially lethal viruses that might be transmitted to humans during a xenotransplant would be nearly impossible.

The Problem of Ethics

The ethical, moral, philosophical and religious concerns over the creation of a "new" species—especially one that is "almost" human—need to be seriously addressed. Is this what we really want as a society? Where does it end? Who controls this process? How human would a transgenic pig be? When does a "non-human" with human genes become human, deserving full human rights? What if our genetic tampering misfires—what have we created? A larger ethical question still is the lesson we are presenting to future generations. Our society does not have a reverence for all life; indeed, many feel that our careless disregard for all living things assisted in the development of our increasingly violent society.

The Problem of Government

On September 20, 1996 the United States Department of Health and Human Services (HHS) released proposed guidelines for xenotransplantation, developed with the Food and Drug Administration (FDA), the Centers for Disease Control and Prevention (CDC), and the National Institutes of Health (NIH). The HHS recommendations included: taking appropriate safety measures to screen animals for diseases; archiving biological samples from the source animals and transplant recipients; expanding transplant teams for specific expertise and conducting appropriate research; having local review boards evaluate infectious disease risks; and monitoring patients after xenotransplants for infectious disease agents.

These guidelines, however, pave the way for a potential public health disaster. First, they warn that infectious agents "may not produce clinically recognizable disease until many years after they enter the host, and some infectious agents are not readily detected or identified in tissue samples by current diagnostic techniques." Secondly, they add that "the full spectrum of infectious agents potentially transmitted via xenograft transplantation is not well known. Infectious agents that produce minimal symptoms in animals may cause severe morbidity and mortality in humans." To make us feel even more nervous they use the example of AIDS/HIV to demonstrate that "persistent viral infections may result in person-to-person transmission for many years before clinical disease develops ..., thereby allowing an emerging infectious agent to become established in the susceptible population before it is recognized."

With the estimate from the Institutes of Medicine report of potentially over 100,000 xenotransplants annually, the surveillance system being established to protect the public is not financially or physically possible. In addition, the system begins to operate only after the xenotransplant occurs, when it may be too late. The suggestion that local medical center review boards can monitor xenotransplantation surgical protocols (including surveillance guidelines) to keep them consistent is unworkable. The HHS seems interested in accelerating the process and pushing as much of the oversight as possible down to the local levels, a poor decision at best.

The Problem of Fame

I believe that most xenotransplant researchers are sincerely interested in saving human lives, rather than pursuing the fame or financial rewards that might accompany research success. But how driven are these very same people by the need to bring funding dollars to their research institution? Or are they so driven to "find the solution" that other considerations become secondary? Can these very same people be the ones making ethical and scientific decisions over their own experimental medical procedures? There is a conflict of interest here, and a strong need for more–independent public oversight.

Alternatives to Xenotransplantation

Happily, there are alternatives to xenotransplantation. The development of new surgical techniques to repair malformed or poorly functioning organs would have substantial long-term benefits. Transplantation with split organs from living human donors may be possible in some cases. The development of synthetic organs would further reduce or potentially eliminate the need for donor organs in the future.

More education in health maintenance and disease prevention has proven to be the most effective use of research dollars. Lifestyle changes, including diet and exercise, have had an enormous impact on preventing and possibly reversing heart disease. Many examples of preventive medicine could greatly reduce the need for xenotransplants, and preventive medicine reduces the need for costly, experimental and often unsuccessful research projects.

Better education regarding the chronic need for donor organs and a strong donor recruitment program could increase the number of available organ donors. Relaxing the medical criteria defining healthy donors, improving the organization of the donor delivery system, and required request legislation with better education and training would all help considerably. A system of mandated choice, as recommended by the American Medical Association, would certainly help in the short run. Again, massive education is needed or the results might backfire as in Texas in 1994, when mandated choice brought an 80 percent refusal rate for organ donors.

The best alternative available now is possibly the presumed–consent law. The successful European model follows the legal presumption that everyone is a potential organ donor, unless he or she has declared otherwise. A system to educate the public, make opting out simple and protect against the fear of early harvesting of organs can easily be established. In Belgium, which enacted its presumed–consent law in 1986, the total number of organs available for transplantation had increased by 183 percent two years after the law was enacted. In Austria, organ availability quadrupled after the presumed–consent law was implemented.

Presumed consent respects the majority opinion regarding donating organs. The United States' current system presumes the absence of consent. Presumed consent shifts the responsibility of decision about organ donation from the relatives to the individual, maximally respecting his or her right to self-determination. Grieving families are spared the stress and trauma of having to make this difficult decision at a time of loss, especially since their response is often to deny permission, in many cases against the unvoiced preference of the deceased.

AIDS and Animal Research

Steven I. Simmons

I am both an AIDS activist and an animal rights activist, two things which in my mind go quite well together. I also have AIDS myself, which makes it a very personal issue for me and has given me perspective on the many sides of these issues and how they fit together. It has been my focus to attempt to bridge the gap that sometimes exists between the AIDS community and the animal rights community—a gap which is unfortunate and has led to some conflict and real misrepresentation of the issues with which we are all concerned.

An Associated Press poll in the early 1990s showed that animal rights has taken hold in the American consciousness. The majority of people surveyed agreed that it is always wrong, for example, to kill animals for fur or to test cosmetics. Most even agreed with the statement that animals have basic rights and that they deserve equal consideration as humans. That is a dramatic shift in opinion in the course of just a few years and represents the inroads the movement has made. There remains, however, the issue of using animals for medical research, which animal advocates have been much less persuasive about. In fact, many allies or potential allies of the animal rights movement—such as those espousing gay rights, feminism, or environmentalism—seem to steer clear of an animal rights position on this particular issue.

We have already established that people are concerned about unnecessary animal suffering and want it eliminated. Obviously, their support for animal research is based on compassion. They believe that using animals in this manner is alleviating more suffering than it is causing and that there is no other way. People want to do what is best and do the greatest good for the most number of beings involved.

One of the reasons that pro-animal research sentiment has remained so strong in the public mind is that those who oppose it are often afraid to tackle this issue. For animal advocates to jump into this debate is to take on Nobel prize-winning doctors and eminent microbiologists with lots of degrees who tell animal advocates that they don't know what they are talking about and that scientific progress depends on using animals. These experts use their status to intimidate and limit debate. The fact is you do not need a Ph.D. to discuss scientific or medical issues or to form opinions about them.

In late 1995 and early 1996, AIDS and animal research was very much in the news. In December, in San Francisco, a man named Jeff Getty[1]—who is suffering from AIDS—received a baboon bone marrow transplant. The idea behind this was that since baboons who are infected with HIV do not appear to develop AIDS, they must have some kind of inherent resistance to it. Since bone marrow is a vital component of the immune system, went the reasoning, giving this AIDS patient baboon bone marrow might create, in effect, a parallel immune system that would fight the virus. On January 30 1996, the Yerkes Regional Primate Research Center in Atlanta, Georgia announced that a chimpanzee had developed AIDS, ten years after being infected with HIV by Yerkes researchers. Only two weeks later, on February 13, Yerkes announced that the chimp, Jerom, had been put to death. The reason, according to Yerkes, was severe and untreatable anemia. Before Jerom died, another chimpanzee, Nathan, was injected with Jerom's blood. The infection of Jerom and Nathan was considered a breakthrough, because for years scientists had attempted to infect chimpanzees in particular with the HIV virus but none of them had actually become sick. According to the scientists, this infection would bring us closer to an animal model of the disease that could be used to test new treatments and vaccines.

What was more alarming for me than either of these two stories themselves was the general support this kind of research has been receiving from the AIDS community. In fact, when Physicians Committee for Responsible Medicine (PCRM) came out opposing the baboon bone marrow transplant, the San Francisco chapter of the group AIDS Coalition To Unleash Power (ACT-UP) issued a press release attacking PCRM and its director, Dr. Neal Barnard. I was shocked to hear this because when I worked for People for the Ethical Treatment of Animals (PETA) a few years ago, I organized a series of protests at the University of Pittsburgh, where a man had received a baboon liver transplant. A few days after the procedure a hospital employee revealed that this man, whose identity had been concealed by the hospital, was actually HIV+. When we learned of this, we contacted ACT-UP in Pittsburgh and they recognized this as a case of AIDS exploitation and joined us in the protest.

The case of Jeff Getty, however, was quite different from the one in Pittsburgh. Instead of concealing the patient's identity, Getty's doctors presented him at news conferences and made him a media figure. Getty himself was a longtime AIDS activist in San Francisco who had fought very long and hard for improved access to medical treatments for AIDS patients. Therefore, when his doctors proposed this pioneering experiment with the baboon bone marrow, it fit in with his desire to push the envelope of science. Meanwhile, the scientific community was raising some very serious concerns about this procedure. In 1996, experts in immunology who testified at a conference held by the Food and Drug Administration (FDA) were in general agreement that this procedure was more likely to kill Getty than to help him. This opposition only added to Getty's rising image as a hero to those living with AIDS and seemed to strengthen his determination. In the end, it was the emotional pleas of his family that led the FDA to give the green light to the experiment.

The issue of xenotransplantation has to be put in a historical context. In this century about 35 animal-to-human transplants have been attempted—everything from pig kidneys to chimpanzee livers. Baboons have been the most recent source of organs for xenografts or cross-species transplantation. Not a single one of these procedures has been successful. In 1963, one person lived for about nine months after receiving a chimpanzee kidney, but most patients have died within a few hours or days. In 1984, Baby Fae made headlines as an infant who received a baboon's heart and died about 20 days later. Xenografts simply do not work and there is no evidence they ever will.

They are, moreover, very dangerous and a portion of the scientific community is sounding an alarm about this topic. Many microbes that are pathogenic in one kind of species are harmless in another, and vice versa. HIV itself probably originated in the Rhesus monkey, where it apparently causes no immunodeficiency. We know that non-human primates carry many bacteria, viruses and parasites which are harmful or even deadly to humans. Included among these are Y. pestis (the bacteria which causes bubonic plague) as well as the deadly Hantaa and Ebola viruses. The fact that baboons are apparently resistant to HIV actually points to the greatest danger about the procedure rather than to its potential benefit. Through this kind of procedure, new illnesses may jump from the donor species to the human population and cause epidemics we cannot even imagine.

Each xenograft is also a cruel waste of money, costing at least $300,000 for the operation alone, not to mention the millions of dollars allocated to research in this area. Meanwhile, programs we know save lives—such as AIDS prevention, housing and primary care—are vastly underfunded. Many promising alternative treatments are not explored because there are not the resources available to study them.

Finally, it is important to look at the issue of informed consent regarding this kind of human experimentation. As with any hazardous medical procedure, Getty was required to sign an informed consent document before he received the baboon bone marrow. This document states that one is aware of the risks and also of the alternatives available. Interestingly, Getty himself told the *New York Times*, "I know this may kill me but I know I will die if I do nothing." Somehow he had been convinced that he had exhausted every other option and that this was his only hope. This is not unusual. In 1984, after the Baby Fae incident, an independent review panel determined there were at least four other procedures that could have been tried to save that child's life, about which the parents were never informed. It is ludicrous for us to think that baboon bone marrow really represents the greatest hope for people with late-stage AIDS.

As for the issue of the chimpanzees Jerom and Nathan developing AIDS, we have to question what this really means scientifically. Over the years the definition of AIDS has changed and blurred quite significantly. The term AIDS was coined before the discovery of the HIV virus. It was simply based on the observation of a group of young gay men who were becoming very sick. After the discovery of the virus it was obvious that many people had the virus without having AIDS, so criteria were established. For years, being HIV+ simply meant that you were infected with the virus, while AIDS or the term "full-blown AIDS" was used to indicate specific opportunistic infections had taken place, such as pneumocystis pneumonia or Kaposi sarcoma. A middle stage of ARC, or AIDS-Related Complex, was used to describe a symptomatic stage between the two. Then, a few years ago, the definitions again changed because of the development of prophylactic treatments which prevent some of the life-threatening infections. Once these therapies became common, people could progress to a very advanced stage of the disease without qualifying for the definition of AIDS. The Centers for Disease Control and Prevention therefore determined that anyone who is HIV+ with a T-cell count below 200/mm^3 of blood now has AIDS.

According to the current criteria, then, for Jerom to develop AIDS simply means he was infected with the HIV virus (which we already knew) and that he was seriously immune-compromised. We have to wonder if we are really surprised that a chimpanzee who has been living for at least a decade in a laboratory has a problem with his immune system and whether we are sure that this is because he is infected with HIV. Of course there are hundreds of other chimpanzees who have been infected with the virus for over a decade who are not exhibiting any of the symptoms of AIDS.

What this brings us to is the conclusion that animals simply cannot model human disease. Research in recent years, particularly in the fields of psycho-neuro-immunology—which studies the interaction between mind and body—has shown us that human illness is a very dynamic process involving many factors. It has been difficult enough simply to create a chemistry in animals similar to that observed in humans. But we will never be able to create the complex context in which this illness arises and progresses. The reason researchers claim we need an animal model for this and other diseases is so they can test new treatments without risking human lives. Yet we know that more than half of the drugs approved every year—all of which have been through extensive animal testing for both toxicity and efficacy—are later pulled from the market because of unpredicted dangerous or even lethal side effects in humans.

The primary focus of AIDS activist groups has been to speed the process of drug approval in this country, and they have been very successful in doing that. But the most obvious way to accomplish this would be to eliminate the animal testing stage from the drug development process. Not only would this hasten the accessibility of new drugs but it would also free up millions of dollars which could be directed into more effective channels. Most animal rights activists are in agreement about the ethics of this situation. It is simply wrong

170

to use animals for research. While it is important, therefore, to argue the scientific grounds for an anti-vivisectionist position, there is still a basic ethical issue which should be stated. Even if xenografts were actually safe, effective and economically feasible, there would still remain the question of whether we have the right to kill non-human beings for the benefit of human beings. I value my life no more than a baboon values his or hers. Fortunately, the facts do not force us to make such complicated ethical judgments. Respect for all life can only hasten scientific progress.

AIDS is a very emotionally charged issue. We have all seen ACT-UP protests, and people are angry and caught up in the emotion. That can be very intimidating in terms of challenging people. Of course, I too am very personally involved in it: I have many friends who are sick and I myself suffer from the disease. I want progress to be made more than anything. I want this disease to be cured or managed. That is the point to which we must stick: AIDS and animal rights activists are on the same side. It is our respect for life and our compassion that has influenced us to take such positions on these issues. The fact is, the current approach is not saving lives. It is costing lives, and that is why it is wrong.

Mad Cow Disease

Martin Rowe

It was the 19th century German chancellor Otto von Bismarck who perhaps summed it up best: "Laws are like sausages. It's better not to see them being made." While it is likely that Bismarck thought the end products of government and the slaughterhouse justified the means, no matter how unsavory, the crisis of mad cow disease that rocked Britain and America in the early 1990s—and is still not over—reveals not only just how very unsavory the processes are, but also how inextricably the two are linked.

For roughly a ten-year period, from 1985 to 1995, a degenerative brain disease called Bovine Spongiform Encephalopathy or "mad cow disease" ravaged British cattle.[1] The disease was particularly unpleasant, causing the infected animals to foam at the mouth, stumble when they walked, show increasingly erratic behavior, and die. Autopsies revealed that the brains of these animals had been perforated like sponges. While transmissible spongiform encephalopathies (the scientific term for these contagious degenerative brain diseases) had been around for years—there have been regular outbreaks of the sheep variety of this disease, known as "scrapie," for centuries—the bovine form seemed new. Scientists were initially puzzled as to what was causing it. By the late 1980s, however, they believed that British farmers' practice of feeding ground-up or rendered animal parts to the same animal species, in this case cows, was contributing to an increase in the spread and virulence of this disease.

Rendering—using the inedible parts of dead food animals for other products, including animal food—is a large business that has grown parallel to factory farming as a way of efficiently using as much of the products of the animals' bodies as possible. By 1989, those parts of the animal considered both inedible or industrially useless were being fed to animals as "protein feed." Not only was it an efficient way of dealing with the waste products of animals (for instance, only 60 percent of a steer is edible), but it offered a way to maximize the growth potential of both the animals and the slaughter and rendering industries. Nevertheless, in 1989, in the face of increasing evidence that such cannibalism was helping spread BSE, the British government banned this practice.

What was especially troubling about this disease was the possibility that human consumption of certain parts of infected cattle was leading to the rise of a similarly degenerative disease in humans called Creutzfeldt-Jakob disease, or CJD. CJD is an extremely rare disease, usually affecting the old, and has the same symptoms as BSE and scrapie: disorientation, fatigue, muscle mass and co-ordination loss, and eventually death. During the early 1990s, doctors noticed that more and much younger people than usual were dying of this disease. Because this form of CJD was slightly different from the normal form, scientists called it new variant CJD (nvCJD). It was discovered that all the victims had consumed meat between 1984 and 1989, which has now been determined as the period of greatest infectivity.

Even now, scientists do not know fully how the disease spreads, although it does appear to be more prevalent than might be imagined (lots of other species can catch their particular versions of the disease). Nor, for that matter, do scientists know definitively what parts of cattle are infectious, or even whether other animals we consume also have forms of brain disease and whether they too are infectious. Scientists have focused on something called a prion—which has all the infectious properties of a virus without its nucleic structure—as the active agent, although nobody has yet provided conclusive evidence that prions exist as independent units. Some scientists have discounted the theory that BSE is caused by prions at all, arguing that it is a common infective agent found in the natural world to which some people may be more genetically susceptible than others. So far, over 20 people in Britain have died of nvCJD.

One of the major tragedies of these deaths in the saga of CJD in Britain—one which is still only a potential tragedy in the United States, where no cases of BSE have been reported—is that it could easily have been avoided. In the mid-1950s, anthropologists in Papua New Guinea came across a human transmissible disease that had all the properties of CJD. The Papuans called it "kuru" and it seemed to come from nowhere, affecting almost exclusively women and children. It was invariably fatal. The anthropologists discovered that early in the century Papuan women had taken to eating the brains of the dead of the tribe (mainly because their social customs kept the better game meat for the men, leaving women to fill their diet with vegetables and small animals). Men were generally not affected by kuru because when men did eat human bodies, they consumed the desirable parts, leaving the brains and the remains to the women. It may be obvious in hindsight, but intraspecies cannibalism clearly intensifies the spread and infectivity of latent diseases. It happened with kuru and it happened with BSE. The question remains whether it will happen with CJD.

Open Question

The reason the question is still open is that, until 1997, the U.S. government was still allowing rendered animals to be fed back to food animals as protein feed. While the British government banned the practice nearly a decade earlier, it had constantly refused to alert the British people to the possibility that there may have been a connection between BSE and nvCJD. The British government claimed at first that BSE was species-specific, much like scrapie, until it was discovered that many other species were coming down with the disease after they were fed BSE-infected animal protein. Even after the ban the British government continued to placate the public (and, more significantly for the governing Conservatives, the farming constituency) by pronouncing that BSE was not a problem and that British beef was entirely safe. Statistics, however, told a different story. In April 1988 there were 455 cases of BSE. By June that year there were over 600. A governmental committee meeting in November 1988 estimated that 17,000 to 20,000 cases would be in existence by 1993. They underestimated by a factor of ten. Likewise, the incidence of nvCJD began rising. In 1995 alone, five farmers died of the disease. The British government resorted to publicity stunts: the Minister of Agriculture forced his daughter to eat a hamburger in front of cameras to assure the public that there was nothing to worry about. Meanwhile, the scientific advice became more and more serious—even the country's leading neurologist announced that he feared a connection between BSE and CJD. The pressure on the government to make a statement admitting there was a problem became overwhelming, and finally, in March 1996, it did. There may be a link, it announced to a stunned House of Commons, and special efforts will be made to cull all cattle which may have BSE.

In spite of all the evidence suggesting that feeding natural herbivores their own kind was not a sound agricultural practice, the United States Department of Agriculture did not suggest that farmers should stop feeding animals back to animals until 1996, and only in 1997 banned it: a full ten years after the cause of BSE became known in Britain. While there have to date been no actual reports of BSE in the United States (although the States also has its transmissible encephalopathies), numerous cows die each year of "downer cow syndrome"—a sporadic and mysterious ailment, some cases of which may be due to BSE, and which has unsurprisingly been virtually ignored by farming and governmental agencies.

One of the reasons such a situation was ignored until deaths occurred is surely the enormous costs involved in changing the agricultural system. When news about the possible connection between BSE and CJD became known in Britain, the beef industry collapsed overnight. Farmers killed themselves; the European Union banned British beef, leading to a crisis which is still not over. In December 1997, European Union scientists called for a ban on British lamb and beef still on the bone, since there is a chance it is infected. These bans have only recently been lifted. In March 1998, it was reported that the true number of cows infected with BSE may have been hidden by farmers burying or burning their livestock without reporting it.

In the United States, when Howard Lyman, a former-rancher-turned-vegetarian, went on the Oprah Winfrey show in April 1996 and announced that BSE was not only in the United States—hidden in "downer cow syndrome"—but had the potential to be an epidemic even more devastating than AIDS, the cattle futures on the Chicago Mercantile Exchange briefly dipped. In a case that went to court

174

in January 1998 and was settled a month later in Oprah Winfrey's favor, Texas cattle-farmers sued the talk show host and Lyman under "agricultural product disparagement laws" to the tune of $2 million. Winfrey clearly f elt the case was a matter of the right of the media to present information they feel is in the public interest, and that it was wrong to be intimidated by monied interests. The price of such freedom of speech, Winfrey knew, was high: the day after Lyman was on "Oprah," the beef industry pulled $600,000 worth of advertising from the show.[2]

Not the Only Disease

Mad cow disease is, however, not the only disease one can catch from consuming animals killed in today's slaughterhouses. Just about any infection latent in the animal in question can make it through to the consumer. Independent research has shown that 80 percent of all chickens sold for human consumption show traces of salmonella, with an even higher percentage showing traces of the less virulent disease campylobacter. The E-coli bacteria, virtually unknown in the early 1980s, have now killed adults and children around the world. The Centers for Disease Control and Prevention estimates that the United States has between 6.5. and 8.1 million cases of food poisoning each year, and that as many as one in every three Americans suffers a food-borne illness in the same period. In the ten years to 1994, deaths from food poisoning more than quadrupled, to 9,000. The major source for this is food of animal origin.[3]

Much of this increase is due to government deregulation of the slaughter industry. In 1978, USDA slaughterhouse inspectors were told they did not have to automatically condemn any bird with fecal contamination, they merely had to wash that bird off as it passed along the disassembly line. The result of this decision was that the tanks in which the birds were washed became "fecal soup," and far from washing the birds actually soaked disease into them. In 1985, the government imposed nationwide a two-year-old pilot program known as Streamlined Inspection. Inspectors would no longer be stopping the production line to inspect for the many contaminants. Instead, employees would do the job—employees who were, of course, subject to firing if they stopped the line and thereby held up processing. At that stage, 450 fewer USDA poultry inspectors were examining a billion and a half more birds than in 1975, and were effectively being allowed one and a half seconds to inspect fully each bird for contamination or inedible matter. Deemed a success in the poultry industry, Streamlined Inspection was then transplanted to the cattle industry. Today, although all beef is stamped "U.S. Inspected" or passed, only 0.03 percent of the meat some of us eat is thoroughly inspected by government inspectors. Everything from bruises, bone, fecal matter, hair, mucous and blood clots ends up on our plates.

Conditions in some of today's slaughterhouses are literally inhuman. The slaughter industry has an almost unprecedented staff-turnover rate of nearly 100 percent per year. Of those who have come forward, many tell of the alcohol problems and marital strife they and others have experienced because of the stress of their jobs. Others recall workers being unable to leave the slaughter line when they needed to go to the bathroom and being forced to relieve themselves on the floor. They tell of four-inch roaches and rats infesting slaughterhouse floors, where offal and animal waste often accumulates.

The animals being killed fare no better. Because of the type of deregulation mentioned already, the shockers or bolts used to render an animal either unconscious or dead before slaughter routinely lack the voltage to complete the task. The results are horrendous: conscious animals, kicking and screaming as they are skinned or scalded alive; animals wounding workers by kicking knives back into their faces or bodies; animals rampaging through the plant, getting caught in machinery. The effect on workers is always desensitizing, and sometimes alarming. Workers relate how they either beat the heads of hogs with concrete bars until they died, sawed or torched off legs of live steers; they speak of cattle repeatedly stunned, choked, dragged—all of it in contravention of the Humane Slaughter Act that, even to those required to enforce it, is not worth the paper it is written on.

Over 90 years after *The Jungle*, Upton Sinclair's exposé of the slaughterhouse industry which galvanized the American public to demand cleaner food, conditions do not seem to have improved. On the assembly line, inspectors still use their five senses to assess contamination of meat—even though much more sophisticated equipment exists to trace the multiple diseases which our senses are unaware that this flesh is heir to. And the scale of slaughter is so much greater than in 1906. In one year in the United States, 93 million pigs, 37 million cattle, two million calves, six million horses, goats and sheep, and a staggering eight billion chickens and turkeys are killed. In such a situation, you would think the government would be tightening regulations, not loosening them; and making the industry more and not less accountable. But as long as citizens can be sued for raising a question about a public-health danger, this seems unlikely. In 1997 in the United States, the President promised to allocate more resources to protecting the safety of America's food. He initiated a campaign to educate the consumer to cook his or her meat more thoroughly to avoid infection, thus contributing to the impression that it was not industry's fault that so many people were getting—and continue to get—sick from eating the dead flesh of diseased animals. It was ours.

I have a personal interest in all of the above. Between 1985 and 1989 (the period of greatest infectivity), I was eating British beef, blissfully oblivious of how animals were killed and what was fed to them before they were sent to the slaughterhouse. In April 1998, Clare Tompkins, who had been a vegetarian for 13 years, died of nvCJD. Because of the deaths of people like Clare, scientists have now had to revise the possible incubation time for nvCJD to 15 years and beyond—much as has had to be done with the AIDS virus. According to Carleton Gajdusek, the anthropologist who first discovered kuru, the transmissible agent that causes BSE and nvCJD could be present in manure from animals who may carry the agent genetically or in their milk. Thus, even a strict vegetarian born today who eats organic vegetables fertilized by manure could catch nvCJD. It could be in gelatin capsules (common vitamin casings), in tallow and in all the other by-products of the slaughterhouse industry.

Some scientists have suggested that the increasing rates of Alzheimer's disease could be masking a much higher rate of nvCJD than previously imagined. Because BSE's incubation rate is so long, we do not know how many people will die in the end; indeed, we routinely slaughter all pigs before they show whether they are infected with the porcine version—who knows what bizarre version of brucellosis we could get? Scientists are still debating the number of people who will die of nvCJD in the years to come. The rate could increase ten-, a hundred-, even a thousand-fold. What is certain, at a most conservative estimate, is that the public on both sides of the Atlantic is going to experience greater sickness as a result of mechanized slaughter and feeding practices that have nothing to do with nature, nothing to do with the health and welfare of people and absolutely nothing to do with even a modicum of respect for the welfare of non-human animals.

Hope, Lily, and Jessie
Towards Vegan Kinship
Lorri Bauston

Since my partner Gene and I began Farm Sanctuary in 1986, we have investigated hundreds of stockyards, factory farms and slaughterhouses. People often ask us how we cope with seeing so much suffering and death. Whenever I am asked that question, I find myself thinking about what inspires me and gives me hope, and I think about a pig I have dearly loved, a pig named Hope. Hope had been dumped at a livestock market because she had a crippled leg and was no longer "marketable." Hope was just a baby, barely two months old. I remember how frightened she was, and how frantically she crawled away as we approached her. Hope had never known a kind touch. Humans had only kicked, dragged and abandoned her. Gene and I spoke gently to her, and wrapped a blanket around her shivering body. She let out one small grunt as we picked her up, and then nestled into my arms as if she had always known me.

For seven years Hope was a part of our lives. We cared for all her special needs, and she filled our hearts with love. Hope touched many other people too. Over the years, she taught thousands of Farm Sanctuary visitors that farm animals are just as capable of suffering from isolation, fear and neglect as a dog or cat, or you and I. It is comforting to know that Hope reached so many people, especially now that she is no longer with us.

Hope passed away at our shelter, surrounded by those who loved her. I still find myself glancing in the direction of her favorite corner. I will never forget how she rolled over for belly rubs at the touch of my hand, or her distinct "thank you" grunt when I placed her food bowl in front of her. Most of all though, I will always remember how her life inspired us to continue to fight for farm animal rights.

It's easy to lose hope when you've just been to a slaughterhouse or factory farm and witnessed so much cruelty. I will never forget the first time I went to an egg factory and saw the horror of modern-day egg production. To produce eggs, four to five hens are crammed into a cage about the size of a folded newspaper. The birds endure this misery for two to three years, unable to stretch their wings, walk or even lie down comfortably. After months of intensive confinement, the birds lose most of their feathers because their bodies are constantly rubbing against the barbed-wire cages. Eventually, their skin becomes covered with painful bruises and sores. When hens become too sick or injured to produce eggs at peak levels, they are literally thrown out of the cage and left on the floor to die slowly from starvation.

Lily

We found Lily on the floor of an egg factory, waiting for death to end her nightmare. She was standing in a corner, trying desperately to keep from falling onto a mound of feces and decaying feathers and bones. Lily had given up all hope. Her entire body was hunched over, and her head drooped close to the ground. She was covered with sores and her left eye was swollen shut. I reached out, and gently lifted her into my hands. She trembled as I lifted her. I kept whispering to her, softly telling her I was a vegan and her misery was over. My "vegan reassurance speeches" always seem ridiculous to me after a rescue, but no matter how foolish I feel the next day, it's become one of my rescue rituals.

For two weeks, Lily received intensive rehabilitation care. Lily was too weak to walk, and throughout the day, I would hold her up to help her regain strength in her legs. She had bruising over 75 percent of her body, and four times a day we wrapped heating pads around her to reduce the swelling. Since Lily was severely emaciated, she could eat only small amounts of liquid food through a dropper every few hours. On more than one occasion, I wondered if we were doing the right thing, or whether we were just prolonging her suffering: this is *the* shelter question whenever an animal is near death. But one morning I had the answer. I opened the door to Lily's rehabilitation pen, and she walked over to me and looked up. I immediately sat down to get as close as I could to chicken height, and Lily climbed onto my lap. I reached down, and this time, I was the one trembling as I stroked her chin. Lily gave me her love in a way I could understand, just like a dog "talking" with his or her tail, or a cat's smooth purring.

Jessie

Vegan kinship is very powerful, and it will touch you and change your life forever. You may notice strange and wonderful things happening to you when you become a vegan. Like the time we rescued Jessie—well actually, the time Jessie rescued herself. Gene and I were making a cross-country trip with several turkeys during one of our annual Thanksgiving Adopt a Turkey projects. We were going through Colorado (a major beef-producing state) when I spotted her along the interstate—a young Angus calf just a few feet from whizzing cars. We pulled over, threw on our boots, and started toward her. She was extremely frightened and started running away from us. An injured leg prevented her from moving too fast and we had her within a few minutes.

Our new "baby" weighed about 150 pounds. As we struggled to get her into the van, we heard angry shouting and saw a man running towards us. We soon learned that Jessie had jumped out of a trailer while it was traveling 60 miles an hour. When I realized what she had done to escape her fate, I felt like an angry mother cow, ready to tear her horns into anyone who tried to take her calf away. Finding it difficult to keep calm, I explained to the owner that we were anti-cruelty agents and would be willing to take this calf off his hands, because, of course, he couldn't take her to the auction now. To my surprise, the owner agreed. I was gearing up for a major battle, since injured and sick animals are legally sold at auctions all the time. To this day, I don't know if he agreed because he was in shock, or because he saw a raging cow in my eyes. Or maybe, just maybe, he got a dose of vegan kinship.

The next feat was getting Jessie through the California border for treatment at a veterinary clinic in northern California. We drove all night with her and four turkeys, through a severe snowstorm. Just as daylight was breaking, we came to the California border and the agriculture checkpoint. Now, every turkey mother knows that daylight is the time when turkeys wake up and start chirping, and we knew we didn't have much time. We turned up the radio, and inched cautiously toward the checker. He asked us if we had any apples or oranges. I smiled sweetly and replied, "No," and drove on with the biggest grin I've ever worn. Jessie survived and is now a big, healthy cow. I've never considered myself a very religious person, nor one who thinks everything happens for a reason. Still, I can't help wondering if Jessie knew we were behind her when she jumped out of the trailer—at least I'd like to think she did.

Broadening Bonds

Farm animals are living, feeling animals. They are not breakfast, lunch and dinner. Americans have drawn an imaginary line and classified some animals as pets and some animals as dinner. Our society is horrified (and rightly so) when we hear of other cultures eating dogs and cats, and most people would never be intentionally cruel to one of these animals. I have to hope they would never be intentionally cruel to a cow or a chicken either. People who love animals called pets would not eat animals called dinner if they would only look into the eyes of a suffering farm animal. If you saw a laying hen like Lily, or a "downer" pig like Hope, wouldn't you do everything you could in your power to stop their suffering?

Every person can stop farm animal suffering, because every person can be a vegan. When you stop consuming animals and animal by-products, you stop the slaughter of hundreds of animals. Your action saves lives, and it is as direct as going to a factory farm or stockyard and rescuing an animal like Hope yourself. When you become a vegan, you begin to share a special bond with farm animals.

As a vegan, I have experienced so many incredible things, so many extraordinary relationships with farm animals. Like many other people, I am fortunate to have the love and companionship of dogs and cats, animals who are truly a part of my family. But unlike many people, I have also known the love and friendship of cows and pigs, and turkeys and chickens—farm animals who suffered horribly at factory farms, slaughterhouses and stockyards. And I was the one to blame: every time I ate a pizza with cheese or had a muffin with eggs in it; every time I didn't care enough to feel their pain. We need to always remember the animals' pain, because that is how we find the love we need to stop it.

180

The production of "food animals" is the single largest and most institutionalized form of animal abuse. Billions of animals suffer tormented lives, and millions of people participate in the cruelty. But Hope's life, and now her memory, remind me that we can stop "food animal" production—one life, one law and one more person at a time every time she or he becomes a vegan because they met an animal like Hope.

Ginger

Antonia Gorman

I should have known better than to go out in such weather. The winter of 1994 had been the worst in memory and the unplowed streets were treacherous beyond navigation. If the snow, which was then falling, had not been enough to dissuade me from my planned trip, my inability to come to a complete stop at the first intersection should have sent me around the block and back to my front door. But I had never been in a car accident, so I not only thought nothing of beginning a three-hour trip during a snowstorm, but blithely chose a route over a narrow and winding mountain road.

The first hour and a half of the trip were uneventful. While it is true that the car, despite its slow speed, had several small skids and near misses, I never felt in danger of a collision. So when I crested the top of High Point, a mountain claiming the highest elevation in New Jersey, and was thrown by a patch of ice into the lane of an oncoming truck, I calmly assumed the other driver would claim for himself the control I lacked and maneuver himself out of my way. That was the last thought I had until the pain of being extricated from the car by emergency workers roused me to consciousness half an hour later. It wasn't until I was inside the ambulance and on my way to the hospital that I was able to regain enough presence of mind to ask about Ginger, my beloved golden retriever, who had been on the floor of the back seat. Nobody had seen her. I begged the paramedics to return to the car to see if she was trapped there and, to calm my agitation, one of them agreed to go back later.

What follows is Ginger's story as told to me by that paramedic, by the driver of the truck that collided with us, by the nurses at the hospital where I was rushed, by the people of the nearby town who read about Ginger's plight in the local paper, and by my husband, Patrick. To the best of my knowledge, it happened this way.

Having been tightly wedged on the floor of the back seat, Ginger was held safely in place during the collision. The force of the impact had collapsed the car's hood and shattered its windshield, but Ginger's body was uninjured and she was able to leap safely out of a broken window and into the surrounding woods. The driver of the truck later told me that he was more concerned with my seemingly lifeless body than with a perfectly healthy, though clearly frightened, dog. He made no effort to chase after Ginger—assuming, he said, that she would keep running and be impossible to catch. But Ginger had not kept running. She had stopped behind a boulder at the top of the road's embankment and had kept watch on the proceedings below. The moment the ambulance pulled away with me inside, Ginger darted down the hill and began to chase after it.

The ambulance driver, oblivious to Ginger's pursuit, increased his speed until he had disappeared completely from her sight. Ginger was now alone in an unfamiliar wilderness during a storm more severe than her coat—thin from a life spent indoors—could easily handle. Rather than lose courage as others might have, Ginger took action and began to sniff along the road until she picked up the scent of the ambulance.

At first the trail was easy to follow; few drivers were foolish enough to be on the mountain in that weather and the road itself was temporarily unintersected by side streets. After three or four miles, however, the road reached the edge of the town of Port Jervis, where the flatter terrain and the increased population meant more cars were on the road. This made Ginger's tracking more difficult. Soon the route was intersected by a feed from a major highway and here Ginger temporarily lost her way. Unable to pick up the scent of ambulance tires beneath the more recent smell of heavy traffic, and forced off her road by the increasingly plentiful cars, Ginger turned right and followed the feed toward the highway. For a quarter of a mile Ginger searched in vain for some clue that she was heading in the right direction. Then, perhaps suspecting she had made an error in judgment, she turned around and returned to the intersection where she'd gone wrong. Knowing that behind her lay a road where she had had no success, and to her left the path back to the mountain, Ginger turned right and began to search for the ambulance again. This time her persistence was rewarded when, several yards away, she once more picked up the elusive scent. Encouraged by her success and again facing an uninterrupted stretch of road, Ginger broke into a run. But as the hours passed and the light began to fail, so did Ginger's energy.

She had traveled nine and a half miles, managing along the way to avoid dangerous vehicles and additional wrong turns, and was worn out by the physical and emotional stress. She had no way of knowing she was a mere half mile from her goal. She only knew she was exhausted and in need of a place where she could sleep—a place safe from cars, malevolent strangers and the cold night air. When she passed a wooded cemetery, she knew she had found such a place.

In the cemetery were several unpruned evergreen trees. Ginger found one whose branches hung below the snow, then she tunneled beneath the branches and in toward the tree's center. When she came up on the other side, she found herself inside a cozy den, with a warm pine-needle floor and a thick wall of snow-covered branches keeping the wind and the cold at bay. Here she slept comfortably until early the next morning.

Ginger woke up hungry. It had been 36 hours since her last meal and she decided to look for breakfast before continuing on her journey. Remembering the smell of food from her travels the day before, Ginger retraced her steps to a small diner where she sat patiently until the owners arrived at 5:30 to open the shop. Hungry as she was, however, she was unwilling to be detained, so when the owners of the diner tried to coax her inside, she bared her teeth and ran back toward the cemetery. There she was spotted by Jill, a woman whose house overlooked the cemetery. Jill promptly called the Port Jervis dog catcher.

I do not know if Ginger managed to find any food that day, nor do I know how she managed to avoid the dog catcher, nor how, 20 hours after the accident, she ferreted out the ambulance scent. But I do know that somewhere around 11:30 that morning a nurse entered my room and asked me what type of dog I had said I had lost.

"A golden retriever," I responded.

"Well," she said. "There's been a golden retriever sitting outside the emergency room door for the last hour, but it runs away every time someone comes near it."

Ginger sat outside the emergency room door the rest of that day, growling and running away every time someone tried to catch her. I wanted the nurses to take me down to her, but I was in an unstable condition and they refused to move me. I kept hoping Patrick would call so I could tell him to come to the hospital to get her, but he and two of his friends were out trying to follow her trail, never thinking she had found me before they had found her. Patrick did, however, call the local dog catcher, who told him of Jill's phone call earlier that morning. When Patrick drove over to the cemetery, he quickly spotted Ginger's tracks in the snow. As he followed her tracks, whistling and calling her name, Jill overheard him and came over to see if she could help. It was Jill who suggested that Patrick leave his scarf tied to the cemetery fence so that Ginger, if she returned to her den that night, would know he was nearby. This proved a stroke of genius, for the next morning when Jill looked out her window she saw Ginger sitting next to the scarf, patiently awaiting the return of Patrick.

Jill immediately called Patrick and the dog catcher. Then she set off across the street with a bag of dog food under her arm. Ginger eyed her suspiciously, baring her teeth and growling menacingly when Jill came too close, but refusing to budge from her spot near Patrick's scarf. Jill put a layer of food on top of the snow, and then backed away. Ginger inched toward the food cautiously, eating it ravenously, but abandoning it the moment Jill tried to approach her. As she laid down more food, the dog catcher arrived and the two tried to capture Ginger by backing her up against the cemetery fence. Ginger was too fast for them, however, and they soon decided to give up their chase and await Patrick's arrival.

Ginger didn't notice Patrick at first, standing upwind of him and focusing her attention on the two intruders who seemed intent on separating her from his scarf. But when Patrick called her name, a change went instantly and visibly through her. Every muscle in her body, taut from hunger, cold and nerves, suddenly relaxed and then rebounded in a frenzy of joy and relief. She rushed to him, licked his lowered face and wound her body in excited circles around his. Then, eager to share her happiness with all around her, she turned to Jill and the dog catcher and at last allowed them to pet her.

Patrick told me that, in spite of Ginger's return to her own home, Ginger's anxiety remained high. She refused, he said, to sleep in her customary spot in the bedroom, choosing instead to stay next to the front door and asking, during the day, to be allowed to sit in the yard and watch the cars. She was, he felt, looking for me. It took two weeks for me to be discharged from the hospital, but Ginger was waiting for me when I pulled into the driveway.

Taking a Stand
Vicki and Tony Moore

Vicki and Tony Moore have been working to document and end the abuse of animals—cows, bulls, birds, donkeys, goats and others—in fiestas and bullfights throughout Spain for more than ten years. Their small organization, FAACE (Fight Against Animal Cruelty in Europe), works in alliance with Spanish activists to educate the public about the cruelties involved in these events. In 1995, while videotaping a "bull" festival, Vicki was gored severely by a bull. Undaunted, Vicki and Tony are back in Spain recording abuses of the animals in the fiestas and bullfights. Among the sights they have videotaped are a live goat being thrown from a church bell tower and blindfolded teenage girls trying to knock the heads off live chickens hung upside-down. The Moores have tapes of bulls with flames attached to their horns running through a village; a bull being stabbed and blinded by large numbers of spears; and a drunken donkey being forced to stand up and be ridden. The Moores make the point that the majority of these festivals are not historic remembrances, but have been invented in the last 20 years.

"Even animal-loving people in Europe think we and our Spanish compatriots are battering our heads against a brick wall. "Why waste time?" they ask. "We hate it, but it's going to go on forever." We feel that this has been the attitude for far too long and that unless people make some sort of stand now, it will go on forever."

Why did you start doing this work?
VM: It truly chose us. In 1987, I read a small newspaper article about a donkey in Spain who was about to be crushed by a crowd. Once we knew, we couldn't turn our backs. I began by writing letters and then I felt I had to go. I went to Spain and pleaded for a donkey's life. Soon after, I was receiving death threats. I have

Spanish blood, so in a way I have a feeling that it is something in my heritage that I have to try and redress. I can tell you it is a terribly complex situation. We are still learning about it.

Can you describe the village festivals you have seen and videotaped that center on animal torture?
VM: Bullfighting in Spain actually encompasses what are called *fiestas populares*, which take place all over Spain. According to recent government statistics, there are 15,000 of these events every year. There are about 37,000 animals killed in the bullrings and on the streets every year; 7,000 are bulls killed in the bullring. In the main the victims are bulls and cows, as well as small calves. It is quite common to see a calf a few weeks old, as well as a full-grown bull four years of age or older, having various instruments of torture thrust into it. A lot of these things will be done to the animals for four or five hours before they are killed. The *fiestas populares* also use chickens, ducks, pigs and birds. Cats have been known to be used, as well as dogs, in very rare instances—virtually any animal that is to hand, even rabbits and squirrels.

When we started working there was a lot of common knowledge but very little visual evidence, so the Spanish government found it very easy to deny any challenge about this cruelty. They said, "Oh, it doesn't happen. These people are exaggerating." Or, "Well, yes, but it happened 50 or 60 years ago. It's not something that's relevant now." So we've devoted ten years to building a massive library of video and photographic evidence. We have challenged the Spanish authorities with this at national and regional levels. We have also taken it to the European Parliament. At present, the Parliament does not have what they call "political competence" to deal with these issues. But we are looking forward to a federal Europe, which will have the legislative powers to issue overall cruelty legislation. That is our aim. It is not what we achieve now, it is what may be achieved in the future. Our work has been done with great difficulty because there is very little money for this. We can all help by applying pressure; but in the end it has got to be Spain that changes it, and the Spanish people who say, "Enough."

What happened when you were gored by the bull?
VM: To be honest, I have had years of hell since it happened, pain you wouldn't wish on any human being. People have often asked me how I feel about the bull, Argentino. He was actually sold to the village because he was too dangerous for a bullfight. The last creature to blame is Argentino. It was just unfortunate that he decided to find the window where I was desperately trying to climb to find a perch to video. He clobbered me. It was quite a miracle that he didn't have a final flick, because that is normal. But I felt there must have been some protective power that got me through all this, because when I got to the hospital I was actually declared dead.

TM: Vicki had eight very badly smashed ribs and a punctured lung. One horn went through her and scratched the backbone. She had a horn go right through her foot. She lost a kidney and a bit of a bowel. She had 11 serious horn wounds and was in intensive care in Spain for four weeks, then in intensive care in the United Kingdom for another week. It was another week after that before they allowed her home.

VM: There doesn't seem to be much breakthrough with the Spanish authorities. In 1995, 16 people died in these fiestas, and that is quite a common figure. So, there are two fronts to fight on, the animal and the human. Often the victims are innocent: they are just caught up in it, not involved in the fiesta. We were told we could have sued for a million or so without too much trouble. But as someone fighting for the animals, I didn't want their money. I didn't want to be bought in any way. Having said that, I encourage any Spanish person who has been injured or had a relative killed to sue them for all they can. Because then the villages won't get insured, and when they don't get insured, it's yet another way to end the *fiestas populares*.

TM: In the town where Vicki was injured, a boy was killed three years ago, and his family is suing, quite rightly, for three million dollars. The mayor at the time of Vicki's injury said to my representative, "I will pay all of the medical fees." I agreed and announced to the newspapers that the mayor was a very generous man, a man of honor, and that he was going to pay all the medical expenses. I didn't see him because I was too upset—enraged actually. I wanted to get out of the car and hit him, but I knew that would be wrong. I sat there with my head in my hands.

Is there a lot of money for this industry?

VM: It *is* an industry. There is an awful lot of money. These animals are sold to villages for thousands of dollars each. The price for a fighting bull is $15,000, for a fiesta animal it is about $6,000. There are salesmen going out to the villages marketing animal fiestas. They say, "We'll put the bulls in, we'll do the posters for you, the barriers, the seating, the advertising." All the mayor has to do is sign the check with municipal money and get maybe a kickback. There is a lot of money involved, and that is why it is growing.

In Spain they say that bullfights and the *fiestas populares* are a good thing, a safety valve contradicting every study that has been made in the world about the connection between violence to animals and its effects on society and human beings. But it is beginning to get out: the fact that, when they have finished ripping the animals limb from limb, young men go out and uproot all the trees, smash windows, rip the wing mirrors off cars, and knock around and abuse any woman who seems to fall in their way. They call the female animals everything they can think of. You are getting the same sort of degenerative effect on society that every other country has, and the connection is only just being recognized in the rest of the world.

188

What actually happens before a bullfight?

VM: The bullfight is an exceedingly fraudulent spectacle, because the bulls are manipulated in so many ways. They have their horns shaved, they are drugged, they are bloated with water before they even go in the ring, so that they move slowly. The bulls are bred for docility; their feed is engineered. In many cases, they are custom bred for certain matadors.

TM: Shaving the horns means taking about four inches off the end of the horn. This is done within 24 hours of the bullfight. If you do it much earlier, infection can set in quite badly or bulls can get used to the shorter horns and get to know where they are. Because of the shaving, the bull loses his sense of judgment, of where he is going, and there is also the possibility that he is going to feel pain when he hits something. The most important thing of all, as far as the bull is concerned—and this is why they really do it—is that the bull loses a sense of self. Suddenly, his horns have been shortened, and he is not quite sure what he is.

VM: After they shave his horns, the bull is given a massive dose of Immobilon, the same drug that many veterinarians use to euthanize an animal. By the time the bull has had all this, he is in a very debilitated state. In 1992, a bullfighting law was supposed to clean out this corruption. All it actually did was give a legal loophole to practice it: the second article in the law is the promotion and protection of bullfighting by the Spanish state. The definition of bullfighting also includes the bull fiestas. All of this is under the wing of protection of the Spanish government, and is paid for with subsidies by the Spanish government. There is also corporate sponsorship, Coca-Cola mainly, and a lot of Japanese electronics corporations' sponsorship.

Do you see an end to your struggle?

VM: Even animal-loving people in Europe think we and our Spanish compatriots are battering our heads against a brick wall. "Why waste time?" they ask. "We hate it, but it's going to go on forever." We feel that this has been the attitude for far too long and that unless people make some sort of stand now, it will go on forever. So we are making a stand, with our compatriots. The Spanish press is not a great help, because who owns it and the television? The bull breeders. You can imagine what happens to Spanish animal rights activists when they try to speak up—they are totally ignored or ridiculed. Nevertheless, the movement in Spain is growing, slowly but surely. It is still small by American or British standards, but nevertheless it is there. We know that our cumulative effort can be handed on to another generation and, maybe, before all that long—perhaps in our children's time—there will be an end to this sort of tragedy.

Not Waving But Drowning

Jane Goodall

This is a true story. It happened six or seven years ago in North America. It's about a chimpanzee called Jojo who was born in Africa and who came over as a two-year-old with a female, Susie. They lived for a while in a cold square cage in a zoo. Jojo lived for eight or nine years alone in this bleak little prison. Then the zoo raised enough money to build a huge enclosure and it bought 19 other chimpanzees from different parts of the world. The zoo wanted the biggest and best enclosure in North America. It introduced the chimps to each other and surrounded the enclosure with a moat filled with water because chimps don't swim.

One day the zoo let them out. After a while a fight broke out, and Jojo, the oldest male, was challenged by one of the new young males. Of course, Jojo lost the fight, for what did he know about fighting? He had lived all those years alone. In his fear, Jojo ran into the water. What did he know about water? It was something he drank from a cup. He was so frightened he scrambled over the safety barrier and disappeared into the deep water beyond. He came up three times, spluttering for air; then he was gone.

On the other side of the moat was a small group of people. It was rainy and cold, and there was a keeper there. Luckily for Jojo, however, there was a visitor watching: Rick Swope. Rick jumped in, although the keeper actually grabbed him and told him it was dangerous and that he'd probably get killed. Rick had to swim under the water—it was murky from the rain and he couldn't see—until he felt Jojo's inert body (which weighed 130 pounds). Rick didn't know if Jojo was alive but he put the body over his shoulder, scrambled over the safety barrier and pushed Jojo onto the bank.

A woman with a video camera went on filming even though she didn't know she was doing it. You can actually hear and see what happened; as Rick turned to go back to his slightly hysterical family, you hear his wife and children calling "Daddy" and "Rick!" The keeper is yelling, "Run! Run! Come back quickly!" Charging down toward Rick, down the steep bank, are three adult males with hair bristling and teeth showing—probably coming to rescue Jojo from Rick. At the same time, Jojo is sliding back down the bank which has been built too steep.

The camera stays—amazingly—on Rick. He stands and looks toward his family; he looks up at the chimps rearing up enormously above him; and he looks down at where Jojo is disappearing under the water. Rick goes back into the water and he holds Jojo up. The chimpanzees stop to watch. After a while, Jojo raises his head and the water comes from his mouth and then he takes a few tottery steps around where the ground is level. There is no question that Rick saved Jojo's life.

190

That evening that little piece of video was flashed across North America and the director of my institute called Rick and said, "Mr. Swope, that was a tremendously brave thing you did. I really want to congratulate you. But why did you do it?" And Rick said, "Well, I just happened to look into his eyes and it was like looking into the eyes of a man. And the message was: 'Won't anybody help me?' "

If we look around, we see that look in the eyes of so many suffering animals, and people too—suffering in the eyes of those less fortunate than ourselves. Albert Schweitzer summed up exactly what it is all about: for all animals who are overworked, underfed and cruelly treated; for all the beautiful creatures in captivity who beat their wings against bars; for any that are hunted, lost or deserted or frightened or hungry; for all who must be put to death and for those who deal with them—for all these we offer help, compassion, a gentle hand and kindly words.

My Brother's Keeper
A Reflection on Booee
Roger S. Fouts and Deborah Fouts

In 1995, Hugh Downs of the television program 20/20 took prima-tologist Roger Fouts to the Laboratory for Experimental Medicine and Surgery in Primates (LEMSIP) at the then-operational New York University School of Medicine in upstate New York. There Dr. Fouts met with Booee, the chimpanzee to whom he had taught American Sign Language 17 years previously. Although Fouts and Booee had not seen each other at all in the interim, as soon as he saw Fouts, Booee became very excited and signed to Fouts not only the sign for his, Booee's, name, but also the sign for Fouts's. In addition, Booee remembered much of the sign language he had been taught. Fouts was unable to stay long with Booee: after Fouts left, Booee retreated to a corner of his cage, clearly depressed. Roger Fouts describes how he met Booee and what his life has been like since.

Many people have seen the piece 20/20 did on my reunion with Booee, televised on May 5, 1995. It was something I did not want to do and now I understand why. Booee is in my dreams. I see him over and over again moving away from me, with a heart-wrenching demeanor, as I tell him I must leave. I had hoped he would not recognize me and would see me as just one more lab-coated visitor passing through the facility. But, after 17 years, Booee recognized me immediately and it was as if time had not passed. We were playing the same games and our relationship had not changed. He was still the dear little boy who had taught me so much during my fledgling years as a new Ph.D. I was torn by the joy of finding an old and dear friend and the heartache of knowing I would have to leave him in a few short hours. Was it worth it? I do not know. I can only hope that the number of viewers who watched and became aware of the plight of captive chimpanzees was worth the pain Booee and I suffered when I told him I had to leave. What happened to Booee—his experiences with science—is unfortunately not atypical for chimpanzees.

Booee was born at a biomedical facility. The staff was unaware that his mother had been pregnant, so Booee's arrival was a surprise. It also brought an unexpected addition to the facility. Because his future had not been charted as far as being used in any specific study, he was a "free" chimp, and therefore an unexpected bonus. Having an unexpected baby gives scientists a chance to try out "hot" new procedures that are usually only read about in journals. Booee made his first mistake when he was a few days old. He convulsed, which made some of the researchers feel that he might be epileptic. The hot new operation in those days was "split brain" research, which recently had been discovered to be a treatment for grand mal seizures. Booee had his brain split when he was only a few days old. This operation was relatively benign. It involved cutting all the connections between the two cerebral hemispheres, in essence giving Booee two separate brains. This was accomplished by cutting the corpus collosum. Nevertheless, Booee's surgery had a few problems. The surgeons had to go back and open his cranium to control the edema. In other words, his brain was so swollen because of the operation that they had to open his cranium to relieve the pressure. Not all biomedical types are consumed with overweening ambition. One of the doctors, Fred Schneider, felt pity for the poor little chimp, who was in agonizing pain and with a bandaged head, and took him home to recuperate with Schneider's family of six children.

Booee's new home proved to offer a great life. His surrogate parents enjoyed him and he became very attached to his human mother and his new family. When he was ten months old, his family went wilderness camping and, not thinking they could take him along, they left him with babysitters. He had become so attached to his family that he fell into a depression, developed pneumonia and was close to death when the Schneiders returned. Fortunately he recovered, and continued to grow. When Booee was three, his human parents began to discover that baby chimps are very much like human babies: they demand mothering and develop personalities as they grow up. For Booee, the living-room drapes became vines to climb on, and cupboards had to be locked with strong locks to prevent this inquisitive chimp with a sweet tooth from raiding the larder.

There were other problems. Booee's normal chimp sense of territory got him in trouble. If a stranger walked by the house on the sidewalk or if a dog dared to enter the yard, Booee would do a threat display—as befitting a very proper chimpanzee—to drive the intruder away. Each display would end with a backhand thump hitting a large picture window. One winter after the window had broken yet again, the Schneiders had to board the windows to keep the cold out, and it became obvious to these good people that their house was not a proper home for a chimpanzee. They were, however, faced with a dilemma: if they returned him to the lab, he would surely be used in biomedical experiments. By this time, Dr. Schneider had visited Allen and Beatrice Gardner and the chimp Washoe. From them he had learned of a facility which at that time was devoted to behavioral research. In 1970, shortly before Washoe arrived at the facility, Booee and his entire human family drove in their van from Maryland to the Institute of Primate Studies at the University of Oklahoma. Parting with Booee was traumatic for the entire Schneider family and they wept as they drove to Booee's new home.

When they arrived in Oklahoma, the Schneiders were invited to spend the night as guests of the director of the Institute and his wife. The Schneiders' children were concerned that Booee would not get his favorite foods and told the director's wife to remember that Booee liked brown sugar with his morning oatmeal. The Schneider family reported feeling physical pain when they left Booee to begin his new life the next morning.

Booee became one of the Oklahoma chimps to whom my students and I began teaching American Sign Language. Several years later, the director of the Institute decided to change the direction of the Institute and sought a contract from the pharmaceutical company Merck Sharp and Dome to do hepatitis research. The director did not get that contract, but eventually sent all of the chimps he owned to the lab which received the contract. Thus, yet again, Booee became lost in the biomedical research community from which his human parents had hoped to protect him. He was again subjected to research and spent the next 17 years in conditions like those seen on *20/20*—alone in a bare cage with no stimuli and certainly no-one with whom to speak. Booee is now a carrier of the hepatitis C virus, for which there is presently no cure.

For those who saw the *20/20* piece and were as moved as I was by Booee's plight, it is good to remember that famous statement by Jeremy Bentham [1748-1832]: "The question is not, Can they reason? Nor, Can they talk? But, Can they suffer?"[1] Booee's mastery of American Sign Language does not make him any more or less of a chimpanzee; indeed, I am certain that all chimpanzees have this capacity. The important thing to remember is that there are at least 1,700 other chimpanzees who are living and being exploited by our species in biomedical research institutions around the country. They are prisoners who have never committed a crime. These chimpanzees are tortured for no other reason than they happen to bear a striking resemblance to humans. They are our brothers and sisters, and we are their Cains.

It is unimportant whether or not Booee should happen to know how to sign, or to remember my name. The most important fact to remember about Booee and all the chimpanzees in captivity is that they have the same capacity to suffer as do you and I. Just as our country is ashamed of what our ancestors have done to people who were considered to be different from us, by exploiting them as slaves or as children in our factories, so too someday will our children be ashamed of what we do today to our sibling species, the chimpanzee.

Being an Activist

The Horror of Hegins
Seven Reflections on an Annual Pigeon Shoot

The annual Labor Day weekend pigeon shoot in Hegins, Pennsylvania has been the scene of protests for a number of years. While it is not the only pigeon shoot in the United States, or even Pennsylvania, it is a far cry from the "sportsmanship" supposedly represented by hunting. Hundreds of trapped pigeons are released and then shot a few feet off the ground. The event has provided activists with an example of humankind's cruelty not only to other species, but often its own.

Paul Shapiro

The 1996 Hegins Pigeon Shoot was the worst experience I've had during my short 18 years. As soon as I entered the park, my name was no longer Paul but—according to some of the shoot supporters there, some of whom were sporting pro-KKK caps and wearing T-shirts bearing quotes from Hitler—"city-dwelling, faggot nigger-lover." My job was to rescue injured birds who had been shot and had flown into the spectator area. It seemed easy enough. Just pick up the pigeon, put him or her in your shirt, and walk out of the park to the veterinary van. Not so.

On one occasion, a wounded bird dropped into the children's playground (between the two areas where birds were being systematically murdered). After a long scuffle, I was able to pick her up and place her in my shirt. All of a sudden I felt a fist land on my back and heard shouts of "Get him!" and "Rip the fucker's head off!" I started sprinting for fear of both my and the bird's lives.

As fast as they could in their drunken stupor, approximately seven spectators came after me. After running through thick clouds of smoke from the grill where burgers and chicken were being cooked, I saw the exit. Just as I thought I was safe, I felt a shoulder pummeling my chest and the next thing I knew I was flat on my back screaming in agony. I then felt a boot forcing itself on my rib cage. Still clutching the pigeon, I looked at my shirt and saw that blood had completely soaked one side of it.

I was lifted up by three activists (all of whom had been assaulted in this ordeal as well) and carried to the van where I handed over the pigeon to the vet. Whether she lived or not I have no idea. I do know that even if she died, she did so quietly among people who cared for her. If she survived, I know that she will live the rest of her life free and far away from Hegins, Pennsylvania.

Sue Coe

This is not a fascist country, but proto-fascistic elements exist here. In Hegins, the root of the tree is rotten. Presumably the mob, on days that are not official holidays, taunt and do violence to gays and lesbians, people of color, women and children, and people of the Jewish faith. I am making this assumption based on the comments I heard. I was sitting in the front row of the stands, listening. A black pigeon was shot and wounded, and flew into a bush. Someone in the row behind me said—in a voice loud enough to be heard but not loud enough to be recognized—"There is a black one, it's like a nigger in a woodpile. Kill it!" The mob started to chant: "Kill it! Kill it!" I watched, as a trapper boy, maybe aged 12, with a black T-shirt that said "Army" on it, use a dead bird as a dive bomber, smashing the bird's beak repeatedly into the ground. Will he grow up to be all that he can be?

Bullies have taken over Hegins, I am sure. I wonder where the religious leaders were. On leaving the town, there is a sign on the road: "Eschew All Evil." Do the residents actually need a billboard to do that? Maybe a neon sign would be more effective. A few of the trapper boys were wearing T-shirts that said, "Shoot Pigeons Not Drugs." I would beg to differ with that slogan. In this case, anti-psychotic medication would be very beneficial to Hegins— maybe gently added to the water supply, or slipped into beer cans. Lives would be saved, both avian and human. I felt honored to be with and witness the courage of the activists and the organizers of the rescue effort. Some of these people are from very poor families and cannot afford to pay the fines for being arrested. This is in great contrast to the shooters, who, I heard, pay from $500 to $700 to murder birds. That these activists exist and speak out will ensure that history will not be repeated.

Hillary Morris

I feel strange saying this: the emotion invoked in me was pure love. Love for the birds, of course. But also for the shooters and the spectators—love and compassion tinged with great, deep, unending sadness. Sadness for the children, who will likely (inevitably?) grow up to be adults with the same cold fist around their hearts. Sadness for the women, many of whom were seemingly locked into attending this absurd farce of an "event" under pressure from their boyfriends and husbands. Sadness for Michael, a boy with Down's syndrome, the brother of a rude, drunk and violent spectator, who stayed with us all day, and at the end cried uncontrollably for the birds, the violence, and the drinking. And love for the people there, members of my own species, who are victims and products of their culture and upbringing and the social pressures around them—so much so that spectators who sided with us could barely bring themselves to tell us so, for fear of condemnation or worse from their neighbors and friends.

I also feel compassion for those people who will live never knowing what it feels like to hold a life in your hand and treasure it, who will never know the feeling of seeing the joyful spreading of the wings of an animal whom you set free. These human lives are a sad shadow of their potential, and, deep down, they know it. After looking into the eyes of a bird I rescued after some men had kicked her around, I hope she felt the total love and respect I had for her when I held her in my hands as she was dying. I hope she felt those feelings from the vets, technicians, rescuers and activists surrounding her. I hope she had the chance, if only for a moment, to sense not only cruelty and blind, ugly hatred from humans, but also love.

Bill Dollinger

What can be said about Hegins to relay the experience to one who has not attended? As a rescue volunteer, certain images will stand in my mind forever: the flapping wings and twitching bodies of so many pigeons, of whom a pitifully small percentage were killed immediately. The gleeful enthusiasm of the crew-cut trapper boys, repeatedly rushing the field to stuff wounded and traumatized birds into bags. The lumbering masses of grotesque slobs gnawing on chicken bones and laughing at the crippled birds on the field. The mounting palpability of a dark aura throughout the day, as the levels of death, gunpowder, intoxication and testosterone steadily increased. There was remarkable composure and bravery exhibited by the rescuers, peace-keepers, and the 12 activists who engaged in civil disobedience. One young woman risked her life for a bird by walking about 75 feet along the rear fence of the field, aware that the barrel of a shotgun which emerged from the back door of a house tracked her every step. The bird, a beautiful racing pigeon, survived.

There were numerous stand-offs in which a mob of shoot spectators would gather beneath a tree which held a wounded bird, competing against the rescuers for the fate of the pigeon. The spectators would become engrossed in the confrontations with a determination far more intense than the actual shoot "competition" itself. Throughout the day, the activists nobly suffered the slings and arrows, as well as body slams and death threats, without response. It became apparent that the only thing the pigeon shoot supporters wanted to do more than kill birds was confront and rile activists.

Jean Hollowell

You have to understand the disgust, anger and tremendous hatred that was exhibited to all of us, all day, from all sides: the chanting, the leering, the ridiculing, and the ugly, nasty, hate-filled words. I walked around all day with my stomach in knots and on the verge of tears; but I kept thinking, "This is not 'us' against 'them.' There, but for the grace of God, go I. Let's not build more walls between us. Let's not hate, but understand." Apparently it was a sentiment felt among the activists because they all acted accordingly. I was so proud to stand with them. It was a great learning experience for me and I gained more than I could have ever hoped to have given. But I hope that when at least one participant laid down his or her head that night, he or she thought, "Those crazy activists out there saving 'rats with wings' are really dedicated and really care. What do I feel that strongly about in my life?" Maybe, just maybe, there will be a small crack in the facade they all fought so strongly to protect.

Laurie Jordan

Although I had heard dreadful things about Hegins, I was still not quite prepared for the bloodthirsty spectacle I observed and the outward hostility of the participants. Equally appalling were rampant displays of racism (KKK symbols) and homophobia (one T-shirt read "Silly fairies—Dix are for Chix"). There was also name-calling: "You fucking faggots! What, are you neutered?" was directed toward a male protester, who did not respond.

Especially tragic is the fact that this day was considered "family entertainment". Young moms were pushing infants in strollers and walking their dogs through the noisy, gunsmoke-filled center, where they could purchase frying chickens, greasy burgers, hot dogs and ice cream. Gunshots and loud blasts echoed everywhere. I needed earplugs to keep my hearing intact. When I couldn't stand any more, I headed out of the park and attempted to speak with some of the shoot supporters. One teenager (he told me he was 16) wore a T-shirt which read "If it flies, it dies." I asked him why he couldn't shoot clay pigeons. He responded, "Clay pigeons just wouldn't be the same. They don't move the same way." His friend wore a T-shirt sporting the words "We've been doing it for 63 years. No honky's gonna stop us! We support live-pigeon shoots."

This kid was one of the trapper boys "hired" to collect the crippled birds and finish them off by either twisting off their heads or stomping them to death. Inebriated spectators cheered in response to this brutality; many birds were thrown into barrels to suffocate, or left to writhe and die on fields. All this sadistic behavior because of "tradition." How unsettling that "tradition" couldn't honor peace and compassion instead.

Deborah Tanzer

Hegins now seems almost unreal, an encapsulated nightmare far away from our ordinary life. But scratch the surface, and it is not so far, really, and God knows, it *is* the "ordinary" life of the birds who die and suffer there. And of so many other animals as well. It was an experience of enormous power and enormous pain—witnessing massive cruelty to animals, and the violence humans do to themselves, too. I myself was hit by a rock thrown at my head. Hegins was a stark dose of reality about where many people are, and what we are up against in our work to change people's minds, which we must do for there to be lasting change.

Connections with other issues were dramatically clear: sexism in the rigid gender roles, with shooters so overwhelmingly male, and the women applauding this display of power known as "masculinity." Sexism in questions to us about our underwear. Racism when people joked that a black pigeon had come out of a woodpile. Fascism was all around, clearest and most frightening in T-shirts boldly quoting Hitler. Mindless anti-gay hatred too, for I got called a "faggot" several times (a first for me).

But there was much love too. Especially for the birds who were so hurt, or scared, or dead. The medical van was truly heaven, and the vets truly angels. But we were all healers, and helpers, and surely brave.

I try to feed pigeons on the street, not always the best way to make human friends in New York City. After Hegins, I vowed never to pass another pigeon by.

Making a Difference
Henry Spira

Henry Spira was Coordinator of Animal Rights International. Before his death in September 1998, he had been an activist for more than 50 years, fighting for union democracy in the merchant marine, reporting on and supporting the Civil Rights movement in the 1950s and 1960s, and winning major battles to reduce animal suffering. He was instrumental in persuading Revlon to stop testing cosmetics on animals and convinced major companies like Procter & Gamble to invest millions in research for alternatives to animal testing. In recent years he focused on the plight of nine billion farm animals, including a successful campaign to get the United States Department of Agriculture (USDA) to end its policy of face-branding steers imported from Mexico. His life and his role in the shaping of the modern animal rights movement are the subjects of a biography by Peter Singer, called *Ethics into Action: Henry Spira and the Animal Rights Movement.*

"The first law of effective activism is:
Stay in touch with reality."

What made you become an activist?
While I was growing up I was farmed out to a variety of relatives in a variety of countries and with a variety of outlooks. This probably encouraged independence and, later, a willingness to question authority.

This was also the period of the Holocaust. There were lots of people who could do something about that, but they didn't. They only expressed the right sentiments—much like our current politically correct do-nothings.

These sorts of personal and political experiences may well have turned me into an activist who wants to make a difference where it matters. And to me, what defines an activist is going beyond the words and sentiments, turning words into productive action that leads to results.

There are all kinds of injustices in the world. How did you end up working on animal rights issues—and why did you select the farm animal issue?
For most of my life I've been active in human rights campaigns including the movements for trade union democracy and for civil rights. Animal rights, for me, was nothing more than a logical extension of these concerns.

For almost two decades we successfully promoted alternatives to the use of lab animals. But however you look at this progress, it did not impact on 95 percent of all animal suffering—the nine billion farm animals raised for dinners every year. A few years ago we began to plan how we could adapt the earlier strategies to the farm animal arena.

How do you respond to those people who say, "We've got all these human problems. Don't you have anything better to do with your time than worry about animals?"
It defies common sense to make it appear that you've got a limited amount of compassion—that if you use it for animals then you don't have it for humans. I think compassion is such that the more you use it, the more of it you have. Once we start excluding certain living, feeling beings from the circle of compassion, the easier it becomes to exclude others as well.

When we see nine billion animals who never have a good day in their lives, and we're the ones responsible for this happening to them, then I think one figures there's nothing one can do but fight in their defense. This does not preclude people from also getting involved in fighting for other vulnerable folks. The big difference with nonhuman animals is that they're incapable of organizing in their own defense. We're the ones who have to do it for them.

Why did you become a vegetarian?
When I was a kid, my grandparents had a cow's tongue hanging in the kitchen, waiting to be cooked. It totally grossed me out and I never ate tongue again. Later on when I worked in Guinea, I was invited to an event in the countryside where I played with a sheep in the grass. Then, at the dinner, the centerpiece was a whole roasted sheep waiting to be carved up. Playing with one and imagining eating another shook me up and I never ate lamb from then on. Years later I was given a cat. Caressing my feline friend while sticking a knife and fork into another animal made me question and made me think. Then I read Peter Singer's essay "Animal Liberation" and it all came together. The discomfort started way back, but it took a long time for my lifestyle to reflect my feelings and for me to realize that animals are not edibles. I think that for many of us, change is a gradual process.

Tell us about the work you're doing on the farm animal issue.
We're working on a number of fronts. One of them is the USDA, which has enormous influence. We've established good rapport with the Department. It takes us seriously and recognizes that we're out to solve problems and are not just looking for a fight. But the USDA also knows that we're capable of conducting a public awareness campaign, as we did on face-branding. The enormous outpouring of public concern in connection with the face-branding campaign made it possible for people at the USDA, many of whom were themselves concerned, to launch a Farm Animal Well-Being Task Group which is working to upgrade current practices.

Another front is the corporate sector. McDonald's has declared that it intends to become a role model for industry in upgrading humane conditions for farm animals. It has created a new corporate position of Director of Farm Animal Welfare and has contracted with Dr. Temple Grandin, a leader in designing less-stressful systems in animal agriculture. And it has developed a formal plan outlining how it plans to proceed in this groundbreaking effort. We're now talking with other major corporations to get them to set standards and also to place the whole issue of animal well-being on the agenda.

At the same time, we're producing generic ads and posters suggesting there's misery in meat, and that for the sake of your health, the animals' health and environmental health one should go meatless or eat less meat. It's a win-win situation. We've also highlighted the inconsistency of petting some animals and eating others. And we're now creating ads that suggest eating meat is as harmful to our health as smoking.

Why are these companies suddenly so willing to take measures to reduce animal suffering?
The fact that McDonald's sets standards for its suppliers is not necessarily because McDonald's suddenly became more sensitive to farm animal misery. What it did become sensitive to is the public's concern with this issue. When I talk to any corporate type, the USDA, or whoever, I just say, "The fact that we're suggesting something doesn't have to concern you at all. It's just that when we suggest something on which we're in sync with the public and you're not, you should start worrying." I don't think animal agriculture today is in sync with what the public wants. But the public doesn't know what's going on. So isn't it our duty to let the public know what's going on? The reason the American Meat Institute put out humane guidelines a few years ago and that everyone we contacted switched over from shackling and hoisting [animals] to an upright-restrainer system was that they figured their practices were indefensible in public debate.

You've said that you look to turn walls into stepping-stones of cooperation. But what about when it's not in someone's best interests to cooperate, as is the case with Frank Perdue [*CEO of Perdue Farms, the nation's fourth largest poultry processor*]?

Most of the time rational discussion does succeed. Sometimes people jerk us around, but you can still see that over the long haul they are going to be responsive. In the case of Perdue, he didn't even think there was a problem, never mind respond to one. But even with Perdue, it was good strategy to attempt to communicate with him, because when we launched our public-awareness campaign, we could legitimately say that Perdue forced us into it. And this negative campaign has probably been very useful in our farm animal initiatives. It reminded those whom we contacted that while we'd rather engage in productive dialogue, we were capable of harming their public image.

You've been active in many different movements for a long time. From your own experience, how is change really made?

It happens a little bit at a time. Many of us are in the animal movement because we identify with the animals who are suffering. Similarly, in politics, I feel it's necessary to be able to look at the situation from the perspective of those you are talking with.

In our campaign which focused on research and testing, we amplified suggestions from the scientific community itself. This helped create a loop of scientific superstars who agreed that it was time to reassess traditional practices. After the scientific community heard the same message from a hundred different sources, it quietly became part of the mainstream.

How are animal rights and human social progress linked?

Any fight for rights, whether it's for human or nonhuman animals, is part of a whole tableau of people willing to speak out in defense of the rights of others, particularly those who are weaker than themselves. People will come to the fight for justice by many different roads.

Why hasn't the left become involved in this?

There's the old leftist view, which has never been updated, that progress requires that we dominate nature, and other animals are considered part of that nature.

Actually, it's rather ironic, since leftist theoreticians maintain that ideologies oftentimes serve to justify oppression. The way it works is that those on top convince themselves that "the other" is somehow different and less than us—as with slavery, or the napalming of the Vietnamese people. Similarly, if a society feels that we need to eat dead animals, then we define ourselves by creating an unbridgeable gap between us and them. It would seem to me that a rational leftist would recognize that the ultimate in exploitation and domination and treating living beings as mere objects for profit is nowhere seen in a purer form than in our relation to animals raised for food.

You've said that you work in an incremental fashion, one step at a time, and that the further you go, the further in the distance you can see. Looking far ahead, what do you see?

I see a coming together of the many movements promoting non-violence and defending the vulnerable. For too long people have viewed the Earth and everything on it as something to be exploited without limits. Now, many of us are beginning to recognize that our planet is not just a quarry to be pillaged and then refilled with garbage. This provides us with an incentive to promote a practical universal ethic—among these, that it's wrong to harm others who, like us, want to avoid pain and get some pleasure out of life.

It seems to me that common sense suggests that our society will be upgraded by shifting from greed and macho violence to doing the least harm and the most good to other humans, to other animals and to our fragile environment. An immediate opportunity is encouraging meat to go the way of tobacco, from fashionable to pariah. I see McVeggies as tomorrow's premier fast–food chain.

What's wrong with the all-or-nothing approach? The atrocities against animals seem to cry out for such an abolitionist policy.

Sometimes this is phrased as, "If humans were vivisected, would you ask for abolition or bigger cages?"—with the all-or-nothings presenting themselves as saints while castigating others as sinners.

But remember, the first law of effective activism is: Stay in touch with reality. And the reality is that nine billion nonhuman animals, not humans, are being raised on farms every year for our dinners. For as long as they remain edibles it is both futile and counterproductive to engage in the blustering bravado of "Abolition now!"

The animal victims can't afford this self-righteous, moralistic stance of all-or-nothing, because so far it has led to nothing. For 100 years people hollered "Abolish vivisection!" while the number of animals in laboratories kept skyrocketing. Reduction came about as a result of campaigns to promote alternatives. If you go for all-or-nothing, it is a good way to get applause, but it is not a good way to make progress. I don't think the suffering animals are well-served by the self-indulgence of the politically correct.

Progress is made stepwise, incrementally. You can have ideals, but, in practical terms, what are you going to do today? What are you going to do tomorrow? You need a program that makes sense in order to move ahead.

Critics accuse you of compromising with injustice—"hobnobbing in the halls with the enemy." How do you respond?

For us, dialoguing with the other side has produced tangible results. When you suggest alternatives that are doable and workable and that lead to progress, and where everybody can come out a winner, you get a change that's a great deal more enduring because it's not begrudging.

I think you always need to start off with dialogue, because if you start off with bashing, it looks like you're looking to fight and not looking to solve problems. The point is to look at issues as problems with solutions, try to figure out solutions, and move ahead. But, where no action is forthcoming, we've been tough and relentless.

What advice would you give someone who wants to make a difference, but doesn't know where to start?
You probably want to select what you're comfortable doing, be it big or small. How much time do you have? What resources are available to you? What are your personal skills, people skills, writing skills? Do you have a talent for organizing protests or for street theater? Anything that makes a difference is valid on its own merits. Droplets turn into streams that can finally turn into tidal waves of change.

Get involved in something that's right for you. Something that's doable, whereby you can achieve planned results. You gain confidence by *doing*. It's good to be impatient with injustice, but you need to be patient with yourself. Start off by writing a letter to the editor, encourage school and company cafeterias to offer more vegetarian options, ask your library to carry *Animal Liberation* and other books dealing with animal protection. Call or write your favorite media personalities and ask them to tell the "meat is misery" story.

It's also important to enjoy what you're doing. That way you're going to be more effective.

You've been at this for a long time, and the problems are enormous. What keeps you going? Do you ever get tired of trying?
No matter how big the problems have been, we've always been able to move forward. It's crucial to have a long-term perspective. Looking back over the past 20 years, I see progress that we've helped achieve. And when a particular initiative causes much frustration, I keep looking at the big picture while pushing obstacles out of the way. There's nothing more energizing than making a difference.

I think that to be effective, you have to enjoy what you're doing. To feel that there's nothing in the world you'd rather do—that you find it personally fulfilling and that it gives meaning to your life. It's a lifestyle where everything is sorted out from the perspective of "What difference does it make?" In which you're not concerned with appearances, popularity, material possessions, social status and trappings of power. You are concerned with results that will endure.

Still, it's been said that we don't live by politics alone. Personally, I also get much pleasure from Nina, my playful feline companion. And I walk in parks and, when I can, hike along the seashore. For me, being in contact with nature is like recharging one's batteries. Which is why I was so comfortable working some 11 years aboard merchant ships oftentimes surrounded by nothing but the seas.

Do you think you've seen a sea change in your lifetime?

I think there's been a revolution in our attitude toward animal suffering. It's totally remarkable that one book, in a couple of decades, has changed our outlook and even our behavior toward non-human animals. But if there hadn't been an *Animal Liberation* by Peter Singer, then I think the same thing might have happened, just more slowly. Once all humans are considered within the circle of our concern, it's just inevitable and natural that the next expansion will be toward non-human animals.

What's your vision?

I'd like to see a world with no violence, no exploitation and no domination, where we live in harmony with other humans, other animals and the environment. But the need is not for grandiose dreams but for careful attention to the real world, followed up with action. Because dreaming or even planning won't get us there. As my favorite button proclaims, "Wearing buttons is not enough."

Are you satisfied with your life?

Yes. Some things I would do differently, but by and large I am comfortable with what I'm doing with my life. And I enjoy it, too. It's exciting and interesting, and I generally feel I'm doing the best I can. I think activism is a lifestyle more people should consider.

I'm not encouraging people to carve out careers for themselves within the animal movement. I earned my living as a teacher while coordinating campaigns that stopped experiments on cats at the Museum of Natural History and pressured Revlon into funding alternatives to animal testing. People can make a lot more time than they imagine once they realize they can get results.

It's energizing to be involved in an initiative that one feels is worthwhile. Working on it, planning it out and then all of a sudden seeing the pieces come together creates an enormous feeling of satisfaction. And you feel better about yourself. I don't think somebody who spends their energies trying to make a difference in the world ends up in therapy.

I think most of us want to be able to look back and figure that, hey, we've done something useful with our lives and, as my current cliché goes, done more than consume products and generate garbage.

Being an Activist
Lawrence Carter-Long

Lawrence Carter-Long has a decade of experience in activism on both grassroots and national levels. From his beginnings as an award-winning writer for his high school newspaper to his later role as a leader of Southeastern Louisiana University's student–disability caucus—which successfully implemented improved accessibility on the campus years before the passage of the Americans with Disabilities Act—he has repeatedly demonstrated his strength and commitment to progressive social change on a variety of fronts.

In recent years, Lawrence has served as a mentor to disabled teens in the Washington, DC area and as the Director of a patient-based project for the Physicians Committee for Responsible Medicine. He has been the education director for Friends of Animals in New York City and the program director for the American Anti-Vivisection Society. In addition to the dozens of radio and television appearances Lawrence has made on behalf of animal protection issues, he has been sought out as an authority on disability and public–health concerns, including a nationally televised appearance on the *Today* show in 1992 which examined the Jerry Lewis Telethon controversy. He is currently the coordinator of science and research issues for the Animal Protection Institute and is an active member of the Buddhist Alliance for Social Engagement.

"I kept asking, 'What's wrong with this picture?'
I decided that if I put myself in the position of that battery hen, it wasn't good enough that I just liked the taste. That was it.
It came back to responsibility: If you don't like it, stop."

You're a communication specialist. How should animal advocates talk to people, especially to those supportive of vivisection?
First, we have to realize that health care, medicine, and science are important issues to a lot of people. Anybody that's ever taken an aspirin can talk about it. Anybody whose mother has suffered through heart disease or arthritis, or

whose uncle has suffered from cancer has an interest in this. Because we are all potential patients, we all have a right to speak out. You don't need the benefit of being a former cerebral palsy poster child to talk about these issues effectively. [*Laughter*]

The most important thing is to build bridges and make connections with people. I can't stress this enough. Talk to them about vivisection in a manner they've never heard before. People are accustomed to hearing the argument of "your baby versus your dog." That's what the animal experimentation industry and people who perform vivisection want them to believe. It makes their work easier.

Take that concept, which is already in people's minds, and rework it, turn it on its ear. Ask whether we want, for instance, to spend $300,000 a year getting monkeys addicted to crack cocaine, or whether we want to treat humans who are suffering with that type of addiction. Where are our priorities? Do we want to be treating people addicted to crack cocaine who want to get off the stuff; or do we want to keep addicting these monkeys? We know about the physiological complications of crack addiction. But experiments with animals are never going to touch the psychological, sociological and financial aspects which go into why someone becomes addicted to crack in the first place. Those are the problems we need to be solving.

For example, let's go back to the question of your baby or the dog. This is what you could say: "In the mid–eighties there was an arthritis drug called Oraflex that was tested on dogs, cats—you name it—on up to nonhuman primates at seven times the maximum tolerated human dosage. No ill side effects were found. When this drug was given to human beings, over 150 people died of fatal liver damage in the U.S. alone and many more died in Europe."

My question to those who support animal testing is: "What do you say to those individuals who lost their mothers, their brothers, their grandmothers, due to this drug?" "Oops, we tried it on a rat?" That's not good enough. We can give the drugs to animals and they are going to react differently physiologically. Then, in the case of a drug such as Oraflex or FIAU, the drug eventually ends up killing people. Are you willing to accept the responsibility for that because you believe that we should be doing animal experimentation?

This type of question applies to your life and the life of the person you're talking with. We need to reframe the standard questions and comments in ways which make it easy for somebody to see what the inaccuracies or inconsistencies of animal tests are. If we start talking about these issues in a way that means something to somebody, people start thinking, "Well, maybe that's not the best way to do it." Then we can make some changes. But we have to have the guts to stand up and be willing to reframe the issue. We have to be able to think on our feet.

Bear in mind that we are all much more similar than we are different. Whether you are talking to non-vegetarians, or vivisectors, or furriers, or whomever it may be, there are probably many more similarities than there are differences between us. We need to work from where those similarities and commonalities are. When I debate with vivisectors, I always end with a question which I want not only the vivisector to think about, but the audience to ponder as well: "Are there any areas, regardless of how you feel about this issue and what we talked about tonight—in entertainment, education, testing, food production—where you feel the use of animals is inappropriate?" My follow–up question to that is "If there are, what will you do to help me stop them?"

What that does is put the onus on them, and lets them move forward from a place where they are most comfortable. When I've asked that question to vivisectors, some have come out and said they're absolutely against product testing and they'd do whatever they could to stop it, while they might feel that cancer research is necessary. Am I going to tell them no? Am I going to say, "Well, don't feel compassionate about this issue because you don't go as far as I think you should go." No. What we have to do is bring people on as much as we can. As we do that the humane community will get bigger and more and more changes will occur.

What are your recommendations for activists avoiding burnout?

When somebody's getting it together on an issue and getting motivated, we say that they're "fired up," or they're "hot." When they're not so "fired up," let's say a year or two later, we say they are "burned out." This happened to me in the fall of 1993, and I started to ask, "How does that happen?" And this is what I discovered: When we go into activism, when we first start learning about what is occurring with animals—or anything really—we become angry and incensed, because we're finding out all this information we never heard about before. We expect that because we're fired up we're going to go out and tell our friends and neighbors and they're going to get just as incensed. What happens is that they are not in the same space we are, spiritually or psychologically, whatever it might be. It is here that our expectations begin to take a beating. It is here that burnout begins. It's good to remember that not everyone's going to go vegan overnight. So don't expect it. It took me two years.

I was raised in Indiana, in farm country, and vegetarianism was the weirdest thing in the world to me. What happened was that I saw an autopsy and they pulled lard out this guy's heart: he was 42 years old and weighed about 400 pounds. I got concerned about my own heart and said to myself, "I don't want to be eating this stuff." The guy who did the autopsy said that it was bacon and eggs and all those kinds of things that did it. I started reading voraciously every thing I could on diet. One of the books I read was *Radical Vegetarianism*. I believe I was still on the preface when the author, Mark Braunstein, asked:

"What right do we have to kill an animal simply to feast on its burnt, dead flesh?" Stopped me cold: I'd never thought about it before. And I asked myself, "Why do I do that?" And I came up with two answers: it was habit, something I'd been raised to do and had always done; and I liked the taste. I kept reading the book, found out about battery hens, veal, the types of production and the suffering that go on. I tried to put myself in that animal's place. I realized it wasn't necessary to eat meat. I had never heard of any vegetarian dropping dead of malnutrition but knew that plenty of people eating flesh foods were dying of heart disease and cancer and obesity. So, I kept asking, "What's wrong with this picture?" I decided that if I put myself in the position of that battery hen, it wasn't good enough that I just liked the taste. That was it. It came back to responsibility: if you don't like it, stop.

How do you prepare for your debates?
Before I speak anywhere I sit down and come up with five points of attack. I don't care what they ask me, I get into those five points of attack. It helps to anticipate what they might throw your way. I once did this TV news segment called "The Hot Seat" on WOR in New York City, in which the interviewer throws all these questions at you, trying to make you nervous. He tried every trick in the book. I remember him yelling, "There were several people naked out there [for a fur protest]. How far are you people willing to go?!" And I looked at him and replied:

"You covered the story, didn't you? Who was hurt? As long as you keep covering the story, we're going to keep doing it. Why? Because it's a way to bring people into the issue, and in a way that maybe they haven't seen or heard before. Why are these people going naked? The fact of the matter is the animals don't get a choice. They're stripped bare of their skin. They're dead. If we can do something to wake somebody up and get them to think about that in a different manner, and you cover us, you are partly responsible for that." It looked natural, but what he couldn't know is that I'd rehearsed that little give-'n'-take with my girlfriend just a few hours before. That's what we need to do: anticipate and prepare.

With anything we do, as we try to communicate with people, we should try to make them aware of their own responsibility. And we also need to know our responsibilities. I'm not of the opinion that all press is good press, that's nonsense. We're not always going to be speaking to other animal rights activists. We could be fine and dandy sitting in our little cloistered rooms talking to each other. But if this movement's ever going to get anywhere, we need to understand how our message is coming across to other people and approach them from that space. We'll never progress if we're always offending those we need to convert.

Sometimes it seems tough feeling so isolated.

Right. It's like a ministry: we can't get away from it. You go to the movies: there's an animal being abused in the movie. You start to go out to eat: they're serving veal. You're on the way home from the movie: you find a stray cat. It's in your life, every day, and that's a very difficult thing. And you can't just turn it off. You have to realize that when you say, "I'm an animal rights activist." You need to know that these pressures are going to build up. First, you have to be aware that this is going to occur and, second, be very mindful of where you're at and what your limits are. Say to yourself, "You know what? I'm going to mail these five letters, and then I'm going to the movies." Because if you're not recharging your batteries or giving yourself a break and bringing something into your life that is empowering and enriching, you're not going to have anything to give to the animals.

What you have to do is to pat yourself on the back for the small gains you can get. Keep working to make each incremental step mean something. That means that if someone changes the brand of toothpaste they buy, that's a great thing. If somebody says, "I'm not going to buy veal anymore," that's a great thing. Maybe after they make that step, they'll make another step. But they're not going to do it if you cram it down their throats.

How do you feel one should approach vegetarianism?

In our culture, vegetarianism and animal advocacy are still a little "out there" and it's difficult for people to make changes because we're all supposed to wear the same jeans with the name on the rear end and we all want the proper haircut or whatever. That's what we're told to get. You step outside of those lines or that paradigm and it becomes difficult. That's why we look for some sort of confirmation for these changes. And it's really crucial we give that to people: "How is that going? Are you having any problems?" People say, "I just can't imagine eating tofu." I mean, I was there once. I looked at this stuff and I said, "Looks like Styrofoam." I tasted it raw, it tasted pretty much like I expect Styrofoam to taste. And I thought, "God, how can anybody eat this?" But I learned more about tofu and how it's an amazing food which will absorb the flavor of anything you put with it if you cook it correctly. And I think we need to tell people what to expect.

It's not necessarily easy to make this change. I was once asked during a debate on the Internet by a woman who was very upset: "Why is it that if a lion is able to go out and eat a gazelle then I can't have a steak?" She was angry about that. And I said, "The question isn't how I can be more like a lion; but how I can be more compassionate as a human. How can I make this world a better place; how can I limit suffering to the greatest degree possible?"

Vegetarians are giving something up, but we're also giving something back and it's more than worth it. The suffering we're not causing is an amazing amount. The self-satisfaction, knowing that you're not contributing to that death, is something we should be very proud of. We as humans are blessed with the capacity to make a choice. We can say, "No, I will not do this." A lion can't, as far as I know. People ask me whether I feel all animals are the same. I don't feel that. I'm not saying that rats should vote, or that dogs should drive cars, or that we should chase down gazelles and rip them open with our bare teeth. But we should recognize the differences and yet understand that the common thread is that we all should have the right to be alive and not be harmed. I come back to the big word: responsibility. When you realize what kind of a mess this planet's in and what our wanton consumerism has done, you begin to realize that we have to develop and cultivate and facilitate something greater. My vegetarianism and animal activism are a large part of that. It's not the whole pie, but it's a big chunk.

If we're able to look at that and say, "I'm bringing more life, more verve and less suffering into the world"—is that not a good thing? So when people ask me, "What are you trying to do? Just *what* are you people trying to do?" I tell them straight–out: "My goal is to eliminate suffering. It is to not cause suffering as much as I can. Isn't that a good thing?" At some point we need to stop being defensive and begin to own our choices. If someone asks me why I am a vegetarian, I warn them, "If you really want to talk about this, you're giving me half an hour. You're not asking me why I'm vegetarian, or you're not going to ask me what's going to happen to all the cows, and then turn around and walk away. If you really want to get into this, let's get into it, let's really talk about it."

I do this because often when we talk about vegetarianism and start to give people information they might find uncomfortable, they turn around and want to leave and stay in denial about what really goes on. So I say, "Look, I'll talk if you're willing to dialogue about this, if we really *do* talk," and give them the option to continue. Sometimes they will, sometimes they won't, but at least you're going into it with your eyes open. People need to cultivate a willingness to question everything—not only their old habits but their new habits. We must question our animal rights activism, our self-righteousness; the way we approach other people; the way people hear and see us and we them.

Going for the Dogs
Alyssa Bonilla

At the end of the summer of 1997, Brooklyn's first dog run became fully operational in Carroll Gardens. It is currently the only place in the entire borough where dogs can be legally let off their leashes. A small group of Carroll Gardens residents, brought together by Alyssa Bonilla, worked the political process and built community goodwill to bring about this historic event. Bonilla tells how she and the Dog Owners Group of Carroll Gardens (DOG) pulled this off in nine months, and offers advice to like-minded local organizers.

"To go really local like this—and I mean two blocks away— to go so grassroots and so local has been so satisfying, because it is not pounding on someone's door for something that happens so far away."

What led you to start the crusade for a dog run?
We used to live in a house near a large park which had lots and lots of space. Then we moved from that house to an apartment in Carroll Gardens. One of my dogs is made for long-distance running. He became very depressed and listless, because he was basically in a shoebox. I would walk him, but it wasn't the same. We had even gotten a companion dog, but that wasn't the same as exercise outdoors. I saw the dog runs happening in Manhattan and thought, "Well, why isn't that happening here?"

This was a very grassroots initiative. How did you get started?
In August 1996, I stuck a crayon–and–magic marker drawing in the pet shop, announcing: "Dog Owners Association Forming Now." One woman called me. Then a woman stopped me on the street and said, "Oh I can make signs." The two of us put up signs. So we were up to three people. Some people called as a result of the

signs. We had a meeting of 12 people, of which only one person besides myself is still active in the group, but has become a core person. In our third meeting, only two people showed up, but I just tried to continue step by step, thinking, "I want to bridge gaps between people. I want to create goodwill."

How did the momentum start building?

We paraded with dogs in the Atlantic Antic street fair opening parade in September 1996 and participated in the Blessing of the Animals day that October. It was a great feeling to hear the dogs being cheered, because it fed my sense that people had just forgotten how great dogs are. Word of mouth is pretty good. Dog owners talk to each other, you see each other. So, when I found someone besides myself who was very much an organizer, we were immediately a team, so that multiplied the effect. Later a great couple showed up. They were total animal-rights, dog-rights people and committed to the project completely. That really helped. We formed a nucleus—a critical mass.

My first outside contact was with a dog trainer, Robin Kovary. I learned she had helped start the Washington Square Park dog run. She told me about the community board process—the need for petitions—and to expect opponents. Neighborhood word of mouth led me next to Margaret Cusack, president of the Boerum Hill Association, who is trying to get a dog run in Boerum Hill, a nearby neighborhood. I was very nervous about starting a community project. She was my community–organizing mentor. She took me under her wing. I actually saw someone doing community organizing work in a very nonchalant, matter-of-fact, in-your-home, in-your-living-room way. She had very clear plans, very clear goals—this is what we need to talk about, this is what we need to do.

The turning point was when we had Marty Waxman as a guest speaker at one of our meetings. He founded the dog run on East 51st Street and York Avenue in Manhattan. The man actually created a Web site for dog runs. He knows what's going on in different dog runs all over the world and was Information Central. That's where I got my learning from. Robin helped me get started, Margaret gave me courage, and Marty provided me with the nuts and bolts of details. The dog run wouldn't exist if these local organizers hadn't paved the way and done a lot of work.

When did it start to seem like it was really going to happen?

In September 1996, I went to a community board meeting all by myself. The district manager met me and said, "Go talk to the Parks Committee chair." The Parks Committee chair's first words were, "I don't like dogs. But it's good to know you're doing the right thing." He was completely supportive of this idea because he saw this as a solution to dogs' being where people don't want them, to decreasing dog traffic on the sidewalks, and therefore the mess. It was an answer to a lot of his prayers. That was the key selling point when we made initial contact with the Parks Committee chair of our community board.

What was the approval process?
Projects are reviewed by committees and then are referred to the full community board. The committee makes a recommendation, yes or no, to the Board. We do not speak to the board; the committees address the board. Our opportunity to speak was the Parks Committee meeting in March 1997. We had a schematic drawing of each site, photos of every site, how many feet of fence each site needs, which one has good water access. We made it very clear that we were willing to put out a lot of effort to have this. We tried to answer every possible question beforehand. We got on the full board agenda in April, and got approval in May. It happened so quickly.

How much community organizing did you do?
We had a petition table at a local pet store on Court Street every Saturday for two months. We tabled at a street fair and a local flea market. Also, we attended monthly meetings of the largest area block associations, making presentations about the dog run. Members of these local groups overlap, so we were making important contacts. We were becoming more of a visible group and not just individuals with dogs. We want the dogs and dog owners to be visible, not skulking around the back roads trying to keep from being yelled at.

Had you done community organizing before?
I was a political science major in school and had a summer job working for a labor union. I did door-to-door canvassing for a while and worked on a congressional campaign once. I haven't done anything like that for years, because it felt like too much energy for too little result. To go really local like this—and I mean two blocks away—to go so grassroots and so local has been so satisfying, because it is not pounding on someone's door for something that happens so far away.

I don't think of myself as a community leader at all. I have a job in this group, so to speak, in that I was an initiator of something that wanted to happen, to be born. I was like a midwife for this project, so I can't take credit for it.

What does this process say about dogs in our society?
Dog owners as a group are on the periphery of the community. People have basically lost touch with what animals have to offer us—they see dogs as aggressive and dirty. They've lost sight of Lassie, of the family dog. They've lost touch with [the fact that] dogs can be integrated into the community in a friendly, responsible way. I don't see us as an animal rights group, because we're not really agitating to raise consciousness, but I have to admit that's in my mind. I'm hoping that as a byproduct of the goodwill created around this project, people will open their minds to animals.

What would you say are the key points in community organizing?

1. The most power I have seen in this group came from having faith in people's positive intentions and goodwill.

2. Write out your intentions clearly and be 100 percent committed. A whole lot of energy will sweep behind you.

3. Make sure you include the community. Attend neighborhood meetings of various groups.

4. As you work, gather and renew. It can't just be a linear charge, because you get burned out that way. Personal support is necessary, especially if you're in a leadership role.

5. The process is very organic. It's like tending a garden. You can't do anything about the weather, but you can water, you can feed the soil, you can tend. I guess love is the best.

Civil Disobedience and Direct Action
Standing Up and Being Counted
Ben White

We are the generation on watch when the last wildlife on Earth is being put on the chopping block. We are the culmination of at least 300 years on this land of a war against nature. It is a war that has an external component—the slaughter of animals and wild places—and an internal component—the slaughter of our own sensitivities.

One of the functions of society is to anesthetize and desensitize us. We feel less and less because it is safer to feel nothing. As an animal person, I take on the pain of others. Yet, there is a problem with that. Because if you extrapolate the concern, for instance, from stopping a man beating his dog to life in the neighborhood, the city, the state, and then the world, it is too huge to contemplate.

My personal antidote for that world pain is direct action. Years ago I used to cut down billboards at night and would run giggling into the night. It didn't save the world, but it was very good for my mental health. It does not matter if your action is covered by the media and it does not matter if there is one of you or 30 of you, if you are doing it for yourself and for the critters. For, when it comes down to it, what can they do to you that is anywhere close to what, for instance, they do to the fox, mink, bobcat, lynx and all the other animals on fur farms?

What is the responsibility of the individual in the context of, for example, an institution like the fur industry that is founded and predicated on the suffering of animals? I have participated in lots of civil disobediences and direct action, and have been arrested over 30 times. It is my feeling that what we have to do is stand up personally and say that we will not go along with this. In his book of essays, *What Are People For?*, Wendell Berry writes: "Protest that endures, I think, is moved by a hope far more modest than that of public success: namely, the hope of preserving qualities in one's own heart and spirit that would be destroyed by acquiescence."[1] That is the nut of it. We must ask what it is we do to stand up for ourselves, to say that we will not go along with the mechanism of death, and that we oppose it.

The word "sabotage" derives from the weavers who fought against the industrial revolution when machines were brought in to do the weaving. The weavers, who were called Luddites, did not take this lying down. What they did was take their wooden shoes called *sabots* and jam them into the gears of the machines and destroy them. I would suggest that our task is to take the machinery of death and put our souls into that machinery and grind it down so that it stops. Nothing else works. There are never enough of us doing this. So we have to undertake essentially a homeopathic activism, because courage is contagious.

With civil disobedience you sometimes lose the battle, but win the war. In 1995 and 1996, a group of us fought to save the old growth forest of Rocky Brook from being cut in the Pacific Northwest. We lost and the loggers cut it. But there were 280 other sites that were going to be cut and we pitched such a fit on Rocky Brook that the loggers made whatever deal they had to and all the others were saved. This situation came about because we let the loggers know that it was not going to happen. We need to say to ourselves: I will not go home with this; I will not give my tacit approval; I will put myself in the way, however that works.

Civil disobedience—breaking the law of the day to argue for a greater goal—has been used as a form of activism for many years. Yet there are important rules that need to be understood before undertaking this powerful form of protest used by Mahatma Gandhi and Dr. Martin Luther King, Jr. One vital thing to remember is that challenging the infliction of suffering is the right thing to do, and you should feel proud doing it. If you act like a criminal, you will be treated as one. Likewise, it is important to treat everyone—the police, your opponents, the press—as potential converts, and to be persuasive rather than angry. It is important to look the person arresting or accosting you in the eye and come across as a normal person—otherwise your opinion will be considered by many to be worthless. It is essential to be completely peaceful. If you are verbally attacked, you should smile; if you are physically assaulted, you should protect yourself without responding in kind.

Finally, it is important to be informed about your subject. It is best not to answer any question from the media that you are not sure of. Similarly, in responding to the authorities or the media, it is best to appeal to their inherent sense of fairness. At all times, remember why you are engaging in the civil disobedience: to keep from personally acquiescing to suffering. The more oppressive the treatment of you, the more obvious is the institutional protection of systemic violence. That is why there is power in numbers.

About 25 years ago, I lived with a medicine man named Rolling Thunder, learning traditional Native religion and herbal medicine. To Rolling Thunder the way you gather a plant and your reverence for and connection to the Earth was as important as the actual plant and the prescription to fight disease. I was taught that to gather the plant was to go up to it, make an offering, ask permission of the plant to gather it, and feel what the answer was. If the answer was yes I would gather the plant; if the answer was no I would not. I always felt a little fraudulent because I thought, "What can I take out of my pocket that hasn't been given to me?" Everything is given to us. We live in such a land of plenty, and all of it is given to us.

Now I ask what we can give as an offering of thanksgiving for this magical place in which we live. I would say that all we have to offer is a little discomfort; to inconvenience ourselves for a few hours or a few days to go to jail, or be locked up, or get abuse. What else do we give up, except being home with our feet up in front of the television for one evening? Some people feel—and I am of that frame of mind—that it is better, when you can (and some people cannot and there is no judgment either way), not to plea out or pay the fine when you are arrested. It is better to go ahead and push the authorities to take responsibility for the cruelty of these laws.

If we do not put our souls into the cogs of the machine, it keeps on grinding. I really believe that the reason we cut down old growth forests and capture dolphins, the reason we slaughter millions of animals, is because we allow it. *We* allow it. *All of us.* When we decide we will no longer allow it, it is going to be over.

Freedom from the Cages
Rod Coronado

Rod Coronado was recently released from the Federal Correctional Institution in Tucson, Arizona, having been convicted of aiding and abetting arson at a Michigan State University research facility, in which 32 years of data intended to benefit the fur industry were destroyed. He is the first Native American member of the Animal Liberation Front in United States history to be sent to federal prison.

"The powers of the Earth and the spirits of my ancestors are smiling upon me, and from them I draw tremendous strength and the power to survive anything."

How do you define extremism?
Extremism comes in varying degrees. Most people associate extremism with religion or politics, but the extremism that most concerns me is environmental, social and spiritual, which I differentiate from religious. Extremism to me is not what we as socially conscious individuals do to fight a greater evil. It's what multinational corporations, governments and consumers do to the Earth and animals that pushes the extremes of the Earth's carrying capacity at the expense of other life forms and future generations.

Extremism to me is continuing to manufacture and produce things that we know are destroying our ozone and contaminating our water. Extremism to me is the tyrannical degree of police and military repression that citizens sanction and that results in the imprisonment, torture and death of any who stand in the way of progress. Extremism is also the distance we have allowed ourselves to come from the laws and power of nature that taught us how to live in harmony with other life for millennia. This is an extremism that allows us to label those trying to reverse the destruction of Earth and animals as "extremists" while calling the destroyers legitimate, law-abiding citizens. I consider myself anti-extremist in every sense of the word because extremism tips the scales of all life on Earth precariously close to disaster.

How far should one be willing to press for a cause or belief system?
It depends on the cause and belief. Capitalism and communism are causes and beliefs, as are most institutionalized religions which, I believe, have been pressed to the point that those opposing them and striving to maintain spiritual or cultural autonomy are persecuted. If you believe in something or rally behind a cause, the best you can do is to embody your principles and beliefs in your own life. People recognize sincerity and true faith. Nothing is gained by forcing someone to believe in something. If your cause or belief is true and does not negatively impact the balance of nature, then it is good for the Earth and most likely good for you and all other life.

When the balance of life on Earth is negatively impacted by the actions of others, whose cause and belief come at the expense of ecological integrity and the human spirit and leads to the unnecessary suffering and exploitation of other life striving to live in harmony with us, then we are justified in taking action that would restore balance and preserve life and freedom. We are justified so long as that action is only to the degree of righting wrongs and obtaining true justice, rather than turning into a cause or belief that obstructs the path to peace and harmony with all creation.

Freedom does not mean you have the right to exploit or abuse others. Using physical force to prevent an atrocity has always been commendable throughout history, when fighting a greater evil. If we can direct that force specifically against the tools and machines of life's destruction, with the goal of also liberating the oppressed without causing harm or loss of life, there can be no truer path for those fighting tyrannical oppression.

All we can do is make an example out of our lives. Rather than pointing fingers at others for not being radical enough, we should be asking ourselves this question: Are we conservative enough? Being radical is not about using more and more force. I don't like the word "radical," as the only radicals are those we are trying to stop from destroying the planet. It is about not just what we eat, but what we consume: paper made from forests, plastics which create dioxins, electricity generated by damming rivers, burning coal, nuclear reactors, agricultural products like non-organic cotton and vegetables which result in pesticides and insecticides being introduced into the environment. It is a question of living as simply as possible with minimal impact on the Earth and animals. It is about asking ourselves whether we are paying the rent—not to landlords, but to the Earth. As citizens of a country that consumes most of the Earth's resources and creates most of its pollution, we should be fighting from within the belly of the beast to stop the destruction the United States is responsible for here and abroad. We do that not by blaming others, but by blaming ourselves for supporting evil industries and politicians with our money and our votes; by educating ourselves and others about every impact of our actions. From realizing that buying coffee is helping to steal lands from indigenous peoples living in poverty because they must grow cash crops rather than food, to realizing that driving a car is supporting the destruction of habitat in the quest for oil and sponsoring wars in other countries, we must measure our own impact on the Earth rather than just on animals, and then pay the rent by striking the evil empire where it hurts the most: in the pocketbook.

When is violence acceptable?
That depends on the definition of violence. I define violence as physical force directed at a sentient being or natural creation. I do not believe that violence can be committed against something inanimate whose sole purpose is the destruction of innocent life and natural creation. The violence that is legally committed against animals in laboratories, in fur and factory farms, and in the wild is totally unjustified and unacceptable, as is the violence committed when the remaining wild places are destroyed. The violence committed against women, people of color, indigenous peoples, and anyone who opposes the loss of human rights and freedoms to governments and corporations, is especially despicable. It prevents those with a close relationship with the Earth from displaying the path of harmony we all might learn from.

Self-defense is not violence. Should anyone defend themselves from violence with violence, I believe it is acceptable. But as a movement whose fundamental belief is respect and reverence for all life, there is no place for violence as a means to preserve life, especially when we have yet to exhaust the avenues of non-violent illegal direct action against the tools and institutions of life's destruction.

What do you think is the future for direct–action movements like Earth First! (EF!), the Animal Liberation Front (ALF) and People for the Ethical Treatment of Animals (PETA)?
For Earth First! I see a wider body of support as more and more people become disenchanted with mainstream environmentalism. I also see Earth First! gaining more respectability, which I do not necessarily think is a good thing. When any movement gains respectability it tends to want to retain it by focusing on the more legitimate and legal avenues for obtaining its goals and objectives. I have always loved EF! because of its primitive edge and its uncompromising support of illegal direct action or "monkeywrenching." But now EF! sometimes seems to become preoccupied with the corporations they oppose by placing too much faith in media-orchestrated actions rather than in actions that cost corporations profits. Still, I have total faith and allegiance to EF! and have incredible hope for

224

the young warriors they attract who must face their own trials and tribulations before deciding whether to place their faith in the powers of the Earth, or the powers of the media, courts and Congress.

For the Animal Liberation Front, I see an escalation in its attacks on institutions of Earth and animal abuse, and a greater emphasis on economic sabotage as police repression and physical security prevent the more popular tactics like live-animal liberations. I see the ALF being treated in the future as the domestic terrorist organization the Justice Department has labeled it, meaning wider persecution of anyone who publicly supports the ALF. Basically, I see the ALF leading other direct-action underground movements to defend Earth and animals into the 21st century. I believe that in order to survive, the ALF must learn the lessons of their British counterparts, hopefully without the costs of imprisoned warriors. If the ALF can grow only through continued imprisonment of its members, then it is everyone else's obligation to ensure that strong prisoner-support exists for them. Either way, illegal direct action will continue to grow as more people realize that governments and corporations whose very existence is based on animal abuse will never afford legal protection to animals. If we truly believe in animal liberation, we had better be ready to break society's laws and do some time for it if necessary.

For PETA, I see the mainstreaming of animal liberation. Whereas other large organizations compromise their more "radical" beliefs to gain acceptance, I have yet to see PETA compromise in this fashion. They have pushed animal rights into every home, and have brought the idea of respect and reverence for animals past the stage of ridicule and onto the borders of acceptance. They also have never shied away from recognizing or supporting their troops—the ALF—which I think is vital. Above-ground organizations like PETA and EF! have an obligation to support illegal direct action because so many of the things both groups believe in can be won only by breaking the law. Very rarely, if ever, have struggles for justice and liberation been won without breaking establishment laws.

Do you think there is a "too far" that can be reached in defending animals and the environment?
It depends on how far humans are willing to go to destroy the Earth and animals. Right now, I have complete faith that we can stem the tide of animal abuse and ecological destruction with non-violent illegal direct action should all other tactics fail (which they are doing). But when we are talking about the preservation of our life-support system, the Earth, and prevention of the extinction of literally thousands of species which play an integral role in a healthy environment, allowing that to happen is what has gone too far. To stop it, whatever we are forced to do now may seem extreme, but will be appreciated by future generations who will be able to live and survive thanks to this generation's actions on behalf of the Earth and animals.

The question is whether we have already gone too far by allowing governments and corporations to play Russian roulette with the fate of this planet and our future, without taking greater personal responsibility to stop it at all costs. We, as citizens of the Earth and the guardians of the planet for future generations, can never go too far in preserving the Earth and the many nations of life upon it. Such is our obligation.

How do you respond to those who say that releasing ranch-raised or laboratory animals into the wild is consigning them to death in a world they are not used to?
Had I been born in this prison I am now in with my only future being a certain, painful death, I think I would accept the slightest chance of survival, knowing the worst that could happen would be the same fate I was destined to meet in the first place. If I knew what my captors knew, as is the case with mink farmers, that many prisoners who have escaped have indeed survived and lived natural lives, then definitely any chance of survival is better than a certain death. When we are talking about a species such as mink, fox, lynx, bobcat or any other animal which contains in its DNA the memory of natural survival, there can be no form of liberation that is acceptable beyond rescue, rehabilitation and release back to their natural environment. Many species have the ability to survive without human help.

More and more species are ending up in laboratories and farms where human beings are attempting to domesticate them for economic exploitation. These efforts should be sabotaged before we have created yet another species whose sole existence is to serve our needs. Mink, foxes, bobcats and lynx belong in the forest. Primates belong in the rainforest. If we fought not only for the protection of animals but also for the environment in which they naturally belong, then we wouldn't have to be asking ourselves this question. When it comes to species already domesticated, we have an obligation as the species which created their dependency to provide them with a life much better than that of their abusers. Otherwise, we are not living up to our own beliefs.

Do you feel that there is pressure within animal advocacy and environmental movements to get arrested? If so, do you think it is helpful pressure?
I'm assuming you mean civil disobedience (CD). Rather than pressure activists simply to get arrested, we should first ask ourselves if the impact of the action we plan has an impact on our target. I have seen a lot of activists get arrested doing CD mostly out of peer pressure, or guilt-tripping people into believing that if they don't get arrested they are not doing enough "for the animals" or "for the Earth." I also see many activists participating in CD with the sole objective of gaining media attention for their cause when deep down inside they feel their impact is insignificant. I believe we should participate only in

226

actions that we honestly believe will accomplish our goals. Any action should speak for itself without the necessity of media coverage to make it a success. When the ALF raids a laboratory and burns it down, it doesn't matter whether it is reported or not. The animals are rescued and that lab won't be torturing any animals for a long time.

I also have never seen intentionally getting arrested result in any major victories in protecting the Earth or animals. Here in the United States, targets for CD usually are hit only once a year, and business is interrupted for only a few hours, while for the other 364 days of the year it is business as usual. Road blockades to preserve forests are undoubtedly noble actions, but when the police arrive and the bulldozers come, within hours we are defeated. I also do not believe we can ever achieve victory by clogging the court system with non-violent protesters. Maybe if tens of thousands of people were willing to get arrested or even rally for the Earth and animals, as was the case during the Vietnam War with peace protesters, it would be different. But even the well-organized March for the Animals on Washington, DC in 1996 brought together only about 5,000 people, who spent thousands of dollars traveling there. I believe a lot more could have been accomplished by those same activists had each one done one act of anonymous direct action on a local animal-abuse target such as a fur shop, or given the money spent to travel to grassroots groups participating in effective campaigns. Instead, our energies were expended with the hopes of proving to politicians that we are a force to be reckoned with, and we are not when it comes to politics. More letters are written to politicians in Washington concerning animal issues than on all other topics. If politicians acted on behalf of the citizenry of this country, those letters would be responded to with political action. But our voice will never be heard as long as politicians are allowed to accept money from special interests like the food, medical, sport, mining, timber, oil and military industries, whom they ultimately serve and answer to.

Rarely in history has it ever been citizen outrage alone that changed immoral or unjust laws; rather it has been a handful of direct-action activists' willingness to give their all in their fight for liberty. Such was the case with slavery. It wasn't the polite abolitionists who brought about change; it was Washington's fears that the John Browns, Nat Turners and Harriet Tubmans would continue direct action attacks against the institutions of slavery. Likewise, the only way we will ever convince big business to stop destroying the Earth and her animal people is when we make it economically unfeasible for them to continue. As long as there is a buck to be made, no one is going to be concerned with the long-term impact of their actions. They don't even care about their own children's future. All they care about is material satisfaction in the here and now.

How have you coped with incarceration? What resources do you draw upon?
Right now I consider my imprisonment the only vacation I am ever going to get
from my social, ecological and spiritual responsibilities. It is a time to rethink
my strategies and prepare for a lifetime of service to save what little is left. It
is a time to study the structure of our enemies to understand them better and
discover their Achilles' heel. I also consider prison a rite of passage for anyone
who is serious about achieving animal and Earth liberation, because it is one of
society's fears that if you step out of line, you will be punished by prison. And if
we are serious, then we have to overcome our fears of imprisonment. After all, it
is little compared with the price paid by freedom fighters in other countries who
are tortured or given ridiculously long sentences for the least degree of resistance.
And it is nothing compared with the animals in zoos and aquariums who are
sentenced to solitary confinement without hope of parole, or the animals sitting
in laboratories, factories and fur farms whose only escape is death.

Spending a few years in prison where I am able to read and write is such a
small price to pay for what I believe, for what my own ancestors were butchered,
raped and sold into slavery for doing. I now believe that freedom is something
we can achieve only by following the laws of nature, not those of man. Freedom is doing what we know in our hearts is right, and to hell with the physical
consequences of not obeying tyranny. As the Mexican revolutionary Emiliano
Zapata [1879-1919] so aptly put it, "It is better to die on your feet than live on
your knees. . . ." I am free, and no amount of imprisonment is going to change
that. I've tasted true freedom, and I know it is much better by far than anything
this government has to offer me. So if prison for a few years is the price for that,
then I gladly accept it. The powers of the Earth and the spirits of my ancestors
are smiling upon me, and from them I draw tremendous strength and the power
to survive anything. When I hear coyotes singing from the other side of the ra-
zor-wire fences, my heart soars, because I know my animal relations know why I
am here, and are blessing me with their friendship and brother- and sisterhood.
Hopefully I've proven to them that I am more like them than I am like the two-
leggeds who wage war upon them.

I have more hope now than I ever had before. I am not saying we will ever
see complete victory and the return to global ecological harmony, but that does
not matter. Having utopian visions is important, but what really gives me hope
and inspiration is to have discovered a power that only the Earth and animals
can give us. Victory for me is never betraying the powers I have been blessed
to represent. Hope comes from seeing more and more activists turn away from
the material comforts of the dominant society and look for something ancient
and true that I believe they can find in wilderness and in the eyes of a wild lynx.
The spirit of the Earth is alive, and through her animal people we have much
to learn. I have hope that as more of us restore our faith in our power, rather

than giving strength to our opposition by believing and fearing them, we will remember the wildness buried in our own DNA. I believe the wild spirit is the only hope for preserving planet Earth and all life. But hope does not necessarily mean we will ever win, it just means we will never surrender. We can't. Too much depends on our unwillingness to compromise. It is time to take a stand, and choose where our allegiance lies: with the Earth and animals, or with those destroying them. My hope is that many will join me, and follow their wildest desires and live the life that many believe exists only in myths and fairy tales. Reality is what we make it, and my expectation is that more and more warriors will swear allegiance to the liberation of the Animal Nations and the defense of Mother Earth. As long as we live we may never get another chance to make as much difference in the fate of the planet as we now can. My greatest hope is that when I leave these prison walls behind there will be many more warriors to greet me than there were when I entered here.

Notes

Waskow: Eco-Kosher *(Pages 34–36)*
1 "What is Eco-Kosher." *The Jewish Quarterly*, Winter 1992–1993, No. 148, pp. 5–10.
2 For more on Judaism and vegetarianism, see Schwartz (1982), Berman (1981), Kalechovsky (1993) and Rosen (1997).

Robbins: Reclaiming Our Health and Our Earth *(Pages 55–58)*
1 McKibben (1996), p. 3.

Rowe: Becoming a Vegetarian *(Pages 61–64)*
1 For a history of vegetarianism, see Spencer (1995).
2 See Douglas (1982), Fiddes (1991), Curtin and Heldke (1992) and Counihan and Van Esterik (1997) for anthropological studies of the importance of food—and especially meat—in ancient and modern, industrialized and non-industrialized cultures.

McGuire: Let Us Eat Plants *(Pages 70–71)*
1 Letter to Sidney Webb, October 18, 1898, in *Bernard Shaw: Collected Letters, 1898–1910*, ed. Dan H. Lawrence (New York: Dodd, Mead & Co, 1972), p. 67. Quoted in Adams (1990).
2 "The Vegetarian," January 15, 1898.
3 Tompkins and Bird (1989).
4 Cousens (1992), p. 250.
5 *Essay on Man*, Epistle ii., 25.

Berry: Fruitarianism: The Ultimate Diet *(Pages 77–78)*
1 For more on fruitarianism, see Honiball and Fry (1996).
2 Robert Kole is interviewed at length in Berry (1998).

Berry: Hitler and Vegetarianism *(Pages 83–85)*
1 Berry (1996).
2 Kundera (1992).
3 Schwartz (1982).
4 Lucas and Geis (1964), p. 89.
5 Payne (1973), pp. 346–7.
6 Toland (1976), pp. 256, 741, 745, 761, 821, 824-6.
7 See Kalechovsky, Roberta, "Hitler's Vegetarianism: A Question of How You Define Vegetarianism." (Unpublished essay, 1997).

MacDonald: Globalization and Its Discontents *(Pages 89–95)*
1 See Brown, Renner et al. (1998).
2 "Four Changes" by Gary Snyder. *Resurgence*, no. 186, January/February, 1998 pp. 14–18, excerpted from *A Place in Space* by Gary Snyder, Washington, DC: Counterpoint, 1996).
3 "Befriending the Dark Emotions" by Miriam Greenspan. *Common Boundary*, May/June 1998, pp. 37–43.

MacDonald: The Dilemma of Development *(Pages 96–100)*
1 This article is adapted from a 1993 study, *Wildebeests and Wheat: Crafting a Land Policy in Kenya's Maasailand*, prepared by Mia MacDonald and Eric Azumi for the Kenyan Ministry of Planning and National Development.

Goff: Car Culture and the Landscape of Subtraction (*Pages 101–114*)

1 Quoted on "Suburbs: Arcadia for Everyone," Episode Four of *Pride of Place: Building the American Dream*, produced by Robert A. M. Stern and aired on the Public Broadcasting System in 1986.

2 National Transportation Safety Board, cited in the *New York Times*, July 6, 1995, p. B9.

3 "Accident Facts," National Safety Council, 1993.

4 Komanoff, Charles, "Pedestrians in Peril," *New York Times*, January 27, 1998, op-ed page.

5 "Rethinking the Role of the Automobile," Michael Renner, *Worldwatch Report* 84, 6/88.

6 "Smart Highways: An Assessment of Their Potential to Improve Travel," U. S. General Accounting Office, 1991.

7 Komanoff, op. cit.

8 "Highway Statistics," U.S. Federal Highway Administration, 1992.

9 "The Real Cost of Energy," Harold M. Hubbard, *Scientific American*, 4/91.

10 John Pucher, "Urban Travel Behavior at the Outcome of Public Policy," *Journal of the American Planning Association* Autumn 1988.

11 "Cars Are Evil: Automobiles and the Environment," Stefanie Pollack, Conservation Law Foundation, 7/90.

12 These limits have been eased recently. Alliance for a Paving Moratorium Factsheet 1, "The Problem with Paving: An Economic and Environmental Dead End." Summer 1993.

13 Cited in "Going Nowhere Fast," published by the Municipal Arts Society and Lightwheels, New York: NY, 1991, p. 6.

14 Rocky Mt. Institute, Amory Lovins, at the First International Conference on Auto-Free Cities, New York, 1991.

15 Kunstler (1993), pp. 106–107.

16 "Acting in the National Interest: The Transportation Agenda," the Surface Transportation Policy Project.

17 Alliance for Paving Moratorium, op. cit.

18 "Oil and the Future" by Richard Reese from *Auto-Free Times* 13 (Winter 1998), Arcata, CA, p. 24.

19 American Public Transit Association, Fact Sheet: "Public Transportation: The Vehicle for Conserving Energy."

20 Kunstler (1993), pp. 113–118.

21 "Automobile Index," Conservation Law Index of New England.

22 Kostof (1992), p. 243.

23 "In the Biggest, Booming Cities, A Car Population Problem," by Keith Bradsher. *New York Times*, May 11, 1997.

24 Renner, op. cit. "City Cyclist" Transportation Alternatives, Sep/Oct 1996, p. 17.

25 USDA statistics, People for the Ethical Treatment of Animals.

26 "Saving Aquatic Biodiversity," Reed Noss and Allen Cooperider, *Wild Earth Review*, Spring 1994.

27 *Earth Island Institute Journal*, Spring 1995.

28 U.S. Fish and Wildlife Service, via *Predator Project Newsletter*, Bozeman, Montana; Fall 1996.

29 *New York Times Magazine*, July 23, 1995.

30 Quoted in *Industrial Design* magazine, October 1955. Cited in "Packaging Anew: An Exhibit Brochure from the Cooper-Hewitt Museum of Design." Smithsonian Institution, 1994.

31 "Alternatives to the Automobile: Transport for Livable Cities," by Marsha D. Lowe (*Worldwatch Report* 98). WorldWatch Institute: Washington, DC, October 1990, p. 9.

32 "Oil in the Sea: Inputs, Fates, and Effects," National Academy Press, 1985.

33 Greenpeace of Alaska Factsheet.

Cornell: A Localized Food System (Pages 118–120)
1 "Modernization of a Thousand Year Old Culture," *Sun* magazine 260, February 1997.

Rowe: The Dog in the Lifeboat (Pages 139–146)
1 The cartoon is found in *The Far Side* (Futura Publications: London, 1982).
2 For a scholarly analysis of Gary Larson's work, see "Humanimals and Anihumans in Gary Larson's Gallery of the Absurd" by Charles D. Minahen in Ham and Senior (1997).
3 For the different ways in which we view animals, and dogs in particular, see Arluke and Sanders (1996). They point out that dogs can be household pets, guardians of our property, studies we experiment on, animals we bet on in races or in dog-fights. This suggests that while we may see animals in many different ways, their value to us depends mostly on their utility to us.
4 The term is unfortunate, and was coined by Jan Narveson, who disagreed with the argument. For a detailed summary of the arguments for and against, see Pluhar (1995)   and especially Dombrowski (1997). For other examinations of the rights of animals and our responsibilities towards them, see Midgley (1979), Sapontzis (1987) and Clark (1997).
5 See de Waal (1995), p. 215.
6 The most influential of the books dealing with animal rights and animal liberation are Singer (1975) and Regan (1983).
7 *Politics*. Quoted in Singer (1975), p. 196.
8 *Summa Theologica*, Part II, Question 64, Article 1, and Question 65, Article 3, cited in Linzey and Regan (1986). See also *Summa Contra Gentiles*, book 3, part 2, chapter 112, cited in Pluhar (1985).
9 See *Discourse on Method*, Part Five, in Veitch (1989), pp. 44–46, and letters to the Marquess of Newcastle (November 23, 1646) and to Henry More (February 5, 1649) in Kenny (1970).
10 *Foundations of the Metaphysic of Morals*. For a concise summary of Kant's views on animals, see "Persons and Non-Persons" by Mary Midgley in Singer (1985).
11 For instance, in the ancient world, Plutarch and (there is reason to think) Plato considered animals differently. Likewise, Leonardo da Vinci, Jeremy Bentham, and others have valued animals. See Berry (1996).
12 See Arluke and Sanders (1996) and Ham and Senior (1997).
13 See Fouts (1987) for the history of teaching American Sign Language to the Great Apes. See also Goodall (1986), Savage-Rambaugh and Levin (1996), de Waal and Lanting (1997) and Fossey (1983) for other interactions with the Great Apes. For information on the Great Ape Project, which aims to extend basic rights to gorillas, chimpanzees, orangutans and bonobos, see Cavalieri and Singer (1995).
14 See Noske (1997) for more on anthropological and sociological approaches to animals, and the numerous discoveries of animals' skills (esp. pp. 153–157). See Masson and McCarthy (1995) for the numerous ways in which animals have expressed what we would—or used to—consider solely consider human characteristics.
15 For more on anthropomorphism and other issues in cognitive ethology, see Bekoff and Jamieson (1996).
16 See Manes (1997). Manes points out that for the Middle Ages, all animals had a moral importance within the world that not only explained their natures but linked them irreducibly to the human world.
17 See Mason (1996) and Shepard (1997) for the sociocultural and imaginative importance of animals to human beings.

Rowe: Transgressions: Patents on Life (Pages 150–156)

[1] This story is related in detail in Gold (1996). See also "Patent Pending: The Race to Own DNA," by Philip L. Bereano, *The Seattle Times* (August 27, 1995) B5.

[2] For more on biotechnology and the use of animals, see Fox (1992).

[3] See http://www.criver.com/techdocs/transqt.htm/ for more on the Charles River laboratories.

[4] For details on the Human Genome Project and genetic manipulation, see Harpignies (1996), "Sold Out" by James Boyle, *New York Times* (March 31, 1996), sec 4. p. 15., and "Scientists Finish First Phase in Mapping of Human Genes," *New York Times* (March 19, 1996), sec. C. p. 7.

[5] "A Biocidal Tree Begins to Blossom," by R. Stone in *Science* (February 28, 1992) quoted in Shiva (1997), p. 70. Most of the material concerning TRIPs comes from Shiva.

[6] This is particularly the case with private property and animal rights, and how they relate to the law. Rights discourse pertaining to animals is generally impermissible in a court of law because animals are assumed not to be persons and thus not possessed of legal rights. This does not mean that the larger society cannot influence legal decisions in cases concerning animal cruelty, or that the bringing of cases of animal cruelty to the attention of the law does not offer various advantages for animal rights activists. For detailed discussions of this and related issues, see Francione (1995) and Silverstein (1996).

[7] For a comparison between slavery in the antebellum United States and practices of animal abuse today, see Spiegel (1996).

[8] In recent years, several states in the U.S. have amended the general provisions against animal cruelty in their state law to make prosecution more difficult. They have done this by arguing in court that what they are doing is "customary" or "accepted" farming practice—which itself is decided by what the farming community considers to be common. This circular argument provides farmers with exemption from legislation such as the Animal Welfare Act or the Humane Slaughter Act. All domestic fowl (chickens, turkeys, ostriches, emus, ducks and geese)—indeed, the overwhelming number of the nine billion animals killed each year in the U.S. for food—do not have any legal protection whatsoever. See Wolfson (1995). For the legal definitions of an animal, see *Code of Federal Regulations: Animals and Animal Products* (Parts 1 to End), revised as of January 1, 1992, Office of the Federal Register of National Archive and Records Administration. For the legal standing and living conditions of poultry in modern farming, see Davis (1996).

[9] The literature on animal rights and the use of animal rights in research is voluminous. Among those titles that have critiqued animal experimentation from a mainly scientific viewpoint are: Cramer (1995), Fano (1997), and Lafollette and Shanks (1997).

Newman: Frankenstein's Children (Pages 157–161)

[1] For more on this, see "Patent Sought for Part-Human Creatures," by Rick Weiss, *Washington Post*, April 2, 1998, p. A12.

Simmons: AIDS and Animal Research (Pages 167–171)

[1] See "Drug Agency Proposed New Guidelines on Animal Transplants," by Lawrence K. Altman, *The New York Times*, September 21, 1996, sec. 1, p. 10; "Cross-Species Transplants Raise Concerns About Human Safety," by Lawrence K. Altman, *The New York Times*, January 9, 1996, sec. 1, p. 11; "Baboon Cells Fail to Thrive, But AIDS Patient Improves," by Lawrence K. Altman, *The New York Times*, February 9, 1996, sec. A, p. 14; "Fear of Viruses," by Jonathan S. Allen, *The New York Times*, Saturday, January 20, 1996, sec. 1, p. 23; "Transplant: Urgent Step or Step off the Edge?" by Gina Kolata, *The New York Times*, January 9, 1996, sec. 1, p. 16.

Rowe: Mad Cow Disease *(Pages 172–177)*

[1] For more on Bovine Spongiform Encephalopathy, see Rampton and Stauber (1997). Most of the material concerning BSE in this chapter is taken from this book. For more on the conditions of slaughterhouse workers, see Griffith et al. (1995).

[2] See Lyman (1998) for more on this and other related farm animal issues.

[3] These figures and the information on slaughterhouses are taken from Eisnitz (1997).

Fouts: My Brother's Keeper *(Pages 192–194)*

[1] *The Principles of Morals and Legislation*, ch. XVII, Sec. 1.

White: Civil Disobedience and Direct Action *(Pages 219–221)*

[1] "A Poem of Difficult Hope," in Berry (1990), p. 62.

Bibliography

This bibliography includes not only books by the contributors themselves, but also books they allude to or cite in their essays or interviews.

Adams, Carol J. *Neither Man nor Beast: Feminism and the Defense of Animals* (New York: Continuum, 1994).

———. *The Sexual Politics of Meat: A Feminist-Vegetarian Critical Theory* (New York: Continuum, 1990).

——— and Josephine Donovan, editors. *Animals and Women: Feminist Theoretical Explorations* (Raleigh: Duke University Press, 1995).

——— and Josephine Donovan, editors. *Beyond Animal Rights: A Feminist Ethic of Care for the Treatment of Animals* (New York: Continuum, 1995).

Akers, Keith. *A Vegetarian Sourcebook*, revised edition (Baltimore: Vegetarian Resource Group, 1993).

Arluke, Arnold and Clinton R. Saunders. *Regarding Animals* (Philadelphia: Temple University Press, 1996).

Bekoff, Marc and Dale Jamieson, editors. *Readings in Animal Cognition* (Cambridge: MIT Press, 1996).

Berman, Louis. *Vegetarianism and the Jewish Tradition* (New York: KTAV, 1981).

Berry, Rynn. *Famous Vegetarians and Their Favorite Recipes: Lives and Lore from the Buddha to the Beatles*, revised edition (New York: Pythagorean Press, 1996).

———. *Food for the Gods: Vegetarianism and the World's Religions* (New York: Pythagorean Press, 1998).

———. *The New Vegetarians*, revised edition (New York: Pythagorean Press, 1992).

Berry, Wendell. *What Are People For?* (San Francisco: North Point Press, 1990).

Braunstein, Mark M. *Radical Vegetarianism: A Dialectic of Diet and Ethic* (Quaker Hill: Panacea Books, 1993).

Brown, Lester R., Michael Renner and Christopher Flavin. *Vital Signs 1998: The Environmental Trends That Are Shaping Our Future* (Washington: The Worldwatch Institute, 1998).

Carse, James. *Breakfast at the Victory: The Mysticism of Ordinary Experience* (San Francisco: Harper San Francisco, 1995).

Cavalieri, Paola and Peter Singer, editors. *The Great Ape Project* (New York: St. Martin's, 1995).

Chapple, Christopher Key. *Non-Violence to Animals, Earth and Self in Asian Religions* (Albany: State University of New York Press, 1993).

Clark, Stephen R. L. *Animals and Their Moral Standing* (New York: Routledge, 1997).

Coe, Sue. *Dead Meat* (New York: Four Walls, Eight Windows, 1996).

Counihan, Carol and Penny Van Esterik. *Food and Culture: A Reader* (New York: Routledge, 1997).

Cousens, Gabriel. *Conscious Eating* (Patagonia: Essene Vision Books, 1992).

Cramer, Marjorie and Stephen Kaufman et al., "A Critical Look at Animal Experimentation" (Medical Research Modernization Committee: New York, 1995).

Curtin, Deane W. and Lisa M. Heldke, editors. *Cooking, Eating, Thinking: Transformative Philosophies of Food* (Bloomington: Indiana University Press, 1992).

Davis, Karen. *Prisoned Chickens, Poisoned Eggs* (Summerville: Book Publishing Company, 1996).

De Waal, Frans. *Good Natured: The Origins of Right and Wrong in Humans and Other Animals* (Cambridge: Harvard University Press, 1996).

_____ and Frans Lanting (photog.). *Bonobo: The Forgotten Ape* (Berkeley: University of California Press, 1997).

Dombrowski, Daniel A. *Babies and Beasts: The Argument from Marginal Cases* (Urbana: University of Illinois Press, 1997).

Douglas, Mary. *Purity and Danger*, reprinted edition (New York: Routledge, 1993).

Eisnitz, Gail. *Slaughterhouse: The Shocking Story of Greed, Neglect and Inhumane Treatment Inside the U.S. Meat Industry* (Buffalo: Prometheus Books, 1997).

Fano, Alix. *Lethal Laws: Animal Testing, Human Health and Environmental Policy* (London/New York: Zed Books/St. Martin's, 1997).

Fiddes, Nick. *Meat: A Natural Symbol* (London: Routledge, 1991).

Fossey, Dian. *Gorillas in the Mist* (Boston: Houghton Mifflin, 1988).

Fouts, Roger (with Stephen Tukel Mills). *Next of Kin: What Chimpanzees Have Taught Me About Who We Are* (New York: William Morrow, 1997).

Fox, Michael W. *Superpigs and Wondercorn: The Brave New World of Biotechnology. . .and Where It May Lead* (New York: Lyons & Burford, 1992).

Francione, Gary. *Animals, Property and the Law* (Philadelphia: Temple University Press, 1995).

Gold, E. Richard. *Body Parts: Property Rights and the Ownership of Human Biological Materials* (Washington: Georgetown University Press, 1996).

Goodall, Jane. *Through a Window: My Thirty Years with the Chimpanzees of Gombe* (Boston: Houghton Mifflin, 1991).

Gould, Stephen Jay. *Dinosaurs and Haystacks: Reflections in Natural History* (New York: Crown, 1996).

_____ . *Ever Since Darwin: Reflections in Natural History* (New York: Norton, 1992).

Grandin, Temple. *Thinking in Pictures: And Other Reports from My Life with Autism* (New York: Vintage, 1997).

Gregory, Dick. *Natural Diet for Folks Who Like to Eat: Cookin' with Mother Nature* (New York: HarperCollins, 1983).

Griffith, David Craig, Donald D. Stull et al. *Any Way You Cut It: Meat Processing and Small Town America* (Lawrence: University of Kansas, 1995).

Guha, Ramachandra and Madhav Gadgil. *Ecology and Equity: The Use and Abuse of Nature in Contemporary India* (New York: Routledge, 1995).

_____ . *This Fissured Land: An Ecological History of India* (New York: Oxford University Press, 1994).

Ham, Jennifer and Matthew Senior, editors. *Animal Acts: Configuring the Human in Western History* (New York: Routledge, 1997).

Hanh, Thich Nhat. *The Heart of Understanding* (Berkeley: Parallax Press, 1988).

Harpignies, J. P. *Double Helix Hubris: Against Designer Genes* (Cool Grove Press, 328 Flatbush Avenue, Suite 302, Brooklyn, NY 11238, 1996).

Hillman, James (with Margot McLean). *Dream Animals* (San Francisco: Chronicle, 1997).

_____ . "Going Bugs" (Winstead: Spring Audiotape, 1992).

Honiball, Essie and T. C. Fry. *I Live On Fruit* (Wellsboro: The Wellness Network, 1996).

Kalechofsky, Roberta, editor. *Judaism and Animal Rights: Classical and Contemporary Responses* (Marblehead: Micah Press, 1993).

Kenny, Anthony, translator and editor. *Descartes: Philosophical Letters* (Oxford: Clarendon Press, 1970).

Klaper, Michael. *Vegan Nutrition: Pure and Simple* (Pala: Gentle World, 1987).

Kostof, Spiro. *The City Assembled* (Boston: Bulfinch Press, 1992).

Kundera, Milan. *The Unbearable Lightness of Being* (New York: HarperPerennial, 1992).

Kunstler, James Howard. *The Geography of Nowhere* (Portland: Touchstone, 1993).

Lafollette, Hugh and Niall Shanks. *Brute Science: Dilemmas of Animal Experimentation* (New York: Routledge, 1997).

Larson, Gary. *The Far Side* (Kansas City: Andrews & McMeel, 1982).

Linzey, Andrew. *Animal Theology* (Urbana: University of Illinois Press, 1995).

_____ . *Christianity and the Rights of Animals* (New York: Crossroad, 1987).

_____ and Dan Cohn-Sherbok. *After Noah: Theology and the Liberation of Animals* (London: Cassell, 1997).

_____ and Tom Regan, editors. *Animals and Christianity: A Book of Readings* (New York: Crossroad, 1986).

Lucas, Dione (with Darlene Geis). *The Gourmet Cooking School Cookbook* (New York: Bernard Geis Associates, 1964).

Lyman, Howard (with Glen Merzer). *Mad Cowboy: Plain Truth from the Cattle Rancher Who Won't Eat Meat* (New York: Scribner, 1998).

Manes, Christopher. *Other Creations: Rediscovering the Spirituality of Animals* (New York: Doubleday, 1997).

Marcus, Erik. *Vegan: A New Ethics of Eating* (Ithaca: McBooks, 1997).

Masson, Jeffrey Moussaieff and Susan McCarthy. *When Elephants Weep: The Emotional Lives of Animals* (New York: Delacorte, 1995).

Mason, Jim. *An Unnatural Order: Why We Are Destroying the Planet and Each Other* (New York: Continuum, 1997).

McKibben, Bill. *Hope, Human and Wild: True Stories of Living Lightly on the Earth* (New York: Little, Brown, 1995).

Midgley, Mary. *Beast and Man: The Roots of Human Nature*, revised edition. (New York: Routledge, 1996).

Noske, Barbara. *Beyond Boundaries: Humans and Animals*, revised edition (Buffalo: Black Rose Books, 1997).

Pateman, Carole. *The Sexual Contract* (Stanford: Stanford University Press, 1988).

Pluhar, Evelyn. *Beyond Prejudice: The Moral Significance of Human and Nonhuman Animals* (Durham: Duke University Press, 1995).

Payne, Robert. *The Life and Death of Adolf Hitler* (New York: Praeger, 1973).

Rampton, Shelton and John Stauber. *Mad Cow USA: Could the Nightmare Happen Here?* (Monroe: Common Courage, 1997).

Regan, Tom. *The Case for Animal Rights* (Berkeley: University of California Press, 1983).
____ and Peter Singer, editors. *Animal Rights and Human Obligations* (Englewood Cliffs: Prentice Hall, 1976).
Rifkin, Jeremy. *Beyond Beef: The Rise and Fall of the Cattle Culture* (New York: Dutton, 1992).
Robbins, John. *Diet for a New America*, revised edition (Tiburon: H. J. Kramer, 1998).
____ . *Reclaiming Our Health* (Tiburon: H. J. Kramer, 1997).
Rosen, Steven. *Diet for Transcendence: Vegetarianism and the World Religions* (Badger: Torchlight Publishing, 1997).
Savage-Rambaugh, Sue and Roger Levin. *Kanzi: The Ape at the Brink of the Human Mind* (New York: John Wiley & Sons, 1996).
Schwartz, Richard. *Judaism and Vegetarianism* (Marblehead: Micah Press, 1982).
Shepard, Paul. *The Others: How Animals Made Us Human* (Washington: Island Press, 1997).
Shiva, Vandana. *Biopiracy: The Plunder of Nature and Knowledge* (Boston: South End Press, 1997).
Silverstein, Helena. *Unleashing Rights: Law, Meaning, and the Animal Rights Movement* (Ann Arbor: University of Michigan Press, 1996).
Sinclair, Upton. *The Jungle* (now available in Signet Classics).
Singer, Peter. "Animals and Liberation," *The New York Review of Books*, April 5, 1973.
____ . *Animal Liberation* (Avon Books: NY, 1975). Revised edition (New York: Avon Books, 1991).
____ . *Ethics into Action: Henry Spira and the Animal Rights Movement* (Lanham: Rowman & Littlefield, 1998).
____ and Tom Regan, editors. *In Defense of Animals* (New York: Harper Perennial, 1985).
Spencer, Colin. *The Heretic's Feast: A History of Vegetarianism* (Hanover: University Press of New England, 1995).
Spiegel, Marjorie. *The Dreaded Comparison: Human and Animal Slavery* (New York: Mirror Books, 1996).
Stepaniak, Joanne and Suzanne Havala. *Vegan Vittles: Recipes Inspired by the Critters of Farm Sanctuary* (Summerville: Book Publishing Company, 1996).
Toland, John. *Adolf Hitler* (Garden City: Doubleday, 1976).
Tompkins, Peter and Christopher Bird. *The Secret Life of Plants* (New York: HarperCollins, 1989).
Veitch, John, translator and editor. *Descartes: Discourse on Method and the Meditations* (Buffalo: Prometheus Books, 1989).
Waskow, Arthur. *Down-to-Earth Judaism: Food, Money, Sex and the Rest of Life* (New York: William Morrow, 1995).
Wasserman, Debra and Reed Mangels. *Vegan Handbook* (Baltimore: Vegetarian Resource Group, 1996).
Webb, Stephen H. *On God and Dogs: A Christian Theology of Compassion for Animals* (New York: Oxford, 1998).
Wolfson, David. *Beyond the Law: Agribusiness and the Systemic Abuse of Animals Raised for Food and Food Production* (New York: Archimedean Press, 1995 Box 214, Planetarium Station, New York, NY 10024).

List of Contributors

Matt Ball is co-founder of Vegan Outreach. He lives in Pittsburgh, Pennsylvania.

Lorri Bauston is co-founder, with her husband **Gene**, of Farm Sanctuary, a sanctuary for abused or "downed" farm animals in upstate New York and northern California. She lives in Watkins Glen, New York.

Alan H. Berger works for the Animal Protection Institute, based in Sacramento, California, where he lives.

Rynn Berry is the author of *The New Vegetarians, Famous Vegetarians and Their Favorite Recipes* and *Food for the Gods* which can be ordered from Pythagorean Publishers, P.O. Box 8174, JAF Station, New York, NY 10116. He conducted the interviews with Andrew Linzey, Muni Nandibhushan Vijayji, and Dick Gregory, the first two of which are condensed versions of longer interviews appearing in *Food for the Gods*. He lives in Brooklyn, New York.

Edward Bikales is a writer and ultimate Frisbee player who lives in New York City.

Sue Coe is an internationally known artist and activist who lives in New York City.

Constance Lynn Cornell writes on produce issues for a co-op newsletter, works her front lawn garden, belongs to her CSA and volunteers with Just Food and at the Brooklyn Botanic Garden. She lives in Brooklyn.

Bill Dollinger works for Friends of Animals in their office in Washington, DC, where he lives.

Patrick Donnelly is a person living with AIDS and an advisor to the Whole Foods Project. He has written on nutrition for people with illness for *POZ, Body Positive,* and *Equilibrium* magazines. He lives in Brooklyn, New York.

Roger S. Fouts and **Deborah S. Fouts** teach at the Central Washington University Chimpanzee and Human Communication Institute in Ellensburg, Washington.

Jason Freitag is a doctoral candidate in South Asian Studies at Columbia University. He lives in Brooklyn, New York.

Phil Goff works on urban planning and sustainable transportation issues in Portland, Oregon, where he lives.

Jane Goodall is a world-famous primatologist whose work with the chimpanzees of Gombe, Tanzania has transformed our knowledge of non-human primates.

Antonia Gorman is completing her doctorate in theology at Drew University. She lives in Honesdale, Pennsylvania.

Jessica Graham is a journalist who lives in Brooklyn, New York.

Jean Hollowell is an animal activist who lives in Fremont, North Carolina.

239

Laurie Jordan is a vegan chef who delivers healthy, nutritious meals directly to individual homes and teaches cooking classes in New York City, where she lives.

Susan Kalev is a health care worker, humane educator and activist. She conducts programs offering a healthy, humane and environmentally friendly approach to food and living. She lives in New York City.

Kathy Lawrence is the director of Just Food.

Howard Lyman is the founder of Voice for a Viable Future.

Mia MacDonald is a consultant in international development with a master's degree in public policy from the Kennedy School of Government at Harvard University. She conducted the interviews with Maneka Gandhi and Alyssa Bonilla. She lives in Brooklyn, New York.

Jim Mason is a popular lecturer on our relationship with animals. He lives in Mount Vernon, Missouri.

Tom McGuire is a writer and environmental activist who lives in Oakland, California.

Stephanie Miller is a metalworker and sculptor who tends her garden in Brooklyn, New York.

Hillary Morris is an animal rights activist and is currently training to be an acupuncturist. She lives in New York City.

Steven I. Simmons, who died in 1997, worked for People for the Ethical Treatment of Animals (PETA), and was active in AIDS Coalition to Unleash Power (ACT-UP). This article was edited and cleared for use by his sister, Linda R. Simmons.

Paul Shapiro is a coordinator of Vegan Action and lives in Washington, DC.

Deborah Tanzer, Ph.D., is a psychologist currently writing a book about the psychological connections between human violence, gender issues and relationships between humans and animals. She lives in New York City.

Stacey Triplett lives in Somerville, Massachusetts. She regularly trades recipes with anyone who cooks.

Ben White is Director of the Church of the Earth and lives in Washington State.

Ying Wu is an environmental activist and student who lives in Brooklyn, New York.

Joan Zacharias is chair of the New York City Sierra Club Vegetarian Outings Committee and has been instrumental in pushing the Sierra Club to promote a plant-based diet. She conducted the interview with Henry Spira. She lives in upstate New York.

Resources

ALEPH: Alliance for Jewish Renewal
7000 Lincoln Drive, #B2, Philadelphia, PA 19119-1793. 212-247-0210, www.aleph.org

Alliance for a Paving Moratorium
P.O. Box 4347, Arcata, GA 95518. 707-826-7775, email: alliance@tidepool.com

American Anti-Vivisection Society
801 Old York Road, #204, Jenkintown, PA 19046-1685. 215-887-0816, www.aavs.org/

Animal People
P.O. Box 960, Clinton WA 98236. Tel. 360-579-2505, www.animalpeoplenews.org

Animal Protection Institute
P.O. Box 22505, Sacramento, CA 95822. 1-800-348-7387, www.api4animals.org

Animal Rights International
P.O. Box 214, Planetarium Station, New York, NY 10024. www.ari-online.org

Animals' Agenda
1301 S. Baylis Street, Suite 325, Baltimore, MD 21224. 410-675-4566, www.animalsagenda.org

American Vegan Society
P.O. Box H, 56 Dinshah Lane, Malaga, NJ 08328-0908. www.americanvegan.org

Animal Welfare Institute
P.O. Box 3650, Washington, DC 20007. 202-337-2332. www.animalwelfare.com

Best Friends
5001 Angel Canyon Drive, Kanab, UT 84741-5001. 435-644-2001, www.bestfriends.org

Car Busters Magazine
Regroupement Pour Une Ville Sans Voitures, 4 Rue Bodin, 69001 Lyon, France. Contact: Randy Ghent. Email: rghent@humboldt1.com

Center for a New American Dream
6930 Carroll Ave., Suite 900, Takoma Park, MD 20912. 301-891-ENUF, www.newdream.org

Center for Science in the Public Interest
1875 Connecticut Avenue, NW, Suite 300. 202-332-9110, www.cspinet.org

Central Washington University Chimpanzee and Human Communication Institute
400 East 8th Avenue, Ellensberg, WA 98926-7573. 509-963-1111

Community Supported Agriculture of North America
Indian Line Farm, 57 Jugend Road, Great Barrington, MA 01230. 413-528-4374, www.umass.edu/umext/csa/

Council for Responsible Genetics
5 Upland Road, Suite 3, Cambridge, MA 02140. 617-868-0870, www.gene-watch.org

Earth First!
P.O. Box 3023, Tucson, AZ 85702. 520-620-6900, www.earthfirst.org

Earth Island Institute
300 Broadway, #28, San Francisco, CA 94133. 415-788-3666, www.earthisland.org

EarthSave International
P.O. Box 96, New York, NY 10108. 718-459-7503, www.earthsave.org
The Ecotourism Society
P.O. Box 755, N. Bennington, VT 05257. 802-447-2121
E Magazine
P.O. Box 2047, Marion, OH, 43305. 815-734-1242, www.emagazine.com
Environmental Coalition of Stuyvesant (E.C.O.S.)
Attn: Rich Realmuto (Faculty Advisor), 142-60 56th Road, Flushing, NY 11355
FAACE (Fight Against Animal Cruelty in Europe)
29 Shakespeare Street, Southport, PR8 5AB, U.K., www.faace.co.uk
FARM
10101 Ashburton, Bethesda, MD 20817. 301-530-1737, www.farmusa.org
Farm Sanctuary
P.O. Box 150, Watkins Glen, NY 14891. 607-583-2225, www.farmsanctuary.org
Feminists for Animal Rights
P.O. Box 41355, Tucson AZ 85717. 520-825-6852, www.farinc.org
Friends of Animals
777 Post Road, Suite 205, Darien, CT 06820. 203-656-1522,
www.friendsofanimals.org
Friends of the Earth
1025 Vermont Ave. NW - Washington, DC 20005. 877-843-8687, www.foe.org
The Fruitarian Network
P.O. Box 293, Trinity Beach, N. Queensland 4879, Australia. ++ 61071- 57-7273
Fund for Animals
200 West 57th Street, New York, NY 10019. 212-246-2096, www.fund.org
Gas Guzzler Campaign
c/o The Advocacy Institute, 1707 L Street, NW, #400, Washington, DC 20036.
202-659-8475
Global Exchange
2017 Mission Street #303, San Francisco, CA 94110. 415-255-7296,
www.globalexchange.org
Greenpeace
702 H Street, NW, Washington, DC 20001. 202-462-1177, www.greenpeace.org
Humane Farming Association
P.O. Box 3577, San Rafael, CA 94912. 415-771-CALF. www.hfa.org.
Humane Society of the United States
2100 L Street, NW, Washington, DC 20037. 202-452-1100, www.hsus.org
In Defense of Animals
131 Camino Alto, Suite E, Mill Valley, CA 94941. 415-388-9641, www.idausa.org
International Forum on Globalization,
1009 General Kennedy Avenue, #2, San Francisco, CA 94129. 415-771-3394,
www.ifg.org
International Vegetarian Union
P.O. Box 38130, 28080 Madrid, Spain. www.ivu.org, email: secretary@ivu.org

Jane Goodall Institute
  8700 Georgia Avenue, Suite 500, Silver Spring, MD, 20910. 240-645-4000, www.janegoodall.org

Just Food
  P.O. Box 20444, Greeley Square Street, New York, NY 10025. 212-645-9880, www.justfood.org

Last Chance for Animals
  8033 Sunset Blvd., Suite 35, Los Angeles, CA 90046. 310-271-6096, www.lcanimal.org

League of Conservation Voters
  1920 L Street NW, Suite 800, Washington, DC 20036. 202-785-8683, www.lcv.org

Magnolia Tree Earth Center
  766 Lafayette Avenue, Brooklyn, NY 11216. 718-387-2116

Medical Research Modernization Committee
  3200 Morley Road, Shaker Heights, OH 44122. www.mrmcmed.org

Mothers & Others for a Livable Planet
  40 West 20th Street, New York, NY 10010. 212-242-0010, www.mothers.org/mothers

Natural Resources Defense Council
  1920 L Street, NW, Suite 1600A, Washington, DC 20036. 202-955-1374, www.nrdc.org

Nature Conservancy
  4245 North Fairfax Drive, Suite 100, Arlington, VA 22209. 703-841-5300, http://nature.org

New England Anti-Vivisection Society
  333 Washington Street, Suite 850, Boston, MA 02108. 617-523-6020, www.neavs.org

New York City Environmental Justice Alliance
  271 West 125th Street, Suite 303, New York, NY 10027. 212-866-4120

North American Vegetarian Society
  P.O. Box 72, Dolgeville, NY 13329. 518-568-7970, www.navs-online.org

Northwest Environment Watch
  1402 Third Avenue, #1127, Seattle, WA 98101-2118. 206-447-1880, www.northwestwatch.org

People for the Ethical Treatment of Animals
  501 Front Street, Norfolk, VA 23510. 757-622-7382, www.peta.org

The Pure Food Campaign
  6101 Cliff Estate Rd., Little Marais, MN 55614. 218-226-4164, www.organicconsumers.org

Rainforest Action Network
  221 Pine Street, Suite 500, San Francisco, CA 94104. 415-398-4404, www.ran.org

Sierra Club
  85 Second Street, Second Floor, San Francisco, CA 94105-3441. 415-977-5500, www.sierraclub.org

Time's Up!
P.O. Box 2030, New York, NY 10009. 212-677-9006. www.times-up.org

Transportation Alternatives
115 West 30th Street, 12th fl., New York, NY 10009. 212-629-3311,
www.transalt.org

United Network for Organ Sharing
P.O. Box 2484, Richmond, VA 23225. 804-782-4800, www.unos.org

United Poultry Concerns
P.O. Box 150, Machipongo, VA 23405-0150. 757-678-7875, www.upc-online.org

Vegan Action
P.O. Box 4288, Richmond, VA 23220. www.vegan.org

Vegan Outreach
P.O. Box 38492, Pittsburgh, PA 15238. www.veganoutreach.org

Vegetarian Journal
P.O. Box 1463, Baltimore, MD 21203. 410-366-8343, www.vrg.org/journal

Vegetarian Resource Group
P.O. Box 1463, Baltimore, MD 21203. 410-366-8343, www.vrg.org

Vegetarian Society of United Kingdom
Parkdale, Dunham Road, Altrincham, Cheshire WA14 4QG. www.vegsoc.org,
email: info@vegsoc.demon.co.uk

Vegetarian Times
4 High Ridge Park Stamford, CT 06905. 203-321-1704, www.vegetariantimes.com

Vivavegie Society
P.O. Box 294, New York, NY 10012. www.vivavegie.org

Voice for a Viable Future
11288 Ventura Blvd., #202A, Studio City, CA 91604. 818-509-1255,
www.vegsource.com/lyman/index.htm

The Whole Foods Project
P.O. Box 433, 285 5th Ave., Brooklyn, NY 11215. 718-832-6628, email:
Wfproject@aol.com.

Wildlife Preservation Trust
1520 Locust Street, Suite 704, Philadelphia, PA 19102. 212-854-8185, fax: 212-
853-8188, www.wpti.org

WorldWatch Institute
1776 Massachusetts Avenue, NW, Washington, DC 20036-1904. 202-452-1999,
www.worldwatch.org

World Wildlife Fund
1250 24th Street, NW, Washington, DC 20037. 202-293-4800, www.wwf.org

Yes! A Journal of Positive Futures
P.O. Box 10818, Bainbridge Island, WA 98110. 206-842-0216, www.futurenet.org

About Satya

A Tool for Activism

Satya is a monthly magazine, distributed free of charge to restaurants, bookstores, holistic health centers, places of learning and worship, and elsewhere around New York City. *Satya* has subscribers all over the United States and abroad. *Satya's* website <www.satyamag.com> now attracts the attention of countless readers around the world.

Subscriptions

To subscribe to *Satya*, visit www.satyamag.com, or send your name, address, and a check for $20.00 made payable to Stealth Technologies Inc., 539 1st Street Brooklyn, NY 11215.

Printed in the United States
23452LVS00005B/61-204

9 780966 405606

The Way of Compassion
Vegetarianism, Environmentalism, Animal Advocacy and Social Justice

In a world filled with what seems only bad news, it is easy to become over-whelmed by the extent of environmental degradation, violence to other species, and collective suffering. The problems seem so immense and so intractable that they often lead only to one despairing question: "What can I do?"

The answer, as presented in *The Way of Compassion*, is "a lot." *The Way of Compassion* collects the inspiring, thoughtful, and eminently practical wisdom of contemporary thinkers and activists from all walks of life, working to maintain sustainable lifestyles, practice non-violence in all its forms and create a deeper spiritual appreciation of our place in the world. These pioneers offer timely, sensible and sometimes challenging advice on how we can all play our parts in creating a more harmonious and peaceful planet.

"[An] eloquent, forceful body of writings that forges vital links between vegetarianism, environmentalism and animal rights and the quest for social justice."

—Publishers Weekly

"Sophisticated but not inaccessible… This important and deeply engaging book belongs in all but the smallest libraries."

—Library Journal

"Sturdy and ethically provocative."

—Values and Visions

"People who like ideas, philosophies and a variety of views will enjoy this book cover to cover."

—Animals' Agenda

"The reader who is serious about making major lifestyle changes will find value in [this book's] plentiful advice and insight."

—NAPRA ReView

Martin Rowe has degrees in English and Religious Studies from Oxford University and New York University. He is the editor of *Satya: A Magazine of Vegetarianism, Environmentalism, and Animal Advocacy.*

Jacket design by Stealth Technologies

Stealth Technologies • New York
$19.95

ISBN 0-966405-0-9

9 780966 405606